M A S T E R I N G
GREEK
VOCABULARY

MASTERING

GREEK

VOCABULARY

THOMAS A. ROBINSON

HENDRICKSON
PUBLISHERS
PEABODY, MASSACHUSETTS 01961-3473

Copyright © 1990 by Hendrickson Publishers, Inc.
P.O. Box 3473
Peabody, Massachusetts 01961–3473
All rights reserved.
Printed in the United States of America

ISBN 0–943575–45–1

In memory of my father,
Cecil Arthur Robinson
1923–1974

CONTENTS

PREFACE

Mastering Greek Vocabulary is offered as one approach to learning a working vocabulary of New Testament Greek as quickly as possible. The project started out some years ago when computers were considerably more expensive — and not much more compact — than a stack of several thousand file cards. And file cards came in color; computers did not. But computers improved and became less expensive; file cards remained file cards and became more expensive.

About two years ago, with the help of a Macintosh computer and a grant from the University of Lethbridge Research Fund, students from the Greek class were employed in converting the material on file cards to a computer data base. Along with the students who worked at that level, a number of students from credit and non-credit Greek courses contributed various ideas along the way. I single out the following students for special mention: Kent Brown, Emma Denhoed, Kathryn Gast, Grace Holmes, Mark Hoogerdyk, Arij Langstraat, David Plaxton, Terry Smith, Greg Smith, and Kurt Widmer. Special thanks to Brian Smart, a professor of Latin at the University of Lethbridge, for careful proof-reading of various sections of the Greek lists.

A number of works have been consulted in the preparation of this work. Word statistics are based primarily on Robert Morgenthaler, *Statistik des neutestamentlichen Wortschatzes* (Zürich: Gotthelf-Verlag, 1958, 1982). The cognate groups have been, to some extent, informed by J. Harold Greenlee, *A New Testament Greek Morpheme Lexicon* (Grand Rapids: Zondervan, 1983). This work should be consulted in any serious study of cognates. Also useful was Xavier Jacques, *List of New Testament Words Sharing Common Elements* (Rome: Biblical Institute Press, 1969). For the meaning of the Greek words, I have tried to show wherever possible the influence of the prefixes and roots, though for general meanings I have consulted Barclay M. Newman, Jr., *A Concise Greek-English Dictionary of the New Testament* (London: United Bible Societies, 1971). Any serious study of Greek vocabulary should make use of the new two-volume United Bible Societies work: *Greek-English Lexicon of the New Testament: Based on Semantic Domains,* eds. Johannes P. Louw and Eugene Nida (New York: UBS, 1988). For etymologies, a number of works were useful: Ernest Klein, *A Comprehensive Etymological Dictionary of the English Language* (Amsterdam / London / New York: Elsevier Publishing, 1966), in two volumes; Donald M. Ayers, *English Words from Latin and Greek Elements* (Tucson: University of Arizona Press, 1986), 2nd. ed. revised and expanded by Thomas D. Worthen, with the assistance of R. L. Cherry; and C. A. E. Luschnig and L. J. Luschnig, *Etyma: An Introduction to Vocabulary-Building from Latin & Greek* (Lanham / New York / London: University Press of America,

1982). Also of use is Robert Claiborne's recent book, *The Roots of English: A Reader's Handbook of Word Origins* (New York: Times Books, 1989).

My own work is offered as an easy *first* step into the vocabulary of the New Testament. Such a manual can be improved by the contributions of the users. I thus welcome all lists of errors and typos, and suggestions for making more streamline any aspect of *Mastering Greek Vocabulary*.

Tom Robinson
The University of Lethbridge
August 1990

ABBREVIATIONS

adj.	adjective
acc.	accusative case
cj.	conjunction
adv.	adverb
dat.	dative case
fem.	feminine noun
gen.	genitive case
interj.	interjection
masc.	masculine noun
mid.	middle voice
neut.	neuter noun
pass.	passive voice
pl.	plural
prep.	preposition
pron.	pronoun
pt.	particle
vb.	verb

Even though the student of New Testament Greek rarely wishes to read extensively in Greek literature outside of the New Testament, the New Testament vocabulary is itself quite large and difficult enough to master. Various attempts have been made to give students a "working" vocabulary of the New Testament. Rather than learning the entire vocabulary from alpha to omega, students sometimes learn words in order of their frequency of occurrence within the New Testament. Thus, instead of learning 5,432 words (the total vocabulary of the New Testament), the student would be presented with a much shorter list of words, from which the rarer words would have been deleted. This learning approach is sound. Why require of a student the effort to learn a word that will be encountered only once in the entire New Testament? Over one third of the words in the New Testament vocabulary occur only once—obviously not the most pressing working vocabulary for a reader of the New Testament.

If one were to learn the more frequently occurring words in the New Testament, however, one could make quick gains. For example, the thirty most frequent words in the New Testament represent fully one half of all word occurrences. A minimal effort here would expose the student to a fairly substantial working vocabulary quite quickly. Of course, most of these words would be common prepositions, particles, the definite article, etc. But it illustrates the principle: a working vocabulary is most quickly gained by learning the most frequently occurring words.

Two works have used this principle. One is Bruce Metzger's rightly praised *Lexical Aids for Students of New Testament Greek*. In a matter of thirty-three pages, Metzger lists all the words in the New Testament that occur ten times or more. The other work is J. W. Wenham's standard grammar, *The Elements of New Testament Greek*. By providing vocabulary lists based on frequency of occurrence, Wenham is able to introduce the first-year student to over eighty percent of the total word occurrences (though not eighty percent of the total vocabulary) in the New Testament.

In *Mastering Greek Vocabulary*, I have used the same principle. But rather than basing the order of words to be learned on their frequency of occurrence, I have based the order on the frequency of the occurrence of the cognate root. In many cases, one root will be reflected in dozens of related words. Thus by learning the most frequent roots, one can even more quickly gain a solid working vocabulary. In the main lists of this present volume, all cognate groups with twenty or more occurrences in the New Testament are given.

Two other features help make *Mastering Greek Vocabulary* an effective way to learn Greek vocabulary. First, for the majority of roots, an easy memory aid is provided. For example, for the Greek root ἀκου, which means "to hear,"

the memory aid provided is the English word "acoustic." The English derivative, thus, illustrates the meaning of the Greek word. In this way, the student
learns Greek by finding common ground between Greek and English. In addition, since words have been grouped in terms of their common root, by learning, for example, that the root ἀκου means "to hear," the student has the basic
meaning not just of one word but of all eleven Greek words that are based on
that root.

The final feature of this work is a breakdown of all the Greek words
into their prefixes and suffixes. By learning how a particular prefix or suffix
can affect a root, the student will be able to determine the meaning of a complex word by breaking that word into its root and its prefixes and suffixes. This
arrangement will not only give the student access to a solid working vocabulary, but will, as well, provide the resources for determining the meanings of
words that are encountered for the first time.

All of this aids the student in gaining a working vocabulary quickly. And
that, of course, is the reason for learning Greek vocabulary—to put it to work
in the actual reading of a text. It is to that end that *Mastering Greek Vocabulary*
is offered.

The purpose of this volume is to help the beginning student of New Testament Greek quickly gain a working vocabulary. Various features will appeal to each user differently. Thus the primary advice is simple: use those sections that help; omit those sections that hinder. But some guide to the use of this volume may help. Try the following.

First: Review Section 1 (*Identical Greek/English Words*). From this, the student can gain—without study!—a vocabulary of about 250 words (and an even larger vocabulary, if all the cognates of these words are considered). All the English words listed in Section 1 are merely transliterations of Greek words. In other words, they are spelled the same (with some minor exceptions). But not only are they spelled the same, they mean the same. Here we hardly have a new language at all—the spelling is the same; the meaning is the same; all that is different is that a different alphabet has been used to write out the words.

Second: The Cognate Group:

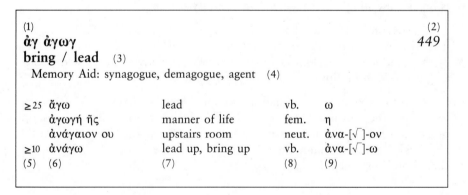

Each Cognate Group has nine main parts:

(1) The Greek root (variant forms are often included)
(2) The frequency of that root in the New Testament
(3) The general meaning of that root (in English)
(4) English words derived from (or suggestive of) the Greek root. These are to serve as Memory Aids.

Following the above general information (contained on the first three lines of the cognate entry) is a list of Greek words sharing that root and aids for prioritizing, defining, and identifying terms.

(5) Symbol column:

> ≥25 indicates that word occurs 25 times or more in the
> New Testament
>
> ≥10 indicates that word occurs 10–24 times
> a blank space indicates that word occurs less that ten
> times

(6) Greek word column
(7) English translation column
(8) Part of speech column (see Abbreviations for details)
(9) Prefix and Suffix column

Roots are included in this section too. Roots that are listed in the Cognate
Lists are enclosed thus: [√]; roots not listed in the Cognate Lists are enclosed
thus: (√).

Third: Study the whole Cognate Group in order to get a sense of the
various relationships of words in this group. Pay particular attention to the Memory Aids (on line three). If the meaning of the derived English words in the Memory Aid section is unfamiliar, look up those words in Section 3 (*Derived English
Words*). If no common English derivative could be found as a memory aid, suggestive words (not cognates) or sentences sometimes have been provided. If they
work, use them. Sometimes nothing seemed to work as a memory aid. The space
is blank—awaiting the student's own memory device.

Fourth: Memorize a basic vocabulary from each Cognate Group. Again,
it is wise to memorize the most frequent words in the list. These are marked
by the symbol ≥25 or ≥10, as explained above. (Note: words are listed in each
Cognate Group in alphabetical order of the Greek words.)

Fifth: Note the prefixes and suffixes. Individual prefixes and suffixes generally alter the root in regular ways. Refer to Section 4 for a detailed description of how the various prefixes and suffixes affect the root. In some cases, Greek
and English share the same prefixes and suffixes. See Section 5 for this list of
shared prefixes and suffixes.

1

Identical Greek/English Words

A number of Greek words have been merely transliterated to create words in the English language. The student should review these words first, since this will give the student some confidence that Greek is not entirely foreign. Words are listed below even if the root occurs less than twenty times (a requirement of all roots that occur in the main Cognate Groups list), since no real effort is required to learn these words (other than for some attention to endings). Proper names are not included. These are capitalized in any New Testament Greek text, and straight transliteration will usually give the rough English equivalent. Names of plants, minerals, and coins are not included either. There should be no trouble with such words when they are met in a text.

One main point to remember is that consonants are considerably more stable than vowels.

ἀββά — abba
ἄβυσσος — abyss
ἄγγελος — angel, messenger
ἄγκυρα — anchor
ἄγνωστος — agnostic, unknown
ἀγωνία — agony
ἀγωνίζομαι — agonize, struggle
ᾅδης — Hades
ἀήρ — air
ἄθλησις — athletics, struggle
αἴνιγμα — enigma, obscurity
αἵρεσις — heresy, faction
αἱρετικός — heretic, division-causing
αἴσθησις — aesthetics, insight
αἰών — eon, age
ἀλάβαστρον — alabaster jar
ἀλληγορέω — allegorize
ἀλληλουϊά — hallelujah

ἄλφα — alpha
ἀμήν — amen
ἀνάθεμα — anathema
ἀναθεματίζω — anathemize
ἀντί — prefix "anti"
ἀντίτυπος — antitype, copy
ἀντίχριστος — antichrist
ἀποκάλυψις — apocalypse
ἀπόκρυφος — apocryphal, secret
ἀπολογία — apology, defense
ἀποστασία — apostasy
ἀπόστολος — apostle
ἀρχάγγελος — archangel
ἀρχαῖος — archaic, old
ἀρχιτέκτων — architect, master builder
ἄρωμα — aroma
ἀστήρ — star

αὐστηρός — austere, severe
αὐτόματος — automatic

βαπτίζω — baptize
βάπτισμα — baptism
βαπτιστής — baptist
βάρβαρος — barbarian
βιβλίον — book (Bible)
βίβλος — book (Bible)
βίος — prefix "bio-," life
βλασφημέω — blaspheme
βλασφημία — blasphemy
βλάσφημος — blasphemous

γάγγραινα — gangrene
γέεννα — gehenna, hell
γενεαλογία — genealogy
γνῶσις — gnosis, knowledge

δαίμων — demon
δέρμα — epidermis, skin
δεσπότης — despot, lord
διάγνωσις — diagnosis, discernment
διάδημα — diadem, crown
διάκονος — deacon, servant
διαλέγομαι — dialogue, discuss
διάλεκτος — dialect, language
διασπορά — diaspora
διδακτικός — didactic
δόγμα — dogma, rule
δράκων — dragon
δυσεντέριον — dysentery
δῶμα — dome, roof

ἐγώ — ego
ἐθνάρχης — ethnarch, governor
εἴδωλον — idol
εἰκών — icon, likeness
εἰρηνικός — irenic, peaceful
ἑκατόν — hecto (metric measure prefix, meaning 100)
ἐκκλησία — ekklesia, church
ἔκστασις — ecstasy
ἐμέω — emit
ἐμπόριον — emporium, market
ἐν — in

ἐνδύω — endue, clothe
ἐνέργεια — energy, working
ἔξοδος — exodus
ἐξορκίζω — exorcize
ἐξορκιστής — exorcist
ἐπιγραφή — epigraph, inscription
ἐπισκοπή — episcopacy
ἐπιστολή — epistle, letter
ἐπιφάνεια — epiphany, appearing
ἔσχατον — eschaton, end
εὐαγγελίζω — evangelize
εὐαγγελιστής — evangelist
εὐγενής — eugenic
εὐλογέω — eulogize
εὐλογία — eulogy
εὐνοῦχος — eunuch
εὐφημία — euphemism, good reputation
εὐχαριστία — eucharist, thanksgiving

ζηλεύω — be zealous
ζῆλος — zeal
ζηλόω — be zealous

ἡγεμονία — hegemony, rule
ἡμι — prefix, like the English prefix "hemi," half

θέατρον — theatre
θεραπεία — therapy
θρόνος — throne
θώραξ — thorax, chest

ἰουδαΐζω — judaize

καθαρισμός — catharsis, cleansing
Καῖσαρ — Kaiser, Caesar
καλέω — call
κάμηλος — camel
κανών — canon, rule
κατακλυσμός — cataclysm
καταλέγω — catalogue, enroll
καταστροφή — catastrophe
καῦσις — caustic, burning
κεντυρίων — centurion
κεραμικός — ceramic, clay

κήρυγμα — kerygma
κίνησις — English suffix "kenesis," meaning "motion"
κοινωνία — koinonia, fellowship
κολωνία — colony
κόσμος — cosmos, world
κρανίον — cranium, skull
κύμβαλον — cymbal

λαμπάς — lamp
λάρυγξ — larynx, throat
λεγιών — legion
λέπρα — leprosy
λεπρός — leper
λέων — lion
λίνον — linen
λογικός — logical, rational

μαγεία — magic
μαγεύω — do magic
μάγος — magi, wise man
μάμμη — mamma, grandmother
μαμωνᾶς — mammon, money
μανία — mania, madness
μάννα — manna
μάρτυς — martyr, witness
μεταμορφόομαι — metamorphose, change
μέτρον — meter, measure
μίλιον — mile
μιμέομαι — mimic
μόρφωσις — English suffix "morph," meaning "form"
μουσικός — musician
μῦθος — myth
μύλος — mill
μυριάς — myriad
μυστήριον — mystery, secret
μωρός — moron, fool

ὀρφανός — orphan

παραβολή — parable
παράδεισος — paradise
παράδοξος — paradoxical, incredible
παράκλητος — Paraclete, comforter

παραλύομαι — be paralyzed
παραλυτικός — paralytic
παρουσία — parousia, coming
πατριάρχης — patriarch
πεντηκοστή — Pentecost
πέτρα — Peter, rock
πλάξ — plaque, tablet
πλαστός — plastic, made-up
πληγή — plague
πλήρωμα — pleroma, fullness
πόλεμος — polemic, war
πόλις — polis, city
πρεσβύτης — presbyter, elderly man
πρόγνωσις — prognosis, foreknowledge
προσήλυτος — proselyte
προφητεία — prophecy
προφητεύω — prophesy
προφήτης — prophet
προφητικός — prophetic
προφῆτις — prophetess
πυλών — pylon, gateway

ῥαββι — rabbi
ῥαίνω — rain, sprinkle

σάββατον — Sabbath
σανδάλιον — sandal
Σατανᾶς — Satan
σκανδαλίζω — scandalize
σκάνδαλον — scandal
σκορπίος — scorpion
σοφία — Sophia, wisdom
σπένδομαι — spend, give one's life
σπέρμα — sperm, seed
σπίλος — spill, spot, stain
σπόγγος — sponge
σπορά — spore, seed
σπόρος — spore, seed
στεῖρα — sterile woman
στίγμα — stigma, mark
στοά — stoa, porch
στόμαχος — stomach
στῦλος — stele, pillar

συκομορέα — sycamore tree
συμπαθής — sympathy
συμπαθέω — sympathize
συμπόσιον — symposium
συμφωνία — symphony, music
συνέδριον — Sanhedrin
συνοδία — synod
σχῆμα — scheme, form
σχίσμα — schism
σχολή — school, lecture hall
σωματικός — somatic, bodily

ταβέρνη — tavern, inn
ταῦρος — Taurus, bull
τέχνη — technique, craft
τεχνίτης — technician
τίτλος — title, notice
τραῦμα — trauma, wound
τραυματίζω — traumatize, wound
τρέμω — tremble
τύπος — type, pattern

ὕβρις — hubris
ὑγιής — hygenic, sound
ὕμνος — hymn
ὑπερβολή — hyperbole, excess
ὑπόκρισις — hypocrisy
ὑποκριτής — hypocrite
ὕσσωπος — hyssop

φαντασία — fantasy, imagination
φάντασμα — phantom
φαρμακεία — pharmacy, sorcery
φάρμακος — pharmacist, sorcerer
   (from use of drugs)
φιλανθρωπία — philanthrophy
φιλοσοφία — philosophy
φιλόσοφος — philosopher
φυλακτήριον — phylactery
φυλή — phylum, tribe
φυσικός — English prefix "physico-,"
   having to do with "nature"

χαρακτήρ — character, likeness
χάρισμα — charism, gift
χάρτης — chart, paper
χάσμα — chasm
χορός — chorus, dancing
χρῖσμα — chrism, anointing
Χριστιανός — Christian
Χριστός — Christ

ψαλμός — psalm
ψευδής — English prefix "pseudo-,"
   false

ὦ — O!
ᾠδή — ode, song
ὥρα — hour, time
ὡσαννά — hosanna

2

Cognate Groups

ὁ ἡ το   *21,117*
the
Memory Aid: See Chart B

≥25	ὁ ἡ τό	the	adj.	
≥10	ὅδε ἥδε τόδε	this	adj.	
≥25	ὅς ἥ ὅ	who, which, what	pron.	ος
	ὅσπερ ἥπερ ὅπερ	who, which	pron.	[√]-περ

καί   *9,039*
and
Memory Aid:

≥25	κἀγώ	and I, I also	cj./pt.	[ἐγω]
≥25	καί	and, also, but	cj./pt.	
	καίπερ	though	cj./pt.	[√]-περ
	καίτοι	yet, though	cj./pt.	
	καίτοιγε	yet, though	cj./pt.	

αὐτο   *5,943*
self
Memory Aid: autobiography, autograph, automatic, autistic

	αὐτόματος η ον	automatic	adj.	[√]-τος
≥25	αὐτός ἥ ό	self	pron.	[√]-ος
≥25	ἑαυτοῦ ἧς οῦ	himself, herself, itself	pron.	
≥25	ἐμαυτοῦ ἧς	myself, my own	pron.	
	ἐξαυτῆς	at once	adv.	ἐκ-[√]
≥25	σεαυτοῦ ἧς	yourself	pron.	[σ]-[√]
	φίλαυτος ον	selfish	adj.	[φιλ]-[√]-ος

δε[1]   *2,771*
but
Memory Aid:

≥25	δέ	but, rather	cj./pt.	

ἐν
in
2,725

Memory Aid: in, include, instill, inside, intake, insert, inscribe

≥25	ἐν (*dat.*)	in	prep.
	ἐνθάδε	here, in this place	adv.
	ἔνθεν	from here	adv.	[√]-θεν
	ἐντός (*gen.*)	within	prep.

εἰμι εἰ¹ ἐσ οὐσ ὀντ
be / exist
2,554

Memory Aid: parousia, ontological, essence

	ἄπειμι	be away	vb.	ἀπο-[√]-μι
	ἀπουσία ας	absence	fem.	ἀπο-[√]-ια
≥25	εἰμί	be, exist	vb.	[√]-μι
	ἔνειμι	be in(side)	vb.	ἐν-[√]-μι
≥25	ἔξεστι	it is proper / possible	vb.	ἐκ-[√]-μι
≥10	ὄντως	really	adv.	[√]-ως
	οὐσία ας	property	fem.	[√]-ια
	πάρειμι	be present	vb.	[√]-μι
≥10	παρουσία ας	coming, parousia	fem.	παρα-[√]-ια
	περιούσιος ον	special	adj.	περι-[√]-ιος
	συμπάρειμι	be present with	vb.	συν-παρα-[√]-μι
	σύνειμι	be with, be present	vb.	συν-[√]-μι

οὐ οὐκ οὐχ
no
1,920

Memory Aid:

≥10	οὔ	no	cj./pt.
≥25	οὐ	not	cj./pt.
	οὐδαμῶς	by no means	adv.	[√]-ως
≥25	οὐδέ	neither, nor	cj./pt.
≥25	οὔτε	not, nor	cj./pt.
≥25	οὐχί	not, no (emphatic)	cj./pt.

εἰς ἐσω
into
1,776

Memory Aid: eisegesis, esophagus

≥25	εἰς (*acc.*)	into, to	prep.
	ἔσω	inside	adv.	[√]-ω
≥10	ἔσωθεν	from within	adv.	[√]-ω-θεν
	ἐσώτερος α ον	inner (adj.), behind / in (prep.)	adj./prep.	[√]-τερος

ἐγω
I
1,713

Memory Aid: ego, egocentric

≥25	ἐγώ	I (first person pronoun)	pron.

οὖτ αὖτ τουτ
this 1,652

Memory Aid:

≥25 οὗτος αὕτη τοῦτο	this, this one	adj.	[√]-ος
≥25 οὕτως [οὕτω]	thus (>in this way)	adv.	[√]-ως
≥25 τοιοῦτος αὕτη οὖτον	such, similar	adj.	[√]-ος

ἐρχ
come 1,392

Memory Aid:

ἀνέρχομαι	go (come) up	vb.	ἀνα-[√]-ω
ἀντιπαρέρχομαι	pass by the other side	vb.	ἀντι-παρα-[√]-ω
≥25 ἀπέρχομαι	go (away)	vb.	ἀπο-[√]-ω
≥25 διέρχομαι	go / come through	vb.	δια-[√]-ω
≥25 εἰσέρχομαι	come, enter, share in	vb.	εἰς-[√]-ω
≥25 ἐξέρχομαι	come / go out, escape	vb.	ἐκ-[√]-ω
ἐπανέρχομαι	return	vb.	ἐπι-ἀνα-[√]-ω
ἐπεισέρχομαι	come upon	vb.	ἐπι-εἰς-[√]-ω
ἐπέρχομαι	come, come upon	vb.	ἐπι-[√]-ω
≥25 ἔρχομαι	come	vb.	[√]-ω
≥10 κατέρχομαι	come / go down	vb.	κατα-[√]-ω
παρεισέρχομαι	come in	vb.	παρα-εἰς-[√]-ω
≥25 παρέρχομαι	pass (by, away)	vb.	παρα-[√]-ω
περιέρχομαι	travel (go) about	vb.	περι-[√]-ω
προέρχομαι	go ahead	vb.	προ-[√]-ω
≥25 προσέρχομαι	come to, agree with	vb.	προς-[√]-ω
συνεισέρχομαι	enter in	vb.	συν-εἰς-[√]-ω
≥25 συνέρχομαι	come together	vb.	συν-[√]-ω

θε[1] θεο θει
god 1,328

Memory Aid: theology, atheist, pantheon, polytheism

ἄθεος ον	without God (>atheist)	adj.	ἀ-[√]-ος
θεά ᾶς	goddess	fem.	[√]-α
θεῖος α ον	divine	adj.	[√]-ιος
θειότης ητος	deity	fem.	[√]-οτης
θεομάχος ον	God-opposing	adj.	[√]-[μαχ]-ος
θεόπνευστος ον	God-inspired	adj.	[√]-[πνευ]-τος
≥25 θεός οῦ	God	masc.	[√]-ος
θεοσέβεια ας	religion	fem.	[√]-[σεβ]-εια
θεοσεβής ές	religious	adj.	[√]-[σεβ]-ης
θεοστυγής ές	God-hating	adj.	[√]-(στύγος)-ης
θεότης ητος	deity	fem.	[√]-οτης
κατάθεμα ματος	God-cursed thing	neut.	κατα-[√]-μα
φιλόθεος ον	God-loving	adj.	[√]-[φιλ]-ος

ὅτι   *1,285*
that / because
Memory Aid: Similar to Greek: τι *Why?*—ὅτι *Because.*
≥25 ὅτι   that, because   cj./pt.

παν πασ παντ   *1,278*
all
Memory Aid: Pan America, panorama, panacea, pantheon
≥25 ἅπας ἅπασα ἅπαν   each, all   adj.
     πανταχῇ   everywhere   adv.   [√]-ῃ
     πανταχοῦ   everywhere   adv.   [√]-ου
     πάντῃ   in every way   adv.
     πάντοθεν   from all directions   adv.   [√]-θεν
     πάντως   by all means   adv.   [√]-ως
≥25 πᾶς πᾶσα πᾶν   each, all   adj.

τι τις τιν²   *1,224*
who / what / any
Memory Aid: See Chart B
≥25 ὅστις ἥτις ὅ τι   whoever, whichever   adj./pron. [ὁ]
≥25 τὶς τὶ   anyone, anything   adj./pron.
≥25 τίς τί   who? what? (τι why?)   adj./pron.

μη   *1,164*
not
Memory Aid:
≥25 μή   not   cj./pt.
     μήγε   otherwise   cj./pt.
     μηδαμῶς   no, by no means   adv.   [√]-ως
≥25 μηδέ   nor   cj./pt.
≥25 μήτε   and not   cj./pt.
≥10 μήτι   (negative answer)   cj./pt.

ἀρ γαρ   *1,085*
then / therefore
Memory Aid:
≥25 ἄρα   then, therefore, thus   cj./pt.
≥25 γάρ   for, since, then   cj./pt.

σ   *1,084*
you
Memory Aid: [S is the sign of the Second person.]
≥25 σός σή σόν   your, yours   adj.   [√]-ος
≥25 σύ   you   pron.

ἐκ ἐξ

out / from 1,006

Memory Aid: exit, Exodus, exorcise, excommunicate, exegesis, exile

≥25	ἐκ (*gen.*)	from, out from	prep.
	ἐκτός (*gen.*)	outside, except	prep. [√]
≥25	ἔξω (*gen.*)	out, outside	adv./prep. [√]-ω
≥10	ἔξωθεν (*gen.*)	from outside	adv./prep. [√]-θεν
	ἐξωθέω	drive out, run aground	vb. [√]-εω (ὠθέω)
	ἐξώτερος α ον	outer	adj. [√]-τερος
	παρεκτός (*gen.*)	except	prep. παρα-[√]

γεν γιν γον

family / birth 949

Memory Aid: genetic, generation, genesis, genealogy, genre, genocide

	ἀγενεαλόγητος ον	without genealogy	adj.	ἀ-[√]-[λεγ]-τος
	ἀγενής ές	insignificant, inferior	adj.	ἀ-[√]-ης
	ἀναγεννάω	give new birth to	vb.	ἀνα-[√]-αω
	ἀπογίνομαι	have no part in	vb.	ἀπο-[√]-ω
	ἀρτιγέννητος ον	newborn	adj.	[ἀρτι]-[√]-τος
≥25	γενεά ᾶς	generation, age, family	fem.	[√]-α
	γενεαλογέομαι	to descend from	vb.	[√]-[λεγ]-εω
	γενεαλογία ας	genealogy	fem.	[√]-[λεγ]-ια
	γενέσια ων (*pl.*)	birthday party	neut.	[√]-ιον
	γένεσις εως	birth, lineage	fem.	[√]-σις
	γενετή ῆς	birth	fem.	[√]-η
	γένημα ματος	harvest, product	neut.	[√]-μα
≥25	γεννάω	be father of, bear	vb.	[√]-αω
	γέννημα ματος	offspring	neut.	[√]-μα
	γέννησις εως	birth	fem.	[√]-σις
	γεννητός ή όν	born	adj.	[√]-τος
≥10	γένος ους	family, race	neut.	[√]-ς
≥25	γίνομαι	become, be, happen	vb.	[√]-ω
≥10	γονεύς έως	parent	masc.	[√]-ευς
	διαγίνομαι	pass (of time)	vb.	δια-[√]-ω
	ἔκγονον ου	grandchild	neut.	ἐκ-[√]-ον
	ἐπιγίνομαι	spring up, come on	vb.	ἐπι-[√]-ω
	εὐγενής ές	high born (>eugenics)	adj.	εὐ-[√]-ης
	μονογενής ές	only, unique born	adj.	[μονο]-[√]-ης
	παλιγγενεσία ας	rebirth	fem.	παλιν-[√]-ια
≥25	παραγίνομαι	come, appear, stand by	vb.	παρα-[√]-ω
	προγίνομαι	happen previously	vb.	προ-[√]-ω
	πρόγονος ου	parent (>progenitor)	masc./fem.	προ-[√]-ος
	συγγένεια ας	relatives	fem.	συν-[√]-εια
	συγγενής οῦς	relative	masc.	συν-[√]-ς

| συγγενίς ίδος | female relative | fem. | συν-[√]-ς |
| συμπαραγίνομαι | assemble | vb. | συν-παρα-[√]-ω |

εἰ² 942
if
Memory Aid:

≥25 ἐάν	if, even if, though	cj./pt.	[√]-[ἀν¹]
ἐάνπερ	if only	cj./pt.	[√]-[ἀν¹]-περ
≥25 εἰ	if	cj./pt.	
εἴπερ	since, if it is true that	cj./pt.	[√]-περ
≥10 εἶτα	then, moreover	adv.	
≥25 εἴτε	if, whether	cj./pt.	

ἀλλ 936
other / change
Memory Aid: allegory, allotrope, parallel, alien

≥25 ἀλλά	but	cj./pt.	
ἀλλάσσω	change	vb.	[√]-σσω
ἀλλαχόθεν	at another place	adv.	[√]-θεν
ἀλλαχοῦ	elsewhere	adv.	[√]-ου
≥25 ἀλλήλων οις ους	one another	pron.	[√]-ος
ἀλλογενής ους	foreigner	masc.	[√]-[γεν]-ς
≥25 ἄλλος η ο	another, other	adj.	[√]-ος
≥10 ἀλλότριος α ον	of another, foreign	adj.	[√]-ιος
ἄλλως	otherwise	adv.	[√]-ως
ἀντάλλαγμα ματος	thing in exchange	neut.	ἀντι-[√]-μα
ἀπαλλάσσω	set free	vb.	ἀπο-[√]-σσω
ἀποκαταλλάσσω	reconcile	vb.	ἀπο-κατα-[√]-σσω
καταλλαγή ῆς	reconciliation	fem.	κατα-[√]-η
καταλλάσσω	reconcile	vb.	κατα-[√]-σσω
μεταλλάσσω	exchange	vb.	μετα-[√]-σσω
παραλλαγή ῆς	variation, change	fem.	παρα-[√]-η
συναλλάσσω	reconcile	vb.	συν-[√]-σσω

ὡς 914
as / how (manner)
Memory Aid: See Chart A.

≥25 καθώς	as, just as	adv.	κατα-[√]
καθώσπερ	as, just as	adv.	κατα-[√]-περ
≥25 ὅπως	that, in order that	cj./pt.	[√]-ως
≥25 πῶς	how? in what way?	cj./pt.	
≥10 πώς	somehow, in some way	cj./pt.	
≥25 ὡς	as, like	cj./pt.	
≥10 ὡσαύτως	likewise	adv.	[√]-[αὐτ]-ως
≥10 ὡσεί	like, as	cj./pt.	

≥25	ὥσπερ	as, just as	cj./pt.	[√]-περ
	ὡσπερεί	as (though)	prep.	[√]-περ
≥25	ὥστε	that, so that, thus	prep.	

ἐπι   896
on
Memory Aid: epidermis, epicenter, epidemic, epitaph

| ≥10 | ἐπάνω (*gen.*) | on, above, over | adv./prep. | [√]-ἀνα-ω |
| ≥25 | ἐπί (*gen., dat., acc.*) | upon, on, over | prep. | |

ἐχ οχ   852
have / hold
Memory Aid: cathexis

≥10	ἀνέχομαι	tolerate (>hold up under)	vb.	ἀνα-[√]-ω
	ἀνοχή ῆς	tolerance	fem.	ἀνα-[√]-η
	ἀντέχομαι	be loyal to, hold firmly	vb.	ἀντι-[√]-ω
≥10	ἀπέχω	receive in full	vb.	ἀπο-[√]-ω
	ἐνέχω	have grudge	vb.	ἐν-[√]-ω
	ἐπέχω	notice	vb.	ἐπι-[√]-ω
≥25	ἔχω	have	vb.	[√]-ω
≥10	κατέχω	hold fast, keep	vb.	κατα-[√]-ω
	μετέχω	share in, eat, have	vb.	μετα-[√]-ω
	μετοχή ῆς	partnership	fem.	μετα-[√]-η
	μέτοχος ου	partner	masc.	μετα-[√]-ος
≥10	παρέχω	cause	vb.	παρα-[√]-ω
	περιέχω	seize, overcome	vb.	περι-[√]-ω
	προέχομαι	be better off	vb.	προ-[√]-ω
	προκατέχω	have previously	vb.	προ-κατα-[√]-ω
	προσανέχω	approach	vb.	προς-ἀνα-[√]-ω
≥10	προσέχω	pay close attention to	vb.	προς-[√]-ω
	συμμέτοχος ου	sharer	masc.	συν-μετα-[√]-ος
≥10	συνέχω	surround, control	vb.	συν-[√]-ω
	ὑπερέχω	surpass, govern	vb.	ὑπερ-[√]-ω
	ὑπεροχή ῆς	position of authority	fem.	ὑπερ-[√]-η
	ὑπέχω	undergo, suffer	vb.	ὑπο-[√]-ω

προσ   744
to / toward
Memory Aid: prosthesis

| ≥25 | ἔμπροσθεν (*gen.*) | before | prep. | ἐν-[√]-θεν |
| ≥25 | πρός (*acc.*) | to, toward | prep. | |

κυρι   737
lord / power
Memory Aid: kyrios [*czar, kaiser, caesar*]

| | κατακυριεύω | have power over | vb. | κατα-[√]-ευω |

κυρία ας	lady	fem.	[√]-ια
κυριακός ή όν	belonging to the Lord	adj.	[√]-ακος
κυριεύω	rule, have power	vb.	[√]-ευω
≥25 κύριος ου	lord, master	masc.	[√]-ιος
κυριότης ητος	power, authority	fem.	[√]-οτης

ἵνα 679
in order that
Memory Aid:

| ≥25 ἵνα | in order that | cj./pt. | |
| ἱνατί | why? | cj./pt. | [√]-[τι] |

λεγ λογ λεκτ 673
say / word
Memory Aid: dialogue, eulogy, prologue, lexicon, dialect, elect

	ἄλογος ον	unreasoning, wild	adj.	ά-[√]-ος
	ἀναλογία ας	proportion	fem.	ἀνα-[√]-ια
	ἀναλογίζομαι	consider closely	vb.	ἀνα-[√]-ιζω
	ἀναπολόγητος ον	without excuse	adj.	ά-ἀπο-[√]-τος
	ἀνθομολογέομαι	give thanks	vb.	ἀντι-[ὁμο]-[√]-εω
	ἀντιλέγω	object to	vb.	ἀντι-[√]-ω
	ἀντιλογία ας	argument, hatred	fem.	ἀντι-[√]-ια
≥10	ἀπολογέομαι	speak in ones defense	vb.	ἀπο-[√]-εω
	ἀπολογία ας	defense (>apology)	fem.	ἀπο-[√]-ια
	βατταλογέω	babble	vb.	(βάττος)-[√]-εω
≥10	διαλέγομαι	discuss	vb.	δια-[√]-ω
	διάλεκτος ου	language (>dialect)	fem.	[√]-τος
	διαλογίζομαι	discuss	vb.	[√]-ιζω
	διαλογισμός οῦ	opinion, thought	masc.	[√]-ισμος
	δίλογος ον	two-faced	adj.	[δευ]-[√]-ος
≥10	ἐκλέγομαι	choose, select (>elect)	vb.	ἐκ-[√]-ω
≥10	ἐκλεκτός ή όν	chosen (>elected)	adj.	ἐκ-[√]-τος
	ἐκλογή ῆς	election, choosing	fem.	ἐκ-[√]-η
	ἐλλογέω	record	vb.	ἐν-[√]-εω
	ἐνευλογέω	bless	vb.	ἐν-[√]-εὐ-[√]-εω
≥10	ἐξομολογέω	agree, consent, admit	vb.	ἐκ-[ὁμο]-[√]-εω
	ἐπιλέγω	call, name	vb.	ἐπι-[√]-ω
≥25	εὐλογέω	bless (>eulogize)	vb.	εὐ-[√]-εω
	εὐλογητός ή όν	blessed, praised	adj.	εὐ-[√]-τος
≥10	εὐλογία ας	blessing (>eulogy)	fem.	εὐ-[√]-ια
	καταλέγω	enroll (>catalogue)	vb.	κατα-[√]-ω
	κατευλογέω	bless	vb.	κατα-εὐ-[√]-εω
≥25	λέγω	say	vb.	[√]-ω
	λόγια ων	oracles, words	neut.	[√]-ια
≥25	λογίζομαι	count, consider	vb.	[√]-ιζω

λογικός ή όν	rational, spiritual	adj.	[√]-ικος
λόγιος α ον	eloquent, learned	adj.	[√]-ιος
λογισμός οῦ	thought, reasoning	masc.	[√]-ισμος
λογομαχέω	fight about words	vb.	[√]-[μαχ]-εω
λογομαχία ας	quarrel about words	fem.	[√]-[μαχ]-ια
≥25 λόγος ου	word, message	masc.	[√]-ος
≥25 ὁμολογέω	confess, declare	vb.	[ὁμο]-[√]-εω
ὁμολογία ας	confession	fem.	[ὁμο]-[√]-ια
ὁμολογουμένως	undeniably	adv.	[ὁμο]-[√]-ως
παραλογίζομαι	deceive	vb.	παρα-[√]-ιζω
προλέγω	say (>prologue)	vb.	προ-[√]-ω
προσλέγω	answer, reply	vb.	προς-[√]-ω
συλλογίζομαι	discuss	vb.	συν-[√]-ιζω

διά 666
through
Memory Aid: diameter, diarrhea

≥25 διά (gen., acc.)	through, on account of	prep.	

ἀπο ἀπ ἀφ 645
from
Memory Aid: apostasy

≥25 ἀπό	from	prep.	

διδ δο δω 644
give
Memory Aid: antidote, dose [donor, donate, dole]

	ἀναδίδωμι	deliver (>give up)	vb.	ἀνα-[√]-μι
	ἀνταποδίδωμι	repay, return	vb.	ἀντι-ἀπο-[√]-μι
	ἀνταπόδομα ματος	repayment	neut.	ἀντι-ἀπο-[√]-μα
	ἀνταπόδοσις εως	repayment	fem.	ἀντι-ἀπο-[√]-σις
≥25	ἀποδίδωμι	give, pay	vb.	ἀπο-[√]-μι
	διαδίδωμι	distribute	vb.	δια-[√]-μι
≥25	δίδωμι	give	vb.	[√]-μι
	δόμα ματος	gift	neut.	[√]-μα
	δόσις εως	gift	fem.	[√]-σις
	δότης ου	giver	masc.	[√]-της
	ἐκδίδομαι	let out, lease	vb.	ἐκ-[√]-μι
	ἔκδοτος ον	given over	adj.	ἐκ-[√]-τος
≥10	ἐπιδίδωμι	deliver, give way	vb.	ἐπι-[√]-μι
	εὐμετάδοτος ον	liberal, generous	adj.	εὐ-μετα-[√]-τος
	μεταδίδωμι	give, share	vb.	μετα-[√]-μι
≥25	παραδίδωμι	hand over, deliver	vb.	παρα-[√]-μι
≥10	παράδοσις εως	tradition	fem.	παρα-[√]-σις
	πατροπαράδοτος ον	handed from ancestors	adj.	[πατρ]-παρα-[√]-τος

προδίδωμι	give first	vb.	προ-[√]-μι
προδότης ου	traitor	masc.	προ-[√]-της

πιστ   602
belief / faith
Memory Aid: epistemology, epistemic

ἀπιστέω	fail to believe	vb.	ἀ-[√]-εω
≥10 ἀπιστία ας	unbelief	fem.	ἀ-[√]-ια
≥10 ἄπιστος ον	unfaithful, unbelieving	adj.	ἀ-[√]-ος
ὀλιγοπιστία ας	little faith	fem.	[ὀλιγ]-[√]-ια
ὀλιγόπιστος ον	of little faith	adj.	[ὀλιγ]-[√]-ος
≥25 πιστεύω	believe	vb.	[√]-ευω
πιστικός ή όν	genuine	adj.	[√]-ικος
≥25 πίστις εως	faith, trust, belief	fem.	[√]-ς
πιστόομαι	firmly believe, entrust	vb.	[√]-οω
≥25 πιστός ή όν	faithful, believing	adj.	[√]-τος

ποι   595
make / do
Memory Aid: poem

ἀχειροποίητος ον	not made by hands	adj.	ἀ-[χειρ]-[√]-τος
εὐποιΐα ας	doing of good	fem.	εὐ-[√]-ια
περιποιέομαι	obtain, preserve	vb.	[περι]-[√]-εω
περιποίησις εως	obtaining, possession	fem.	[περι]-[√]-σις
≥25 ποιέω	make, do	vb.	[√]-εω
ποίημα ματος	something made	neut.	[√]-μα
ποίησις εως	undertaking	fem.	[√]-σις
ποιητής οῦ	one who does, doer	masc.	[√]-της
προσποιέομαι	pretend	vb.	προς-[√]-εω
συζωοποιέω	make alive together	vb.	συν-[ζω]-[√]-εω
χειροποίητος ον	hand / man-made	adj.	[χειρ]-[√]-τος

ἱστη στα στη   568
stand
Memory Aid: static, status, system, ecstasy

ἀκαταστασία ας	disorder	fem.	ἀ-κατα-[√]-ια
ἀκατάστατος ον	unstable	adj.	ἀ-κατα-[√]-τος
≥25 ἀνάστασις εως	resurrection	masc./fem.	ἀνα-[√]-σις
ἀναστατόω	agitate, incite a revolt	vb.	ἀνα-[√]-οω
≥10 ἀνθίστημι	resist	vb.	ἀντι-[√]-μι
≥25 ἀνίστημι	raise up, appoint	vb.	ἀνα-[√]-μι
ἀντικαθίστημι	resist	vb.	ἀντι-κατα-[√]-μι
ἀποκαθίστημι	reestablish, cure	vb.	ἀπο-κατα-[√]-μι
ἀποκατάστασις εως	restoration	fem.	ἀπο-κατα-[√]-σις
ἀποστασία ας	apostasy	fem.	ἀπο-[√]-ια
ἀποστάσιον ου	notice of divorce	neut.	ἀπο-[√]-ιον

ἀστατέω	be homeless, wander	vb.	ἀ-[√]-εω
≥10 ἀφίσταμαι	leave	vb.	ἀπο-[√]-μι
διάστημα ματος	interval	neut.	δια-[√]-μα
διΐστημι	part, past time	vb.	δια-[√]-μι
διχοστασία ας	division	fem.	[δευ]-[√]-ια
ἔκστασις εως	amazement (>ecstasy)	fem.	ἐκ-[√]-σις
ἐνίστημι	be present	vb.	ἐν-[√]-μι
ἐξανάστασις εως	resurrection	fem.	ἐκ-ἀνα-[√]-σις
ἐξανίστημι	have, stand up	vb.	ἐκ-ἀνα-[√]-μι
≥10 ἐξίστημι	be amazed, amaze	vb.	ἐκ-[√]-μι
ἐπανίσταμαι	turn against, rebel	vb.	ἐπι-ἀνα-[√]-μι
≥10 ἐπίσταμαι	know, understand	vb.	ἐπι-[√]-μι
ἐπίστασις εως	pressure, stirring up	fem.	ἐπι-[√]-σις
ἐπιστάτης ου	Master	masc.	ἐπι-[√]-της
ἐπιστήμων ον	understanding	adj.	ἐπι-[√]-μων
εὐπερίστατος ον	holding on tightly	adj.	εὐ-περι-[√]-τος
≥10 ἐφίστημι	come to, approach	vb.	ἐπι-[√]-μι
≥25 ἵστημι	set, stand	vb.	[√]-μι
≥10 καθίστημι	put in charge	vb.	κατα-[√]-μι
κατάστημα ματος	behavior	neut.	κατα-[√]-μα
κατεφίστημι	attack, set upon	vb.	κατα-ἐπι-[√]-μι
μεθίστημι	remove, mislead	vb.	μετα-[√]-μι
≥25 παρίστημι	present	vb.	παρα-[√]-μι
περιΐστημι	stand around	vb.	περι-[√]-μι
προΐστημι	be a leader, manage	vb.	προ-[√]-μι
προστάτις ιδος	helper (>stand before)	fem.	προ-[√]-ς
στασιαστής οῦ	rebel	masc.	[√]-της
στάσις εως	dispute, revolt	fem.	[√]-σις
≥10 στήκω	stand	vb.	[√]-ω
συνεφίστημι	join in an attack	vb.	συν-ἐπι-[√]-μι
≥10 συνίστημι	recommend, show	vb.	συν-[√]-μι
ὑπόστασις εως	conviction, confidence	fem.	ὑπο-[√]-σις

ἀνθρωπ   561
man

Memory Aid: anthropology, anthropomorphic

ἀνθρώπινος η ον	human	adj.	[√]-ινος
ἀνθρωποκτόνος ου	murderer	masc.	[√]-[κτειν]-ος
≥25 ἄνθρωπος ου	man, person	masc.	[√]-ος
φιλανθρωπία ας	kindness	fem.	[φιλ]-[√]-ια
φιλανθρώπως	considerately	adv.	[φιλ]-[√]-ως

κρι   553
judge

Memory Aid: critical, critic, crisis, critique, crime

ἀδιάκριτος ον	without favoritism	adj.	ἀ-δια-[√]-τος

ἀκατάκριτος ον	uncondemned	adj.	ἀ-κατα-[√]-τος
≥10 ἀνακρίνω	question, examine	vb.	ἀνα-[√]-ω
ἀνάκρισις εως	investigation	fem.	ἀνα-[√]-σις
ἀνταποκρίνομαι	reply	vb.	ἀντι-ἀπο-[√]-ω
ἀνυπόκριτος ον	sincere, genuine	adj.	ἀ-ὑπο-[√]-τος
ἀπόκριμα ματος	sentence	neut.	ἀπο-[√]-μα
≥25 ἀποκρίνομαι	answer, reply	vb.	ἀπο-[√]-νω
ἀπόκρισις εως	answer, reply	fem.	ἀπο-[√]-σις
αὐτοκατάκριτος ον	self-condemned	adj.	[αὐτο]-κατα-[√]-τος
≥10 διακρίνω	evaluate (mid. doubt)	vb.	δια-[√]-ω
διάκρισις εως	ability to discriminate	fem.	δια-[√]-σις
ἐγκρίνω	class with	vb.	ἐν-[√]-ω
εἰλικρίνεια ας	sincerity	fem.	(ἕλη)-[√]-εια
εἰλικρινής ές	sincere, pure	adj.	(ἕλη)-[√]-ης
ἐπικρίνω	decide	vb.	ἐπι-[√]-ω
κατάκριμα ματος	condemnation	neut.	κατα-[√]-μα
≥10 κατακρίνω	condemn, judge	vb.	κατα-[√]-ω
κατάκρισις εως	condemnation	fem.	κατα-[√]-σις
≥25 κρίμα τος	judgment, decision	neut.	[√]-μα
≥25 κρίνω	judge, consider	vb.	[√]-ω
≥25 κρίσις εως	judgment	fem.	[√]-σις
κριτήριον ου	court (judgment hall)	neut.	[√]-τηριον
≥10 κριτής οῦ	judge	masc.	[√]-της
κριτικός ή όν	able to judge	adj.	[√]-τικος
πρόκριμα ματος	prejudice (>pre-judging)	neut.	προ-[√]-μα
συγκρίνω	compare, interpret	vb.	συν-[√]-ω
συνυποκρίνομαι	act insincerely with	vb.	συν-ὑπο-[√]-ω
ὑποκρίνομαι	pretend, be a hypocrite	vb.	ὑπο-[√]-ω
ὑπόκρισις εως	hypocrisy	fem.	ὑπο-[√]-σις
≥10 ὑποκριτής οῦ	hypocrite	masc.	ὑπο-[√]-της

χρι χρις   549
anoint
Memory Aid: Christ, christen, chrism

ἀντίχριστος ου	Antichrist	masc.	ἀντι-[√]-τος
ἐγχρίω	rub on	vb.	ἐν-[√]-ω
ἐπιχρίω	smear	vb.	ἐπι-[√]-ω
χρῖσμα ματος	anointing	neut.	[√]-μα
Χριστιανός οῦ	Christian	masc.	[√]-ος
≥25 Χριστός οῦ	Christ	masc.	[√]-τος
χρίω	anoint	vb.	[√]-ω
ψευδόχριστος ου	false Christ	masc.	[ψευδ]-[√]-τος

κατ καθ[1]   523
down / according to
Memory Aid: catacomb, catapult, cataract, cataclysm

καθά	as, just as	cj./pt./adv.
≥10 καθάπερ	as, just as	cj./pt./adv. [√]-περ
καθό	as, according as	adv.
≥25 κατά (*gen., acc.*)	down, according to	prep.
κάτω	down, below	adv. [√]-ω
κατώτερος α ον	lower	adj. [√]-τερος
κατωτέρω	under	adv. [√]-ω
≥10 ὑποκάτω (*gen.*)	under	prep. ὑπο-[√]-ω

οτε   523
when

Memory Aid: See Chart A.

δήποτε	whatever	adv.
μηδέποτε	never	adv. [μη]-[√]
≥25 μήποτε	lest, whether, never	cj./pt. [μη]-[√]
ὁπότε	when	adv. [ὁπ]-[√]
≥25 ὅταν	when, whenever	adv. [√]-[ἀν]
≥25 ὅτε	when, while	cj./pt.
≥10 οὐδέποτε	never	adv. [οὐ]-[√]
≥25 πάντοτε	always, at all times	adv. [παν]-[√]
≥25 ποτέ	once, ever	cj./pt.
≥10 πότε	when?	adv.
πώποτε	ever, at any time	adv.
≥25 τότε	then	adv.

καλ² κλη   515
call

Memory Aid: paraclete, ecclesiastical

ἀνέγκλητος ον	beyond reproach	adj.	ἀ-ἐν-[√]-τος
ἀντικαλέω	invite in return	vb.	ἀντι-[√]-εω
ἐγκαλέω	accuse	vb.	ἐν-[√]-εω
ἔγκλημα ματος	accusation	neut.	ἐν-[√]-μα
εἰσκαλέομαι	invite in	vb.	εἰς-[√]-εω
≥25 ἐκκλησία ας	church, assembly	fem.	ἐκ-[√]-ια
≥25 ἐπικαλέω	call, name	vb.	ἐπι-[√]-εω
≥25 καλέω	call, name	vb.	[√]-εω
≥10 κλῆσις εως	call, calling	fem.	[√]-σις
≥10 κλητός ή όν	called, invited	adj.	[√]-τος
μετακαλέομαι	send for, invite	vb.	μετα-[√]-εω
≥25 παρακαλέω	beg, encourage	vb.	παρα-[√]-εω
≥25 παράκλησις εως	encouragement, help	fem.	παρα-[√]-σις
παράκλητος ου	helper (the Paraclete)	masc.	παρα-[√]-τος
προκαλέομαι	irritate	vb.	προ-[√]-εω
≥25 προσκαλέομαι	summon, invite	vb.	προς-[√]-εω
συγκαλέω	call together, summon	vb.	συν-[√]-εω
συμπαρακαλέομαι	be encouraged together	vb.	συν-παρα-[√]-εω

ἀγγελ   505
message
Memory Aid: angel, evangelist

ἀγγελία ας	message, news	fem.	[√]-ια
ἀγγέλλω	tell	vb.	[√]-ω
≥25 ἄγγελος ου	angel, messenger	masc.	[√]-ος
≥10 ἀναγγέλλω	tell, proclaim	vb.	ἀνα-[√]-ω
≥25 ἀπαγγέλλω	tell, proclaim	vb.	ἀπο-[√]-ω
ἀρχάγγελος ου	archangel	masc.	[ἀρχ]-[√]-ος
διαγγέλλω	preach, proclaim	vb.	δια-[√]-ω
ἐξαγγέλλω	tell, proclaim	vb.	ἐκ-[√]-ω
≥25 ἐπαγγελία ας	promise, decision	fem.	ἐπι-[√]-ια
≥10 ἐπαγγέλλομαι	promise, confess	vb.	ἐπι-[√]-ω
ἐπάγγελμα ματος	promise	neut.	ἐπι-[√]-μα
≥25 εὐαγγελίζω	evangelize	vb.	εὐ-[√]-ιζω
≥25 εὐαγγέλιον ου	good news, gospel	neut.	εὐ-[√]-ιον
εὐαγγελιστής οῦ	evangelist	masc.	εὐ-[√]-ιστης
ἰσάγγελος ον	angel-like	adj.	[ἰσ]-[√]-ος
καταγγελεύς έως	proclaimer	masc.	κατα-[√]-ευς
≥10 καταγγέλλω	proclaim	vb.	κατα-[√]-ω
παραγγελία ας	order, instruction	fem.	παρα-[√]-ια
≥25 παραγγέλλω	command, order	vb.	παρα-[√]-ω
προεπαγγέλλομαι	promise before	vb.	προ-ἐπι-[√]-ω
προευαγγελίζομαι	evangelize before	vb.	προ-εὐ-[√]-ιζω
προκαταγγέλλω	announce before	vb.	προ-κατα-[√]-ω

ἀκο ἀκου   504
hear
Memory Aid: acoustic

≥10 ἀκοή ῆς	hearing, report, news	fem.	[√]-η
≥25 ἀκούω	hear, understand	vb.	[√]-ω
διακούω	hear (legal cases)	vb.	δια-[√]-ω
εἰσακούω	hear, obey (>listen to)	vb.	εἰς-[√]-ω
ἐπακούω	hear, listen to	vb.	ἐπι-[√]-ω
παρακοή ῆς	disobedience, disloyalty	fem.	παρα-[√]-η
παρακούω	refuse to listen, disobey	vb.	παρα-[√]-ω
προακούω	hear before	vb.	προ-[√]-ω
≥10 ὑπακοή ῆς	obedience	fem.	ὑπο-[√]-η
≥10 ὑπακούω	obey	vb.	ὑπο-[√]-ω
ὑπήκοος ον	obedient	adj.	ὑπο-[√]-ος

οὖν   497
therefore
Memory Aid:

οὐκοῦν	so, then	adv.	[οὐ]-[√]

| ≥25 | οὖν | therefore | cj./pt. | |
| | τοιγαροῦν | therefore, then | cj./pt. | [ἀρ]-[√] |

μετα 476
with / after
Memory Aid: metaphysics, metamorphosis

| ≥25 | μετά (*gen., acc.*) | with, after | prep. | |
| | μεταξύ (*gen.*) | between, among | prep. | |

ἀγ ἀγωγ 455
lead / bring
Memory Aid: synagogue, demagogue, agent

≥25	ἄγω	lead	vb.	[√]-ω
	ἀγωγή ῆς	manner of life	fem.	[√]-η
	ἀνάγαιον ου	upstairs room	neut.	ἀνα-[√]-ον
≥10	ἀνάγω	lead up, bring up	vb.	ἀνα-[√]-ω
	ἀνεκδιήγητος ον	indescribable	adj.	ἀ-ἐκ-δια-[√]-τος
≥10	ἀπάγω	lead away, bring before	vb.	ἀπο-[√]-ω
	ἀποσυνάγωγος ον	excommunicated	adj.	ἀπο-συν-[√]-ος
	ἀρχισυνάγωγος ου	chief of a synagogue	masc.	[ἀρχ]-συν-[√]-ος
	διάγω	lead, spend (a life)	vb.	δια-[√]-ω
	διηγέομαι	tell fully	vb.	δια-[√]-εω
	διήγησις εως	account	fem.	δια-[√]-σις
≥10	εἰσάγω	lead / bring in	vb.	εἰς-[√]-ω
	ἐκδιηγέομαι	tell fully	vb.	ἐκ-δια-[√]-εω
≥10	ἐξάγω	lead / bring out	vb.	ἐκ-[√]-ω
	ἐξηγέομαι	tell, explain	vb.	ἐκ-[√]-εω
	ἐπάγω	bring upon	vb.	ἐπι-[√]-ω
	ἐπανάγω	return, put out	vb.	ἐπι-ἀνα-[√]-ω
	ἐπεισαγωγή ῆς	bringing in	fem.	ἐπι-εἰς-[√]-η
	ἐπισυνάγω	gather	vb.	ἐπι-συν-[√]-ω
	ἐπισυναγωγή ῆς	assembly	fem.	ἐπι-συν-[√]-η
	καθηγητής οῦ	teacher	masc.	κατα-[√]-της
	κατάγω	bring (down)	vb.	κατα-[√]-ω
≥10	κατηγορέω	accuse (bring against)	vb.	κατα-[√]-εω
	κατηγορία	accusation	fem.	κατα-[√]-ια
	κατήγορος ου	accuser	masc.	κατα-[√]-ος
	κατήγωρ ορος	accuser	masc.	κατα-[√]-ρ
	μετάγω	guide, direct	vb.	μετα-[√]-ω
≥10	παράγω	pass by (away)	vb.	παρα-[√]-ω
	παρεισάγω	bring in	vb.	παρα-εἰς-[√]-ω
	περιάγω	go around	vb.	περι-[√]-ω
≥10	προάγω	go before	vb.	προ-[√]-ω
	προηγέομαι	outdo, lead the way	vb.	προ-[√]-εω
	προσάγω	bring to or before	vb.	προς-[√]-ω

προσαγωγή ῆς	access	fem.	προς-[√]-η
συλαγωγέω	make captive	vb.	(συλάω)-[√]-εω
≥25 συνάγω	gather	vb.	συν-[√]-ω
≥25 συναγωγή ῆς	synagogue	fem.	συν-[√]-η
συναπάγομαι	be carried away	vb.	συν-ἀπο-[√]-ω
≥25 ὑπάγω	go (away)	vb.	ὑπο-[√]-ω
χειραγωγέω	lead by the hand	vb.	[χειρ]-[√]-εω
χειραγωγός οῦ	one who leads	masc.	[χειρ]-[√]-ος

γνο γνω γινω   445
know

Memory Aid: agnostic, gnosis, gnosticism, diagnosis

≥10 ἀγνοέω	be ignorant, disregard	vb.	ἀ-[√]-εω
ἀγνόημα ματος	sin done in ignorance	neut.	ἀ-[√]-μα
ἄγνοια ας	ignorance	fem.	ἀ-[√]-ια
ἀγνωσία ας	lack of spiritual insight	fem.	ἀ-[√]-ια
ἄγνωστος ον	unknown	adj.	ἀ-[√]-τος
ἀκατάγνωστος ον	above criticism	adj.	ἀ-κατα-[√]-τος
≥25 ἀναγινώσκω	read	vb.	ἀνα-[√]-σκω
ἀναγνωρίζομαι	make known again	vb.	ἀνα-[√]-ιζω
ἀνάγνωσις εως	reading	fem.	ἀνα-[√]-σις
≥25 γινώσκω	know, learn	vb.	[√]-σκω
γνώμη ης	purpose, will, opinion	fem.	[√]-η
≥25 γνωρίζω	make known, know	vb.	[√]-ιζω
≥25 γνῶσις εως	knowledge	fem.	[√]-σις
γνώστης ου	one familiar with	masc.	[√]-της
≥10 γνωστός ή όν	known (acquaintance)	adj.	[√]-τος
διαγινώσκω	investigate, decide	vb.	δια-[√]-σκω
διάγνωσις εως	decision (>diagnosis)	fem.	δια-[√]-σις
≥25 ἐπιγινώσκω	know, perceive	vb.	ἐπι-[√]-σκω
≥10 ἐπίγνωσις εως	knowledge	fem.	ἐπι-[√]-σις
καταγινώσκω	condemn	vb.	κατα-[√]-σκω
προγινώσκω	know already	vb.	προ-[√]-σκω
πρόγνωσις εως	foreknowledge, purpose	fem.	προ-[√]-σις
συγγνώμη ης	permission	fem.	συν-[√]-η

πατρ   436
father

Memory Aid: paternity, patriarch [Father: *see Grimm's Law*.]

ἀπάτωρ ορος	the fatherless	masc.	ἀ-[√]-ρ
≥25 πατήρ πατρός	father	masc.	[√]-ρ
πατριά ᾶς	family, nation	fem.	[√]-ια
πατριάρχης ου	patriarch	masc.	[√]-[ἀρχ]-ης
πατρικός ή όν	paternal	adj.	[√]-ικος
πατρίς ίδος	homeland	fem.	[√]-ς

| πατρῷος α ον | belonging to ancestors | adj. | [√]-ιος |
| προπάτωρ ορος | forefather | masc. | προ-[√]-ρ |

ἀρχ 435
begin / old / rule / chief
Memory Aid: monarch, archangel, archbishop, archetype, archaeology

ἀπαρχή ῆς	first-fruits	fem.	ἀπο-[√]-η
≥10 ἀρχαῖος α ον	old, ancient, former	adj.	[√]-ιος
≥25 ἀρχή ῆς	beginning, rule	fem.	[√]-η
ἀρχηγός οῦ	leader, founder	masc.	[√]-[ἀγ]-ος
ἀρχιερατικός όν	highpriestly	adj.	[√]-τικος
≥25 ἀρχιερεύς έως	high priest	masc.	[√]-ευς
ἀρχιποίμην ενος	chief shepherd	masc.	[√]-[ποιμ]-ην
≥25 ἄρχω	govern (mid. begin)	vb.	[√]-ω
≥25 ἄρχων οντος	ruler	masc.	[√]-ων
≥10 ἑκατοντάρχης ου	centurion	masc.	(ἑκατ)-[√]-ης
ἐνάρχομαι	begin	vb.	ἐν-[√]-ω
ἐπαρχεία ας	province (>thing ruled)	fem.	ἐπι-[√]-εια
προενάρχομαι	begin, begin before	vb.	προ-ἐν-[√]-ω
προϋπάρχω	exist previously	vb.	προ-ὑπο-[√]-ω
ὕπαρξις εως	possession	fem.	ὑπο-[√]-σις
≥25 ὑπάρχω	be under one's rule	vb.	ὑπο-[√]-ω
≥10 χιλίαρχος ου	tribune, officer	masc.	[χιλι]-[√]-ος

ἡμερ 435
day
Memory Aid: ephemeral

ἀνήμερος ον	fierce	adj.	ἀ-[√]-ος
ἐφημερία ας	division	fem.	ἐπι-[√]-ια
ἐφήμερος ον	daily	adj.	ἐπι-[√]-ος
≥25 ἡμέρα ας	day	fem.	[√]-α
καθημερινός ή όν	daily	adj.	κατα-[√]-ινος
ὀκταήμερος ον	on the eighth day	adj.	(ὀκτώ)-[√]-ος
≥25 σήμερον	today	adv.	[√]-ον

πν πνευ 429
spirit / wind / breath
Memory Aid: pneumonia, pneumatic

ἀποπνίγω	choke, drown	vb.	ἀπο-[√]-ω
ἐκπνέω	die	vb.	ἐκ-[√]-ω
ἐμπνέω	breathe	vb.	ἐν-[√]-ω
≥25 πνεῦμα ματος	spirit, self, wind	neut.	[√]-μα
≥25 πνευματικός ή όν	spiritual	adj.	[√]-τικος
πνευματικῶς	spiritually, symbolically	adv.	[√]-τικος-ως
πνέω	blow	vb.	[√]-ω

πνίγω	choke, drown	vb.	[√]-ω
πνικτός ή όν	strangled	adj.	[√]-τος
πνοή ῆς	wind, breath	fem.	[√]-η
ὑποπνέω	blow gently	vb.	ὑπο-[√]-ω

εἷς μια ἑν   424
one
Memory Aid: henotheism

≥25 εἷς μία ἕν	one, only	adj.	
ἑνότης ητος	unity	fem.	[√]-οτης
≥25 μηδείς μηδεμία μηδέν	no one	adj.	[μη]-[√]

λαμβ λημ λαβ   424
take / receive
Memory Aid: syllable, dilemma

≥10 ἀναλαμβάνω	take (up)	vb.	ἀνα-[√]-ανω
ἀνάλημψις εως	ascension (>taking up)	fem.	ἀνα-[√]-σις
ἀνεπίλημπτος ον	above reproach	adj.	ἀ-ἐπι-[√]-τος
ἀντιλαμβάνομαι	help	vb.	ἀντι-[√]-.ανω
ἀντίλημψις εως	ability to help, helper	fem.	ἀντι-[√]-σις
ἀπολαμβάνω	receive, get back	vb.	ἀπο-[√]-ανω
ἀπροσωπολήμπτως	impartially	adv.	ἀ-προς-[ὁρ]-[√]-ως
≥10 ἐπιλαμβάνομαι	take, seize, help	vb.	ἐπι-[√]-ανω
εὐλάβεια ας	godly fear, reverence	fem.	εὐ-[√]-εια
εὐλαβέομαι	act in reverence	vb.	εὐ-[√]-εω
εὐλαβής ές	reverent	adj.	εὐ-[√]-ης
≥10 καταλαμβάνω	obtain, attain, overtake	vb.	κατα-[√]-ανω
≥25 λαμβάνω	take, receive	vb.	[√]-ανω
λῆμψις εως	receiving	fem.	[√]-σις
μεταλαμβάνω	receive, share in	vb.	μετα-[√]-ανω
μετάλημψις εως	receiving, accepting	fem.	μετα-[√]-σις
≥25 παραλαμβάνω	take (along), receive	vb.	παρα-[√]-ανω
προλαμβάνω	do (take) ahead of time	vb.	προ-[√]-ανω
≥10 προσλαμβάνομαι	welcome, accept	vb.	προς-[√]-ανω
πρόσλημψις εως	acceptance	fem.	προς-[√]-σις
≥10 συλλαμβάνω	seize, arrest	vb.	συν-[√]-ανω
συμπαραλαμβάνω	take / bring along with	vb.	συν-παρα-[√]-ανω
συμπεριλαμβάνω	embrace, hug	vb.	συν-περι-[√]-ανω
συναντιλαμβάνομαι	(come to) help	vb.	συν-ἀντι-[√]-ανω
ὑπολαμβάνω	suppose, take away	vb.	ὑπο-[√]-ανω

οἰκ   418
house
Memory Aid: economy, ecology, ecosystem, ecumenical, diocese

| ἀνοικοδομέω | rebuild | vb. | [ἀνα]-[√]-[δημ]-εω |
| ἐγκατοικέω | live among | vb. | ἐν-κατα-[√]-εω |

ἐνοικέω	live in	vb.	ἐν-[√]-εω
ἐποικοδομέω	build on / build up	vb.	ἐπι-[√]-(δέμω)-εω
≥25 κατοικέω	live, inhabit	vb.	κατα-[√]-εω
κατοίκησις εως	home	fem.	κατα-[√]-σις
κατοικητήριον ου	house, home	neut.	κατα-[√]-τηριον
κατοικία ας	place where one lives	fem.	κατα-[√]-ια
κατοικίζω	place, put	vb.	κατα-[√]-ιζω
μετοικεσία ας	carrying off	fem.	μετα-[√]-ια
μετοικίζω	deport / send off	vb.	μετα-[√]-ιζω
οἰκεῖος ου	family member	masc.	[√]-ιος
οἰκετεία ας	household	fem.	[√]-εια
οἰκέτης ου	house servant	masc.	[√]-της
οἰκέω	live, dwell	vb.	[√]-εω
οἴκημα ματος	prison cell	neut.	[√]-μα
οἰκητήριον ου	home, dwelling	neut.	[√]-τηριον
≥25 οἰκία ας	home, family	fem.	[√]-ια
οἰκιακός οῦ	member of household	masc.	[√]-ακος
οἰκοδεσποτέω	run a household	vb.	[√]-(δεσπότης)-εω
≥10 οἰκοδεσπότης ου	master, householder	masc.	[√]-(δεσπότης)-της
≥25 οἰκοδομέω	build, encourage	vb.	[√]-(δέμω)-εω
≥10 οἰκοδομή ῆς	structure	fem.	[√]-(δέμω)-η
οἰκοδόμος ου	builder	masc.	[√]-(δέμω)-ος
οἰκονομέω	be a manager, steward	vb.	[√]-[νομ]-εω
οἰκονομία ας	task, responsibility	fem.	[√]-[νομ]-ια
≥10 οἰκονόμος ου	manager, steward	masc.	[√]-[νομ]-ος
≥25 οἶκος ου	house	masc.	[√]-ος
≥10 οἰκουμένη ης	world (>oikomenia)	fem.	[√]-η
οἰκουργός όν	domestic	adj.	[√]-[ἐργ]-ος
πανοικεί	with one's household	adv.	[παν]-[√]
παροικέω	live in, live as a stranger	vb.	παρα-[√]-εω
παροικία ας	stay, visit	fem.	παρα-[√]-ια
πάροικος ου	alien, stranger	masc.	παρα-[√]-ος
περιοικέω	live in neighborhood	vb.	περι-[√]-εω
περίοικος ου	neighbor	masc.	περι-[√]-ος
συνοικέω	live with	vb.	συν-[√]-εω

ἐκει ἐκειν   411
there
Memory Aid:

≥25 ἐκεῖ	there	adv.	
≥25 ἐκεῖθεν	from there	adv.	[√]-θεν
ἐκείνης	there	adv.	
≥25 ἐκεῖνος η ο	that	adj./pron.	[√]-ος
ἐκεῖσε	there	adv.	

ἐπέκεινα (*gen.*)	beyond	prep.	ἐπι-[√]-α
≥10 κἀκεῖ	and there	adv.	[και]
≥10 κἀκεῖθεν	from there	adv.	[και]-[√]-θεν
≥10 κἀκεῖνος η ο	and that one	pron.	[και]-[√]-ος
ὑπερέκεινα (*gen.*)	beyond	prep.	ὑπερ-[√]-α

βαλ βολ βλη   394
throw

Memory Aid: ballistic, diabolical [One *throws* a *ball*.]

	ἀμφιβάλλω	cast a net	vb.	ἀμφι-[√]-ω
	ἀμφίβληστρον ου	casting net	neut.	ἀμφι-[√]-τρον
	ἀναβάλλομαι	postpone	vb.	ἀνα-[√]-ω
	ἀναβολή ῆς	delay	fem.	ἀνα-[√]-η
	ἀντιβάλλω	exchange	vb.	ἀντι-[√]-ω
	ἀποβάλλω	throw off	vb.	ἀπο-[√]-ω
	ἀπόβλητος ον	rejected	adj.	ἀπο-[√]-τος
	ἀποβολή ῆς	loss, rejection	fem.	ἀπο-[√]-η
≥25	βάλλω	throw	vb.	[√]-ω
	βλητέος α ον	must be put, poured	adj.	[√]-ος
	βολή ῆς	throw	fem.	[√]-η
	βολίζω	measure depth	vb.	[√]-ιζω
	διαβάλλω	accuse (>throw against)	vb.	δια-[√]-ω
	διάβολος ον	accusing (falsely)	adj.	δια-[√]-ος
≥25	διάβολος ου	devil (the accuser)	masc.	δια-[√]-ος
≥25	ἐκβάλλω	force out, exclude	vb.	ἐκ-[√]-ω
	ἐκβολή ῆς	throwing overboard	fem.	ἐκ-[√]-η
	ἐμβάλλω	throw	vb.	ἐν-[√]-ω
≥10	ἐπιβάλλω	lay (hands) on	vb.	ἐπι-[√]-ω
	καταβάλλω	knock down	vb.	κατα-[√]-ω
≥10	καταβολή ῆς	beginning, foundation	fem.	κατα-[√]-η
	μεταβάλλομαι	change one's mind	vb.	μετα-[√]-ω
	παραβάλλω	arrive	vb.	παρα-[√]-ω
	παραβολεύομαι	risk	vb.	παρα-[√]-ευω
≥25	παραβολή ῆς	parable, symbol	fem.	παρα-[√]-η
	παρεμβάλλω	set up	vb.	παρα-ἐν-[√]-ω
≥10	παρεμβολή ῆς	barracks, camp	fem.	παρα-ἐν-[√]-η
≥10	περιβάλλω	put on, clothe	vb.	περι-[√]-ω
	περιβόλαιον ου	cloak, covering	neut.	περι-[√]-ιον
	προβάλλω	put forward	vb.	προ-[√]-ω
	συμβάλλω	meet, discuss	vb.	συν-[√]-ω
	ὑπερβαλλόντως	much more	adv.	ὑπερ-[√]-ως
	ὑπερβάλλω	surpass (>overthrow)	vb.	ὑπερ-[√]-ω
	ὑπερβολή ῆς	the extreme (>hyperbole)	fem.	ὑπερ-[√]-η
	ὑποβάλλω	bribe	vb.	ὑπο-[√]-ω

δυνα δυναμ   /   388
power / ability
Memory Aid: dynamic, dynamite, dynasty, dynamo

	ἀδυνατεῖ	it is impossible	vb.	ἀ-[√]-εω
≥10	ἀδύνατος ον	impossible, unable	adj.	ἀ-[√]-τος
≥25	δύναμαι	be able	vb.	[√]-μι
≥25	δύναμις εως	power, strength	fem.	[√]-ς
	δυναμόω	make strong	vb.	[√]-οω
	δυνάστης ου	ruler	masc.	[√]-της
	δυνατέω	be able, be strong	vb.	[√]-εω
≥25	δυνατός ή όν	able, possible, strong	adj.	[√]-τος
	ἐνδυναμόω	strengthen	vb.	ἐν-[√]-οω
	καταδυναστεύω	oppress	vb.	κατα-[√]-ευω

ἀδελφ   380
brother / sister
Memory Aid: Philadelphia

≥25	ἀδελφή ῆς	sister	fem.	[√]-η
≥25	ἀδελφός οῦ	brother, countryman	masc.	[√]-ος
	ἀδελφότης ητος	brotherhood	fem.	[√]-οτης
	φιλαδελφία ας	brotherly love	fem.	[φιλ]-[√]-ια
	φιλάδελφος ον	brother-loving	adj.	[φιλ]-[√]-ος
	ψευδάδελφος ου	false brother	masc.	[ψευδ]-[√]-ος

υἱ   380
son
Memory Aid:

	υἱοθεσία ας	adoption	fem.	[√]-[τιθ]-ια
≥25	υἱός οῦ	son, descendant	masc.	[√]-ος

πολλ πολυ   367
much / many
Memory Aid: polytheistic, polygamy

	πολλάκις	often	adv.	[√]-κις
	πολλαπλασίων ον	more	adj.	[√]-(πλασίων)-ων
	πολυλογία ας	many words	fem.	[√]-[λεγ]-ια
	πολυμερῶς	many times, bit by bit	adv.	[√]-[μερ]-ως
	πολυποίκιλος ον	in varied forms	adj.	[√]-(ποικίλος)-ος
≥25	πολύς πολλή πολύ	much, many	adj.	[√]-υς
	πολύσπλαγχνος ον	very compassionate	adj.	[√]-(σπλάγχνον)-ος
	πολυτελής ές	expensive	adj.	[√]-[τελ]-ης
	πολύτιμος ον	expensive	adj.	[√]-[τιμ]-ος
	πολυτρόπως	in many ways, variously	adv.	[√]-[τρεπ]-ως

ἐργ οὐργ   360
work

Memory Aid: liturgy, energy

	ἀργέω	be idle (>not working)	vb.	ἀ-[√]-εω
	ἀργός ή όν	idle, unemployed	adj.	ἀ-[√]-ος
	δημιουργός οῦ	builder	masc.	[δημ]-[√]-ος
	ἐνέργεια ας	work (>energy)	fem.	ἐν-[√]-εια
≥10	ἐνεργέω	work	vb.	ἐν-[√]-εω
	ἐνέργημα ματος	working, activity	neut.	ἐν-[√]-μα
	ἐνεργής ές	active, effective	adj.	ἐν-[√]-ης
≥25	ἐργάζομαι	work, do	vb.	[√]-αζω
	ἐργασία ας	gain, doing	fem.	[√]-σια
≥10	ἐργάτης ου	worker	masc.	[√]-της
≥25	ἔργον ου	work, action	neut.	[√]-ον
	εὐεργεσία ας	service, kind act	fem.	εὐ-[√]-ια
	εὐεργετέω	do good	vb.	εὐ-[√]-εω
	εὐεργέτης ου	benefactor	masc.	εὐ-[√]-της
≥25	καταργέω	destroy	vb.	κατα-[√]-εω
≥10	κατεργάζομαι	do, accomplish	vb.	κατα-[√]-αζω
	πανουργία ας	trickery	fem.	[παν]-[√]-ια
	πανοῦργος ον	tricky	adj.	[παν]-[√]-ος
	περιεργάζομαι	be a busybody	vb.	περι-[√]-αζω
	περίεργος ου	busybody	masc.	περι-[√]-ος
	προσεργάζομαι	make more	vb.	προς-[√]-αζω
	ῥαδιούργημα ματος	wrongdoing	neut.	ῥά]-[√]-μα
	ῥᾳδιουργία ας	wrongdoing	fem.	ῥά]-[√]-ια
	συνεργέω	work with	vb.	συν-[√]-εω
≥10	συνεργός οῦ	fellow-worker	masc.	συν-[√]-ος
	συνυπουργέω	join in, help	vb.	συν-ὑπο-[√]-εω

γραφ γραπ γραμ   345
write

Memory Aid: geography, calligraphy, graphite, grammar

	ἀγράμματος ον	uneducated	adj.	ἀ-[√]-τος
	ἀπογραφή ῆς	registration, census	fem.	ἀπο-[√]-η
	ἀπογράφω	register	vb.	ἀπο-[√]-ω
≥10	γράμμα ματος	letter, Scripture, account	neut.	[√]-μα
≥25	γραμματεύς έως	scribe	masc.	[√]-ευς
	γραπτός ή όν	written	adj.	[√]-τος
≥25	γραφή ῆς	Scripture	fem.	[√]-η
≥25	γράφω	write	vb.	[√]-ω
	ἐγγράφω	write, record	vb.	ἐν-[√]-ω
	ἐπιγραφή ῆς	inscription (>epigraph)	fem.	ἐπι-[√]-η
	ἐπιγράφω	write on	vb.	ἐπι-[√]-ω

καταγράφω	write	vb.	κατα-[√]-ω
προγράφω	write beforehand	vb.	προ-[√]-ω
ὑπογραμμός οῦ	example	masc.	ὑπο-[√]-ος
χειρόγραφον ου	record of debt	neut.	[χειρ]-[√]-ον

ἤ
or / than
Memory Aid:

≥25	ἤ	or, than	cj./pt.	
	ἤπερ	than	cj./pt.	[√]-περ
	ἤτοι	or	cj./pt.	

344

τιθ θε² θη
put / place
Memory Aid: synthesis, epithet, bibliotheca, thesis

	ἄθεσμος ον	lawless	adj.	ἀ-[√]-μος
≥10	ἀθετέω	reject, ignore (>not put)	vb.	ἀ-[√]-εω
	ἀθέτησις εως	nullification (>not put)	fem.	ἀ-[√]-σις
	ἀμετάθετος ον	unchangeable	adj.	ἀ-μετα-[√]-τος
	ἀνάθεμα ματος	cursed, anathematized	neut.	ἀνα-[√]-μα
	ἀναθεματίζω	curse, anathematize	vb.	ἀνα-[√]-ιζω
	ἀνάθημα ματος	offering, gift	neut.	ἀνα-[√]-μα
	ἀνατίθεμαι	present	vb.	ἀνα-[√]-μι
	ἀνεύθετος ον	unsuitable (>not well put)	adj.	ἀ-εὐ-[√]-τος
	ἀντιδιατίθεμαι	oppose	vb.	ἀντι-δια-[√]-μι
	ἀντίθεσις εως	antithesis, contradiction	fem.	ἀντι-[√]-σις
	ἀπόθεσις εως	removal	fem.	ἀπο-[√]-σις
	ἀποθήκη ης	barn	fem.	ἀπο-[√]-η
	ἀποτίθημι	throw (take) off	vb.	ἀπο-[√]-μι
	ἀσύνθετος ον	faithless, disloyal	adj.	ἀ-συν-[√]-τος
≥25	διαθήκη ης	covenant	fem.	δια-[√]-η
	διατίθεμαι	make (a covenant)	vb.	δια-[√]-μι
	ἔκθετος ον	abandoned	adj.	ἐκ-[√]-τος
	ἐκτίθεμαι	explain, expound	vb.	ἐκ-[√]-μι
	ἐπίθεσις εως	laying on (of hands)	fem.	ἐπι-[√]-σις
≥25	ἐπιτίθημι	put on, place	vb.	ἐπι-[√]-μι
	εὔθετος ον	suitable (>well placed)	adj.	εὐ-[√]-τος
	θήκη ης	sheath	fem.	[√]-η
	κ αταθεματίζω	curse	vb.	κατα-[√]-ιζω
	κατατίθημι	lay, place	vb.	κατα-[√]-μι
	μετάθεσις εως	removal, change	fem.	μετα-[√]-σις
	μετατίθημι	remove, change	vb.	μετα-[√]-μι
	παραθήκη ης	something entrusted	fem.	παρα-[√]-η
≥10	παρατίθημι	place before, give	vb.	παρα-[√]-μι
	περίθεσις εως	wearing (of jewelry)	fem.	περι-[√]-σις

336

περιτίθημι	put around	vb.	περι-[√]-μι
≥10 πρόθεσις εως	purpose, plan	fem.	προ-[√]-σις
προσανατίθεμαι	go for advice, add to	vb.	προς-ἀνα-[√]-μι
≥10 προστίθημι	add, increase, continue	vb.	προς-[√]-μι
προτίθεμαι	plan, intend	vb.	προ-[√]-μι
συγκατάθεσις εως	joint agreement	fem.	συν-κατα-[√]-σις
συγκατατίθεμαι	agree with	vb.	συν-κατα-[√]-μι
συνεπιτίθεμαι	join in the attack	vb.	συν-ἐπι-[√]-μι
συντίθεμαι	agree, arrange	vb.	συν-[√]-μι
≥25 τίθημι	put, place, lay	vb.	[√]-μι
ὑποτίθημι	risk (>place under)	vb.	ὑπο-[√]-μι

περι
around
Memory Aid: perimeter, peripheral

≥25 περί (gen., acc.)	about, concerning	prep.
πέριξ	around	adv.

λαλ
speak
Memory Aid: glossolalia

ἀλαλάζω	wail (>not speaking)	vb.	ἀ-[√]-αζω
ἀλάλητος ον	inexpressible	adj.	ἀ-[√]-τος
ἄλαλος ον	unable to speak, dumb	adj.	ἀ-[√]-ος
ἀνεκλάλητος ον	inexpressible in words	adj.	ἀ-ἐκ-[√]-τος
διαλαλέω	discuss	vb.	δια-[√]-εω
ἐκλαλέω	tell (>speak out)	vb.	ἐκ-[√]-εω
καταλαλέω	slander (>speak against)	vb.	κατα-[√]-εω
καταλαλιά ᾶς	slander	fem.	κατα-[√]-ια
κατάλαλος ου	slanderer	masc.	κατα-[√]-ος
≥25 λαλέω	speak	vb.	[√]-εω
λαλιά ᾶς	what is said, accent	fem.	[√]-ια
μογιλάλος ον	mute, dumb	adj.	(μόγος)-[√]-ος
προσλαλέω	speak to	vb.	προς-[√]-εω
συλλαλέω	talk with	vb.	συν-[√]-εω

οἰδ
know
Memory Aid:

≥25 οἶδα	know	vb.	[√]-ω
σύνοιδα	share knowledge with	vb.	συν-[√]-ω

ἀγαπ
love
Memory Aid: agape

≥25 ἀγαπάω	love	vb.	[√]-αω

332

328

322

318

≥25	ἀγάπη ης	love	fem.	[√]-η
≥25	ἀγαπητός ή όν	beloved	adj.	[√]-τος

ζω ζα
life

317

Memory Aid: zoology, zoo, protozoa

	ἀναζάω	revive	vb.	ἀνα-[√]-ω
≥25	ζάω	live	vb.	[√]-ω
≥25	ζωή ῆς	life	fem.	[√]-η
	ζῳογονέω	save life	vb.	[√]-[γεν]-εω
≥10	ζῷον ου	animal (>living thing)	neut.	[√]-ον
≥10	ζῳοποιέω	make alive	vb.	[√]-[ποι]-εω
	συζάω	live with	vb.	συν-[√]-ω

βασιλ
royal

311

Memory Aid: basilica

≥25	βασιλεία ας	reign, kingdom	fem.	[√]-εια
	βασίλειος ον	royal	adj.	[√]-ιος
≥25	βασιλεύς έως	king	masc.	[√]-ευς
≥10	βασιλεύω	rule, reign	vb.	[√]-ευω
	βασιλικός ή όν	royal	adj.	[√]-ικος
	βασίλισσα ης	queen	fem.	[√]-ισσα
	συμβασιλεύω	live together as kings	vb.	συν-[√]-ευω

δικ
just / judgment

309

Memory Aid: syndicate

≥25	ἀδικέω	wrong	vb.	ἀ-[√]-εω
	ἀδίκημα ματος	crime, sin, wrong	neut.	ἀ-[√]-μα
	ἀδικία ας	wrongdoing, evil	fem.	ἀ-[√]-ια
≥10	ἄδικος ον	evil, sinful	adj.	ἀ-[√]-ος
	ἀδίκως	unjustly	adv.	ἀ-[√]-ως
	ἀντίδικος ου	opponent at law, enemy	masc.	ἀντι-[√]-ος
	δικαιοκρισία ας	just judgment	fem.	[√]-[κρι]-ια
≥25	δίκαιος α ον	just, right	adj.	[√]-ιος
≥25	δικαιοσύνη ης	righteousness, justice	fem.	[√]-συνη
≥25	δικαιόω	acquit, make righteous	vb.	[√]-οω
≥10	δικαίωμα ματος	judgment, acquittal	neut.	[√]-μα
	δικαίως	justly	adv.	[√]-ως
	δικαίωσις εως	acquittal	fem.	[√]-σις
	δικαστής οῦ	judge	masc.	[√]-της
	δίκη ης	justice, punishment	fem.	[√]-η
	ἐκδικέω	avenge, punish	vb.	ἐκ-[√]-εω
	ἐκδίκησις εως	punishment	fem.	ἐκ-[√]-σις
	ἔκδικος ου	one who punishes	masc.	ἐκ-[√]-ος

ἔνδικος ον	just, deserved	adj.	ἐν-[√]-ος
καταδικάζω	condemn	vb.	κατα-[√]-αζω
καταδίκη ης	sentence, condemnation	fem.	κατα-[√]-η
ὑπόδικος ον	answerable to	adj.	ὑπο-[√]-ος

οὐραν 301
heaven
Memory Aid: Uranus

≥10 ἐπουράνιος ον	heavenly	adj.	ἐπι-[√]-ιος
οὐράνιος ον	heavenly	adj.	[√]-ιος
οὐρανόθεν	from heaven	adv.	[√]-θεν
≥25 οὐρανός οῦ	heaven	masc.	[√]-ος

ἁγι ἁγν 296
holy / sacred
Memory Aid: hagiology, Hapia Sophia

≥25 ἁγιάζω	make holy, purify	vb.	[√]-αζω
≥10 ἁγιασμός οῦ	consecration	masc.	[√]-σμος
≥25 ἅγιος α ον	holy, consecrated	adj.	[√]-ιος
ἁγιότης ητος	holiness	fem.	[√]-οτης
ἁγιωσύνη ης	holiness, consecration	fem.	[√]-συνη
ἁγνεία ας	moral purity	fem.	[√]-εια
ἁγνίζω	purify (>holy + ize)	vb.	[√]-ιζω
ἁγνισμός οῦ	purification	masc.	[√]-ισμος
ἁγνός ή όν	holy, pure	adj.	[√]-ος
ἁγνότης ητος	purity, sincerity	fem.	[√]-οτης
ἁγνῶς	purely	adv.	[√]-ως

μαθ μανθ 295
learn
Memory Aid: math

ἀμαθής ές	ignorant	adj.	ἀ-[√]-ης
καταμανθάνω	consider, observe	vb.	κατα-[√]-ανω
μαθητεύω	make a disciple	vb.	[√]-ευω
≥25 μαθητής οῦ	disciple, pupil	masc.	[√]-της
μαθήτρια ας	woman disciple	fem.	[√]-τρια
≥25 μανθάνω	learn, discover	vb.	[√]-ανω
συμμαθητής οῦ	fellow disciple	masc.	συν-[√]-της

πατ 290
walk
Memory Aid: Peripatetic

≥25 ἐμπεριπατέω	live among	vb.	ἐν-περι-[√]-εω
≥25 καταπατέω	trample on, despise	vb.	κατα-[√]-εω
πατέω	walk, trample	vb.	[√]-εω
≥25 περιπατέω	walk, move about, live	vb.	περι-[√]-εω

φα φη φημ   *286*
say / report
Memory Aid: prophet, euphemistic, blaspheme [*fame*]

	διαφημίζω	spread around	vb.	δια-[√]-ιζω
	δυσφημέω	slander	vb.	δυσ-[√]-εω
	δυσφημία ας	slander	fem.	δυσ-[√]-ια
	εὐφημία ας	good reputation	fem.	εὐ-[√]-ια
	εὔφημος ον	worthy of praise	adj.	εὐ-[√]-ος
≥10	προφητεία ας	prophesying	fem.	προ-[√]-εια
≥25	προφητεύω	prophesy, preach	vb.	προ-[√]-ευω
≥25	προφήτης ου	prophet	masc.	προ-[√]-της
	προφητικός ή όν	prophetic	adj.	προ-[√]-τικος
	προφῆτις ιδος	prophetess	fem.	προ-[√]-ς
	σύμφημι	agree with	vb.	συν-[√]-μι
	φάσις εως	news, report	fem.	[√]-σις
	φάσκω	claim, assert	vb.	[√]-σκω
	φήμη ης	report, news	fem.	[√]-η
≥25	φημί	say	vb.	[√]-μι
≥10	ψευδοπροφήτης ου	false prophet	masc.	[ψευδ]-προ-[√]-της

γη γε¹   *276*
earth
Memory Aid: geography, George

	γεωργέω	cultivate (>work earth)	vb.	[√]-[ἐργ]-εω
	γεώργιον ου	field (>worked earth)	neut.	[√]-[ἐργ]-ιον
≥10	γεωργός οῦ	farmer (>earth-worker)	masc.	[√]-[ἐργ]-ος
≥25	γῆ γῆς	earth, land, region	fem.	[√]-η
	ἐπίγειος ον	earthly	adj.	ἐπι-[√]-ιος

στελ στολ   *275*
send / equip
Memory Aid: apostle

≥25	ἀποστέλλω	send	vb.	ἀπο-[√]-ω
	ἀποστολή ῆς	apostleship	fem.	ἀπο-[√]-η
≥25	ἀπόστολος ου	apostle, messenger	masc.	ἀπο-[√]-ος
	διαστέλλομαι	order	vb.	δια-[√]-ω
	διαστολή ῆς	distinction	fem.	δια-[√]-η
≥10	ἐξαποστέλλω	send off	vb.	ἐκ-ἀπο-[√]-ω
	ἐπιστέλλω	write	vb.	ἐπι-[√]-ω
≥10	ἐπιστολή ῆς	letter	fem.	ἐπι-[√]-η
	καταστέλλω	quiet	vb.	κατα-[√]-ω
	στέλλομαι	avoid	vb.	[√]-ω
	συναποστέλλω	send along with	vb.	συν-ἀπο-[√]-ω
	συστέλλω	carry out	vb.	συν-[√]-ω
	ὑποστέλλω	draw back, hold back	vb.	ὑπο-[√]-ω
	ὑποστολή ῆς	shrinking / turning back	fem.	ὑπο-[√]-η

ἁμαρτ   270
sin
Memory Aid: hamartiology

≥25 ἁμαρτάνω	sin	vb.	[√]-ανω
ἁμάρτημα ματος	sin	neut.	[√]-μα
≥25 ἁμαρτία ας	sin	fem.	[√]-ια
≥25 ἁμαρτωλός όν	sinful	adj.	[√]-λος
ἀναμάρτητος ον	sinless	adj.	ἀ-[√]-τος
προαμαρτάνω	sin previously	vb.	προ-[√]-ανω

θελ   270
will
Memory Aid: monothelite

≥25 θέλημα ματος	will, desire	neut.	[√]-μα
θέλησις εως	will	fem.	[√]-σις
≥25 θέλω	wish, want	vb.	[√]-ω

θαν θνη   269
death
Memory Aid: euthanasia

ἀθανασία ας	immortality	fem.	ἀ-[√]-ια
≥25 ἀποθνήσκω	die, face death	vb.	ἀπο-[√]-σκω
ἐπιθανάτιος ον	sentenced to death	adj.	ἐπι-[√]-ιος
ἡμιθανής ές	half dead	adj.	[ἡμι]-[√]-ης
θανάσιμον ου	deadly poison	neut.	[√]-ιμος
θανατηφόρος ον	deadly	adj.	[√]-[φερ]-ος
≥25 θάνατος ου	death	masc.	[√]-ος
≥10 θανατόω	kill (>make dead)	vb.	[√]-οω
θνήσκω	die	vb.	[√]-σκω
θνητός ή όν	mortal	adj.	[√]-τος
συναποθνήσκω	die with	vb.	συν-ἀπο-[√]-σκω

χαρι χαριστ   262
gift
Memory Aid: charismatic, charity, Eucharist

ἀχάριστος ον	ungrateful	adj.	ἀ-[√]-τος
≥25 εὐχαριστέω	thank, be thankful	vb.	εὐ-[√]-εω
≥10 εὐχαριστία ας	thanksgiving (eucharist)	fem.	εὐ-[√]-ια
εὐχάριστος ον	thankful	adj.	εὐ-[√]-τος
≥10 χαρίζομαι	give, forgive	vb.	[√]-ιζω
χάριν	for sake of, because of	prep.	
≥25 χάρις ιτος	grace, favor, kindness	fem.	[√]-ς
≥10 χάρισμα ματος	gift	neut.	[√]-μα
χαριτόω	give freely (>make a gift)	vb.	[√]-οω

βαιν βα βη βασ   *261*
go / foot

Memory Aid: Anabasis, acrobat, base

≥25 ἀναβαίνω	go up, ascend, grow	vb.	ἀνα-[√]-ω
ἀναβιβάζω	make to go, draw, drag	vb.	ἀνα-[√]-αζω
ἀπαράβατος ον	permanent	adj.	ἀ-παρα-[√]-τος
ἀποβαίνω	get out, go from	vb.	ἀπο-[√]-ω
βαθμός οῦ	standing, position	masc.	[√]-μος
βάσις εως	foot (>base)	fem.	[√]-ς
≥10 βῆμα ματος	judgment bench	neut.	[√]-μα
διαβαίνω	cross, cross over	vb.	δια-[√]-ω
ἐκβαίνω	leave, go out	vb.	ἐκ-[√]-ω
≥10 ἐμβαίνω	get in, embark	vb.	ἐν-[√]-ω
ἐπιβαίνω	embark, arrive	vb.	ἐπι-[√]-ω
≥25 καταβαίνω	descend, fall	vb.	κατα-[√]-ω
κατάβασις εως	descent, slope	fem.	[√]-ς
≥10 μεταβαίνω	leave, move	vb.	μετα-[√]-ω
παραβαίνω	break, disobey	vb.	παρα-[√]-ω
παράβασις εως	disobedience	fem.	παρα-[√]-ς
παραβάτης ου	one who disobeys	masc.	παρα-[√]-της
προβαίνω	go on	vb.	προ-[√]-ω
προσαναβαίνω	move up	vb.	προς-ἀνα-[√]-ω
συγκαταβαίνω	come down with	vb.	συν-κατα-[√]-ω
συμβαίνω	happen, come about	vb.	συν-[√]-ω
συμβιβάζω	bring together	vb.	συν-[√]-αζω
συναναβαίνω	come up together	vb.	συν-ἀνα-[√]-ω
ὑπερβαίνω	do wrong to	vb.	ὑπερ-[√]-ω

προ πρω πρωτ   *254*
before / first

Memory Aid: prologue, prophesy, prototype, prognosis

≥10 πρίν	before	cj./pt.	
≥25 πρό (*gen.*)	before	prep.	
≥10 πρότερος α ον	former, earlier	adj.	[√]-τερος
≥10 πρωΐ	morning	adv.	
πρωΐα ας	morning	fem.	[√]-ια
πρωϊνός ή όν	morning	adj.	[√]-ινος
πρῷρα ης	prow, bow	fem.	[√]-α
πρωτεύω	have first place	vb.	[√]-ευω
≥25 πρῶτον	in the first place, earlier	adv.	[√]-ον
≥25 πρῶτος η ον	first, earlier, leading	adj.	[√]-τος
πρωτοστάτης ου	ring-leader	masc.	[√]-[ίστη]-της
πρωτοτόκια ων	birthright	neut.	[√]-[τεκν]-ια

πρωτότοκος ον	first-born	adj.	[√]-[τεκν]-ος
πρώτως	for the first time, firstly	adv.	[√]-ως
φιλοπρωτεύω	desire to be first	vb.	[√]-[φιλ]-ευω

νομ 253
law

Memory Aid: nomos, antinomian, astronomy, Deuteronomy

≥10	ἀνομία ας	lawlessness, wickedness	fem.	ἀ-[√]-ια
	ἄνομος ον	lawless	adj.	ἀ-[√]-ος
	ἀνόμως	lawlessly, without law	adv.	ἀ-[√]-ως
	ἔννομος ον	legal, subject to law	adj.	ἐν-[√]-ος
≥10	νομίζω	suppose	vb.	[√]-ιζω
	νομικός ή όν	legal	adj.	[√]-ικος
	νομίμως	lawfully	adv.	[√]-ως
	νόμισμα ματος	coin (>legal tender)	neut.	[√]-μα
	νομοδιδάσκαλος ου	teacher of law	masc.	[√]-[διδασκ]-ος
	νομοθεσία ας	giving of the law	fem.	[√]-[τιθ]-ια
	νομοθετέομαι	be given the law	vb.	[√]-[τιθ]-εω
	νομοθέτης ου	lawgiver	masc.	[√]-[τιθ]-της
≥25	νόμος ου	law	masc.	[√]-ος
	παρανομέω	act contrary to the law	vb.	παρα-[√]-εω
	παρανομία ας	offense	fem.	παρα-[√]-ια

πορ 240
journey

Memory Aid: emporium, pore [Fare, far: see *Grimm's Law*.]

	διαπορεύομαι	go through	vb.	δια-[√]-ευω
≥10	εἰσπορεύομαι	go / come in, enter	vb.	εἰς-[√]-ευω
≥25	ἐκπορεύομαι	go / come out	vb.	ἐκ-[√]-ευω
	ἐμπορεύομαι	be in business, exploit	vb.	ἐν-[√]-ευω
	ἐμπορία ας	business	fem.	ἐν-[√]-ια
	ἐμπόριον ου	market (>emporium)	neut.	ἐν-[√]-ιον
	ἔμπορος ου	merchant	masc.	ἐν-[√]-ος
	ἐπιπορεύομαι	come to	vb.	ἐπι-[√]-ευω
	εὐπορέομαι	have financial means	vb.	εὐ-[√]-εω
	εὐπορία ας	wealth	fem.	εὐ-[√]-ια
	παραπορεύομαι	pass by, go	vb.	παρα-[√]-ευω
	πορεία ας	journey	fem.	[√]-εια
≥25	πορεύομαι	journey, go, live	vb.	[√]-ευω
	πόρρω	far away	adv.	[√]-ω
	πόρρωθεν	from a distance	adv.	[√]-θεν
	πορρώτερον	farther	adv.	[√]-τερος
	προπορεύομαι	go before	vb.	προ-[√]-ευω
	προσπορεύομαι	come to	vb.	προς-[√]-ευω
	συμπορεύομαι	go along with	vb.	συν-[√]-ευω

ὀνομ 239
name

Memory Aid: onomatopoeia, synonym, pseudonym

ἐπονομάζομαι	call oneself	vb.	ἐπι-[√]-αζω
≥25 ὄνομα ματος	name	neut.	[√]-μα
ὀνομάζω	name, call	vb.	[√]-αζω
ψευδώνυμος ον	so-called	adj.	[ψευδ]-[√]-ος

δοξ 235
glory

Memory Aid: doxology

≥25 δόξα ης	glory, power	fem.	[√]-α
≥25 δοξάζω	praise, honor	vb.	[√]-αζω
ἐνδοξάζομαι	receive glory	vb.	ἐν-[√]-αζω
ἔνδοξος ον	glorious, fine	adj.	ἐν-[√]-ος
κενοδοξία ας	conceit (>empty glory)	fem.	[κενο]-[√]-ια
κενόδοξος ον	conceited	adj.	[κενο]-[√]-ος
συνδοξάζομαι	share in glory	vb.	συν-[√]-αζω

πλη πληθ πληρ 232
full

Memory Aid: plethora, pleroma, plenary

ἀναπληρόω	meet requirements	vb.	ἀνα-[√]-οω
ἀνταναπληρόω	complete (>make full)	vb.	ἀντι-ἀνα-[√]-οω
ἀποπληρόω	meet requirements	vb.	ἀπο-[√]-οω
ἐκπληρόω	fulfill (>make happen)	vb.	ἐκ-[√]-οω
≥10 ἐκπλήρωσις εως	completion, end	fem.	ἐκ-[√]-σις
ἐμπίμπλημι	fill, satisfy, enjoy	vb.	ἐν-[√]-μι
παμπληθεί	together	adv.	[παν]-[√]
≥10 πίμπλημι	fill, end	vb.	[√]-μι
≥25 πλῆθος ους	crowd	neut.	[√]-ς
≥10 πληθύνω	increase	vb.	[√]-υνω
πλήμμυρα ης	flood	fem.	[√]-α
≥10 πλήρης ες	full	adj.	[√]-ης
πληροφορέω	accomplish	vb.	[√]-[φερ]-εω
πληροφορία ας	certainty	fem.	[√]-[φερ]-ια
≥25 πληρόω	fulfill (>make happen)	vb.	[√]-οω
≥10 πλήρωμα ματος	fullness	neut.	[√]-μα
πλησμονή ῆς	satisfaction	fem.	[√]-η
προσαναπληρόω	supply, provide	vb.	προς-ἀνα-[√]-οω
συμπληρόω	draw near, end	vb.	συν-[√]-οω

φερ φορ 231
bring / bear / carry

Memory Aid: euphoria, paraphernalia [Bear: *see Grimm's Law.*]

	ἀναφέρω	offer (>bring up)	vb.	ἀνα-[√]-ω
	ἀποφέρω	take, carry away	vb.	ἀπο-[√]-ω
	ἀποφορτίζομαι	unload	vb.	ἀπο-[√]-ιζω
≥10	διαφέρω	be superior, carry through	vb.	δια-[√]-ω
	δωροφορία ας	a bearing of gifts	fem.	[δωρ]-[√]-ια
	εἰσφέρω	bring in	vb.	εἰς-[√]-ω
	ἐκφέρω	carry out, yield	vb.	ἐκ-[√]-ω
	ἐπιφέρω	bring upon, inflict	vb.	ἐπι-[√]-ω
	εὐφορέω	produce good crops	vb.	εὐ-[√]-εω
	καταφέρω	bring against	vb.	κατα-[√]-ω
	παραφέρω	remove, carry away	vb.	παρα-[√]-ω
	παρεισφέρω	exert	vb.	παρα-εἰς-[√]-ω
	περιφέρω	carry about, bring	vb.	περι-[√]-ω
≥25	προσφέρω	offer, do	vb.	προς-[√]-ω
	προσφορά ᾶς	offering, sacrifice	fem.	προς-[√]-α
	προφέρω	progress, produce	vb.	προ-[√]-ω
≥10	συμφέρω	be helpful / useful	vb.	συν-[√]-ω
	σύμφορον ου	advantage, benefit	neut.	συν-[√]-ον
	τροφοφορέω	care for	vb.	[τρεφ]-[√]-εω
	ὑποφέρω	endure, bear up under	vb.	ὑπο-[√]-ω
≥25	φέρω	bring, carry	vb.	[√]-ω
	φορέω	wear	vb.	[√]-εω
	φόρος ου	tax (>burden)	masc.	[√]-ος
	φορτίζω	burden, load	vb.	[√]-ιζω
	φορτίον ου	burden, cargo	neut.	[√]-ιον

ἰδ   229
see
Memory Aid: idea, idol

	εἰδέα ας	appearance, form	fem.	[√]-α
	εἶδος ους	visible form, sight	neut.	[√]-ς
≥25	ἴδε	Behold! here is	interj.	
≥25	ἰδού	Behold! here is	interj.	

ἀνηρ ἀνδρ   221
man
Memory Aid: android, androgynous

	ἀνδραποδιστής οῦ	kidnapper, slave dealer	masc.	[√]-[πο²]-ιστης
	ἀνδρίζομαι	act like a man	vb.	[√]-ιζω
	ἀνδροφόνος ου	murderer	masc.	[√]-(φενω)-ος
≥25	ἀνήρ ἀνδρός	man, husband	masc.	[√]-ρ
	ὕπανδρος ον	married (>under + man)	adj.	ὑπο-[√]-ος
	φίλανδρος ον	husband-loving	adj.	[φιλ]-[√]-ος

ὑπο
under / by means of
Memory Aid: hypodermic

≥25	ὑπό (*gen., acc.*)	under, by means of	prep.

217

μεγ μεγαλ
great
Memory Aid: megaphone, megaton, megalomania

	μεγαλεῖον ου	great / mighty act	neut.	[√]-ιον
	μεγαλειότης ητος	greatness, majesty	fem.	[√]-οτης
	μεγαλύνω	enlarge	vb.	[√]-υνω
	μεγαλωσύνη ης	greatness, majesty	fem.	[√]-συνη
	μεγάλως	greatly	adv.	[√]-ως
≥25	μέγας μεγάλη μέγα	great, large	adj.	
	μέγεθος ους	greatness	neut.	[√]-ς
	μεγιστάν ᾶνος	person of high position	masc.	[√]-ς
	μέγιστος η ον	very great, greatest	adj.	[√]-ιστος

215

διδασκ διδακ διδαχ
teach
Memory Aid: didactic, Didache

	διδακτικός ή όν	able to teach	adj.	[√]-τικος
	διδακτός ή όν	taught	adj.	[√]-τος
≥10	διδασκαλία ας	teaching, instruction	fem.	[√]-ια
≥25	διδάσκαλος ου	teacher	masc.	[√]-ος
≥25	διδάσκω	teach	vb.	[√]-ω
≥25	διδαχή ῆς	instruction	fem.	[√]-η
	ἑτεροδιδασκαλέω	teach different doctrine	vb.	[ἑτερ]-[√]-εω
	θεοδίδακτος ον	taught by God	adj.	[θε]-[√]-τος
	καλοδιδάσκαλος ον	teaching what is good	adj.	[καλ¹]-[√]-ος

214

γυνη γυναικ
woman
Memory Aid: gynecology, polygyny, androgynous

	γυναικάριον ου	foolish woman	neut.	[√]-αριον
	γυναικεῖος α ον	female	adj.	[√]-ιος
≥25	γυνή αικός	woman, wife	fem.	[√]-ς

211

μεν² μον
wait / remain
Memory Aid: remain

	ἀναμένω	wait expectantly	vb.	ἀνα-[√]-ω
	διαμένω	remain, stay	vb.	δια-[√]-ω
	ἐμμένω	remain faithful	vb.	ἐν-[√]-ω

207

≥10	ἐπιμένω	remain, continue	vb.	ἐπι-[√]-ω
	καταμένω	remain, stay, live	vb.	κατα-[√]-ω
≥25	μένω	remain	vb.	[√]-ω
	μονή ῆς	room	fem.	[√]-η
	παραμένω	remain, stay	vb.	παρα-[√]-ω
	περιμένω	wait for	vb.	περι-[√]-ω
	προσμένω	remain (with)	vb.	προς-[√]-ω
≥10	ὑπομένω	endure (>stay under)	vb.	ὑπο-[√]-ω
≥25	ὑπομονή ῆς	endurance (>stay under)	fem.	ὑπο-[√]-η

φων   207
voice
Memory Aid: symphony, telephone, phonetics, euphony, phoneme

	ἀναφωνέω	call out	vb.	ἀνα-[√]-εω
	ἀσύμφωνος ον	in disagreement	adj.	ἀ-συν-[√]-ος
	ἄφωνος ον	dumb, silent	adj.	ἀ-[√]-ος
	ἐπιφωνέω	shout	vb.	ἐπι-[√]-εω
	κενοφωνία ας	foolish (empty) talk	fem.	[κενο]-[√]-ια
	προσφωνέω	call to, address	vb.	προς-[√]-εω
	συμφωνέω	agree with	vb.	συν-[√]-εω
	συμφώνησις εως	agreement	fem.	συν-[√]-σις
	συμφωνία ας	music (>symphony)	fem.	συν-[√]-ια
	σύμφωνον ου	mutual consent	neut.	συν-[√]-ον
≥25	φωνέω	call	vb.	[√]-εω
≥25	φωνή ῆς	voice, sound	fem.	[√]-η

κοσμ   200
world / order
Memory Aid: cosmos, cosmetics, cosmopolitan

≥10	κοσμέω	adorn, put in order	vb.	[√]-εω
	κοσμικός ή όν	worldly, man-made	adj.	[√]-ικος
	κόσμιος ον	ordered, well-behaved	adj.	[√]-ιος
	κοσμοκράτωρ ορος	world-ruler	masc.	[√]-[κρατ]-τωρ
≥25	κόσμος ου	world, universe	masc.	[√]-ος

μαρτυρ   198
witness
Memory Aid: martyr

	ἀμάρτυρος ον	without witness	adj.	ἀ-[√]-ος
≥10	διαμαρτύρομαι	declare solemnly	vb.	δια-[√]-ω
	ἐπιμαρτυρέω	witness, declare	vb.	ἐπι-[√]-εω
	καταμαρτυρέω	witness against	vb.	κατα-[√]-εω
≥25	μαρτυρέω	testify, affirm	vb.	[√]-εω
≥25	μαρτυρία ας	witness, testimony	fem.	[√]-ια
≥10	μαρτύριον ου	witness, testimony	neut.	[√]-ιον
	μαρτύρομαι	witness, testify, urge	vb.	[√]-ω

≥25	μάρτυς μάρτυρος	witness, martyr	masc.	[√]-ς
	προμαρτύρομαι	predict	vb.	προ-[√]-ω
	συμμαρτυρέω	testify in support of	vb.	συν-[√]-εω
	συνεπιμαρτυρέω	add further witness	vb.	συν-ἐπι-[√]-εω

αἰών
age
193

Memory Aid: aeon

≥25	αἰών ῶνος	age, eternity	masc.	[√]-ων
≥25	αἰώνιος ον	eternal	adj.	[√]-ιος

μεν¹
particle of contrast
193

Memory Aid:

≥25	μέν	(used to show contrast)	cj./pt.	
	μενοῦν	rather	cj./pt.	[√]-[ουν]
	μέντοι	but	cj./pt.	

παρα
by
191

Memory Aid: parallel, paramedic

≥25	παρά (*gen., dat., acc.*) by, with	prep.	

ἀν¹
particle indicating contingency
187

Memory Aid:

≥25	ἄν	(signals contingency)	cj./pt.	
	ἐπάν	when	cj./pt.	ἐπι-[√]
≥10	κἄν (καὶ ἐάν)	even if	cj./pt.	[καὶ]-[√]-[εἰ]

ου
where
187

Memory Aid: Sounds like French *où: where.* See Chart A.

	δήπου	of course	adv.	
≥25	ὅπου	where	adv.	
≥10	οὗ	where	adv.	
≥25	πόθεν	from where, where	adv.	[√]-θεν
	πού	somewhere	adv.	
≥25	ποῦ	where?	adv.	

χειρ
hand
186

Memory Aid: chiropractic, enchiridion

	αὐτόχειρ ος	doer	masc./fem.	[αὐτ]-[√]-ρ
	διαχειρίζομαι	seize and kill	vb.	δια-[√]-ιζω
	ἐπιχειρέω	undertake	vb.	ἐπι-[√]-εω
	προχειρίζομαι	choose in advance	vb.	προ-[√]-ιζω

	προχειροτονέω	choose in advance	vb.	προ-[√]-[τεν]-εω
≥25	χείρ χειρός	hand	fem.	[√]-ρ

βλεπ βλεψ βλεμ   185
see

Memory Aid: A *blemish* is a *visible* flaw.

≥25	ἀναβλέπω	look up, regain sight	vb.	ἀνα-[√]-ω
	ἀνάβλεψις εως	restoration of sight	fem.	ἀνα-[√]-σις
	ἀποβλέπω	keep ones eyes on	vb.	ἀπο-[√]-ω
	βλέμμα ματος	what is seen, sight	neut.	[√]-μα
≥25	βλέπω	see, look	vb.	[√]-ω
	διαβλέπω	see clearly	vb.	δια-[√]-ω
≥10	ἐμβλέπω	look at, consider	vb.	ἐν-[√]-ω
	ἐπιβλέπω	look upon (with care)	vb.	ἐπι-[√]-ω
	περιβλέπομαι	look around	vb.	περι-[√]-ω
	προβλέπομαι	provide	vb.	προ-[√]-ω

ἀληθ   183
true

Memory Aid:

≥25	ἀλήθεια ας	truth, truthfulness	fem.	[√]-εια
	ἀληθεύω	be truthful, honest	vb.	[√]-ευω
≥25	ἀληθής ές	true, truthful, genuine	adj.	[√]-ης
≥25	ἀληθινός ή όν	real, true, genuine	adj.	[√]-ινος
≥10	ἀληθῶς	truly, actually	adv.	[√]-ως

δευτερ δυο   182
two

Memory Aid: duo, duet

	δευτεραῖος α ον	in two days	adj.	[√]-ιος
	δευτερόπρωτος ον	the next	adj.	[√]-[προ]-ος
≥25	δεύτερος α ον	second	adj.	[√]-ος
≥25	δύο	two	adj.	

δουλ   180
slave

Memory Aid: *Slaves do lots.*

	δουλαγωγέω	bring under control	vb.	[√]-[ἀγ]-εω
	δουλεία ας	slavery	fem.	[√]-εια
≥25	δουλεύω	serve, be enslaved	vb.	[√]-ευω
	δούλη ης	female servant	fem.	[√]-η
	δοῦλος η ον	slave-like	adj.	[√]-ος
≥25	δοῦλος ου	servant, slave	masc.	[√]-ος
	δουλόω	enslave (>make a slave)	vb.	[√]-οω
	καταδουλόω	make a slave of	vb.	κατα-[√]-οω
≥10	σύνδουλος ου	fellow-slave (servant)	masc.	συν-[√]-ος

ἐγειρ ἐγερ γρηγορ   *180*
raise / rouse
Memory Aid: *Gregory* the Great *raised* the papal office.

≥10	γρηγορέω	be awake, watch	vb.	[√]-εω
	διαγρηγορέω	become fully awake	vb.	δια-[√]-εω
	διεγείρω	awake	vb.	δια-[√]-ω
≥25	ἐγείρω	raise	vb.	[√]-ω
	ἔγερσις εως	resurrection	fem.	[√]-σις
	ἐξεγείρω	raise	vb.	ἐκ-[√]-ω
	ἐπεγείρω	stir up	vb.	ἐπι-[√]-ω
	συνεγείρω	raise together	vb.	συν-[√]-ω

ἱη ε   *180*
let / send
Memory Aid:

	ἄνεσις εως	relief (>let up)	fem.	ἀνα-[√]-σις
	ἀνίημι	loosen, stop, desert	vb.	ἀνα-[√]-μι
	ἀσύνετος ον	without understanding	adj.	ἀ-συν-[√]-τος
≥10	ἄφεσις εως	forgiveness	fem.	ἀπο-[√]-σις
≥25	ἀφίημι	forgive, cancel	vb.	ἀπο-[√]-μι
	ἐγκάθετος ου	spy	masc.	ἐν-κατα-[√]-τος
	καθίημι	let down	vb.	κατα-[√]-μι
	παρίημι	neglect (>let [go] by)	vb.	παρα-[√]-μι

τελ   *180*
end / far
Memory Aid: telescope, telephone, television, teleology, Anatolia

	ἀνατέλλω	rise	vb.	ἀνα-[√]-ω
≥10	ἀνατολή ῆς	rising, dawn, east	fem.	ἀνα-[√]-η
	ἀποτελέω	accomplish	vb.	ἀπο-[√]-εω
	διατελέω	continue	vb.	δια-[√]-εω
	ἐκτελέω	finish, complete	vb.	ἐκ-[√]-εω
	ἐξανατέλλω	sprout, spring up	vb.	ἐκ-ἀνα-[√]-ω
≥10	ἐπιτελέω	complete	vb.	ἐπι-[√]-εω
	παντελής ές	complete	adj.	[παν]-[√]-ης
	συντέλεια ας	end, completion	fem.	συν-[√]-εια
	συντελέω	end, complete	vb.	συν-[√]-εω
≥10	τέλειος α ον	complete	adj.	[√]-ιος
	τελειότης ητος	completeness	fem.	[√]-οτης
≥10	τελειόω	make perfect	vb.	[√]-οω
	τελείως	fully	adv.	[√]-ως
	τελείωσις εως	fulfillment	fem.	[√]-σις
	τελειωτής οῦ	perfecter	masc.	[√]-της
	τελεσφορέω	produce mature fruit	vb.	[√]-[φερ]-εω
≥10	τελευτάω	die	vb.	[√]-αω

τελευτή ῆς	death	fem.	[√]-η
≥25 τελέω	finish (make an end)	vb.	[√]-εω
≥25 τέλος ους	end	neut.	[√]-ς

εὑρ 179
find

Memory Aid: heuristic, Eureka!

ἀνευρίσκω	find	vb.	ἀνα-[√]-σκω
≥25 εὑρίσκω	find	vb.	[√]-σκω
ἐφευρετής οῦ	inventor	masc.	ἐπι-[√]-της

ὀχλ 179
crowd / mob

Memory Aid: ochlocracy

ἐνοχλέω	trouble (>crowd in)	vb.	ἐν-[√]-εω
ὀχλέομαι	crowd, trouble, harass	vb.	[√]-εω
ὀχλοποιέω	gather a crowd	vb.	[√]-[ποι]-εω
≥25 ὄχλος ου	crowd, mob	masc.	[√]-ος
παρενοχλέω	add extra difficulties	vb.	παρα-ἐν-[√]-εω

πιπτ πτω 176
fall

Memory Aid: symptom [Sounds something like pit, as in *pit-fall*.]

≥10 ἀναπίπτω	sit, lean	vb.	ἀνα-[√]-ω
ἀντιπίπτω	resist, fight against	vb.	ἀντι-[√]-ω
ἀποπίπτω	fall from	vb.	ἀπο-[√]-ω
≥10 ἐκπί ˙ω	fall off, lose	vb.	ἐκ-[√]-ω
ἐμπίπ	fall into or among	vb.	ἐν-[√]-ω
≥10 ἐπιπίπτω	fall upon, close in on	vb.	ἐπι-[√]-ω
καταπίπτω	fall (down)	vb.	κατα-[√]-ω
παραπίπτω	apostatize (>fall away)	vb.	παρα-[√]-ω
≥10 παράπτωμα ματος	sin	neut.	παρα-[√]-μα
περιπίπτω	encounter	vb.	περι-[√]-ω
≥25 πίπτω	fall	vb.	[√]-ω
προσπίπτω	fall at someone's feet	vb.	προς-[√]-ω
πτῶμα ματος	body, corpse	neut.	[√]-μα
πτῶσις εως	fall	fem.	[√]-σις
συμπίπτω	collapse	vb.	συν-[√]-ω

λυ λυτρ 175
loose / redeem

Memory Aid: analysis, paralysis [*loose*]

ἀκατάλυτος ον	indestructible	adj.	ἀ-κατα-[√]-τος
ἀλυσιτελής ές	of no advantage / help	adj.	ἀ-[√]-[τελ]-ης
ἀνάλυσις εως	death (>releasing)	fem.	ἀνα-[√]-σις
ἀναλύω	come back	vb.	ἀνα-[√]-ω

ἀντίλυτρον ου	ransom	neut.	ἀντι-[√]-τρον
≥10 ἀπολύτρωσις εως	deliverance	fem.	ἀπο-[√]-σις
≥25 ἀπολύω	release, send away	vb.	ἀπο-[√]-ω
διαλύω	scatter	vb.	δια-[√]-ω
ἐκλύομαι	give up, faint	vb.	ἐκ-[√]-ω
ἐπίλυσις εως	interpretation	fem.	ἐπι-[√]-σις
ἐπιλύω	explain, settle	vb.	ἐπι-[√]-ω
κατάλυμα ματος	room, guest room	neut.	κατα-[√]-μα
≥10 καταλύω	destroy, stop	vb.	κατα-[√]-ω
λύσις εως	separation (loosed from)	fem.	[√]-σις
λύτρον ου	means of release	neut.	[√]-τρον
λυτρόομαι	redeem, set free	vb.	[√]-οω
λύτρωσις εως	redemption	fem.	[√]-σις
λυτρωτής οῦ	liberator	masc.	[√]-της
≥25 λύω	loose, free	vb.	[√]-ω
παραλύομαι	be paralyzed	vb.	παρα-[√]-ω
≥10 παραλυτικός οῦ	paralytic	masc.	παρα-[√]-τικος

νυν
now
174

Memory Aid: *now*

≥25 νῦν	now	adv.
≥10 νυνί	now	adv.
τοίνυν	therefore, then	prep.

πολι
city
173

Memory Aid: metropolis, political, polis

≥25 πόλις εως	city, town	fem.	[√]-ς
πολιτάρχης ου	city official	masc.	[√]-[ἀρχ]-ης
πολιτεία ας	citizenship, state	fem.	[√]-εια
πολίτευμα ματος	place of citizenship	neut.	[√]-μα
πολιτεύομαι	live, be a citizen	vb.	[√]-ευω
πολίτης ου	citizen	masc.	[√]-της
συμπολίτης ου	fellow citizen	masc.	συν-[√]-της

πορν πονηρ
evil
173

Memory Aid: pornographic [Fornication: *see Grimm's Law.*]

≥25 ἐκπορνεύω	live immorally	vb.	εκ-[√]-ευω
πονηρία ας	wickedness	fem.	[√]-ια
≥25 πονηρός ά όν	evil	adj.	[√]-ρος
≥25 πορνεία ας	fornication	fem.	[√]-εια
πορνεύω	commit fornication	vb.	[√]-ευω
≥10 πόρνη ης	prostitute	fem.	[√]-η
≥10 πόρνος ου	immoral person	masc.	[√]-ος

ἐθν   *168*
nation / gentile
Memory Aid: ethnic, ethnology, ethnarch

	ἐθνάρχης ου	governor, ethnarch	masc.	[√]-[ἀρχ]-ης
	ἐθνικός ή όν	pagan, Gentile	adj.	[√]-ικος
	ἐθνικῶς	like a Gentile	adv.	[√]-ικως
≥25	ἔθνος ους	nation, Gentiles	neut.	[√]-ς

ζητ   *165*
seek / discuss
Memory Aid:

	ἀναζητέω	seek after	vb.	ἀνα-[√]-εω
	ἐκζητέω	seek diligently	vb.	ἐκ-[√]-εω
	ἐκζήτησις εως	speculation	fem.	ἐκ-[√]-σις
≥10	ἐπιζητέω	seek, desire	vb.	ἐπι-[√]-εω
≥25	ζητέω	seek, try	vb.	[√]-εω
	ζήτημα ματος	question	neut.	[√]-μα
	ζήτησις εως	discussion	fem.	[√]-σις
≥10	συζητέω	discuss, argue	vb.	συν-[√]-εω
	συζήτησις εως	discussion, argument	fem.	συν-[√]-σις
	συζητητής οῦ	skillful debater	masc.	συν-[√]-της

καρδ   *161*
heart
Memory Aid: cardiac

≥25	καρδία ας	heart	fem.	[√]-ια
	καρδιογνώστης ου	knower of hearts	masc.	[√]-[γνο]-της
	σκληροκαρδία ας	hard-heartedness	fem.	(σκληρός)-[√]-[ια

ἔτι   *161*
still / yet
Memory Aid:

≥25	ἔτι	still, yet	adv.	
≥10	μηκέτι	no longer	adv.	[μη]
≥25	οὐκέτι	no longer	adv.	[οὐ]

καθ² καθεδρ   *158*
sit (compare with κατ)
Memory Aid: cathedral

	ἀνακαθίζω	sit up	vb.	ἀνα-[√]-ιζω
	ἐπικαθίζω	sit, sit on	vb.	ἐπι-[√]-ιζω
	καθέδρα ας	chair	fem.	[√]-α
	καθέζομαι	sit	vb.	[√]-ω
≥25	κάθημαι	sit, live	vb.	[√]-μι
≥25	καθίζω	sit	vb.	[√]-ιζω

παρακαθέζομαι	sit	vb.	παρα-[√]-ω
πρωτοκαθεδρία ας	place of honor	fem.	[προ]-[√]-ια
συγκάθημαι	sit with	vb.	συν-[√]-μι
συγκαθίζω	sit together with	vb.	συν-[√]-ιζω

σαρξ σαρκ   158
flesh
Memory Aid: sarcophagus, sarcastic

σαρκικός ή όν	belonging to the world	adj.	[√]-ικος
σάρκινος η ον	belonging to the world	adj.	[√]-ινος
≥25 σάρξ σαρκός	flesh, physical body	fem.	[√]-ξ

φοβ   158
fear
Memory Aid: all of the "phobias"

ἀφόβως	without fear	adv.	ἀ-[√]-ως
ἐκφοβέω	frighten, terrify	vb.	ἐκ-[√]-εω
ἔκφοβος ον	frightened	adj.	ἐκ-[√]-ος
ἔμφοβος ον	full of fear	adj.	ἐν-[√]-ος
≥25 φοβέομαι	fear, be afraid, respect	vb.	[√]-εω
φοβερός ά όν	fearful	adj.	[√]-ρος
φόβητρον ου	fearful thing	neut.	[√]-τρον
≥25 φόβος ου	fear	masc.	[√]-ος

ὑπερ   157
over
Memory Aid: hypersensitive, hyperactive, hyperbole

≥25 ὑπέρ (*gen., acc.*)	over	prep./adv.	
ὑπεράνω (*gen.*)	far above, above	prep.	[√]-άνα
ὑπερέκεινα (*gen.*)	beyond	prep.	[√]-[ἐκει]-α
ὑπερῷον ου	upstairs room	neut.	[√]-ιον

τιμ   155
honor / price
Memory Aid: Paul asked Corinth *to honor Timothy.*

ἀτιμάζω	dishonor	vb.	ἀ-[√]-αζω
ἀτιμία ας	dishonor, shame	fem.	ἀ-[√]-ια
ἄτιμος ον	dishonored, despised	adj.	ἀ-[√]-ος
βαρύτιμος ον	very expensive	adj.	[βαρ]-[√]-ος
ἔντιμος ον	valuable, esteemed	adj.	ἐν-[√]-ος
≥25 ἐπιτιμάω	order, rebuke	vb.	ἐπι-[√]-αω
ἐπιτιμία ας	punishment	fem.	ἐπι-[√]-ια
ἰσότιμος ον	equally valuable	adj.	[ἰσο]-[√]-ος
≥10 τιμάω	honor	vb.	[√]-αω
≥25 τιμή ῆς	honor, price	fem.	[√]-η

≥10	τίμιος α ον	precious, respected	adj.	[√]-ιος
	τιμιότης ητος	wealth, abundance	fem.	[√]-οτης
≥10	Τιμόθεος ου	Timothy	masc.	[√]-[θε]-ος

τρι
three

154

Memory Aid: triangle, trilogy, trinity, trio, triplet

≥25	τρεῖς τρία	three	adj.	
≥10	τριάκοντα	thirty	adj.	[√]-κοντα
	τριακόσιοι αι α	three hundred	adj.	[√]-κοσιοι
	τριετία ας	period of three years	fem.	[√]-ια
	τρίμηνον ου	three months	neut.	[√]-[μην]-ον
≥10	τρίς	three times, a third time	adv.	
	τρίστεγον ου	third floor	neut.	[√]-(στέγω)-ον
	τρισχίλιοι αι α	three thousand	adj.	[√]-χιλιοι
	τρίτον	the third time	adv.	[√]-τος
≥25	τρίτος η ον	third	adj.	[√]-τος

δεχ δεκ δοχ δοκ[1]
receive

150

Memory Aid: *Dock*: place where ships *receive* goods onto their *deck*.

	ἀναδέχομαι	receive, welcome	vb.	ἀνα-[√]-ω
	ἀνένδεκτος ον	impossible	adj.	ἀ-ἐν-[√]-τος
	ἀπεκδέχομαι	await	vb.	ἀπο-ἐκ-[√]-ω
	ἀπόδεκτος ον	pleasing	adj.	ἀπο-[√]-τος
	ἀποδέχομαι	welcome, receive	vb.	ἀπο-[√]-ω
	ἀποδοχή ῆς	acceptance	fem.	ἀπο-[√]-η
	δεκτός ή όν	acceptable	adj.	[√]-τος
≥25	δέχομαι	receive, take	vb.	[√]-ω
	διαδέχομαι	receive possession of	vb.	δια-[√]-ω
	διάδοχος ου	successor	masc.	δια-[√]-ος
	δοχή ῆς	reception	fem.	[√]-η
	εἰσδέχομαι	welcome, receive	vb.	εἰς-[√]-ω
	ἐκδέχομαι	wait for, expect	vb.	ἐκ-[√]-ω
	ἐκδοχή ῆς	expectation	fem.	ἐκ-[√]-η
	ἐνδέχεται	it is possible	vb.	ἐν-[√]-ω
	ἐπιδέχομαι	receive, welcome	vb.	ἐπι-[√]-ω
	εὐπρόσδεκτος ον	acceptable	adj.	εὐ-[√]-τος
	πανδοχεῖον ου	inn (>receive all)	neut.	παν-[√]-ειον
	πανδοχεύς έως	inn-keeper	masc.	παν-[√]-ευς
	παραδέχομαι	accept, receive, welcome	vb.	παρα-[√]-ω
≥10	προσδέχομαι	wait for, expect, receive	vb.	προς-[√]-ω
≥10	προσδοκάω	wait for, expect	vb.	προς-[√]-αω
	προσδοκία ας	expectation	fem.	προς-[√]-ια
	ὑποδέχομαι	receive as a guest	vb.	ὑπο-[√]-ω

οσ   *150*
much / many
Memory Aid: See Chart A.

≥25	ὅσος η ον	as much as, as great as	pron.	[√]-ος
	ποσάκις	how often?	adv.	[√]-κις
≥25	πόσος η ον	how much, how many	pron.	[√]-ος
≥10	τοσοῦτος αύτη οῦτον	so much, so great	adj.	[√]-[οὐτ]

ὁρα   *148*
see
Memory Aid: One can *see* as far as the *horizon.*

	ἀόρατος ον	invisible, unseen	adj.	ἀ-[√]-τος
	ἀφοράω	fix one's eyes on	vb.	ἀπο-[√]-ω
	ἐφοράω	take notice of	vb.	ἐπι-[√]-αω
	καθοράω	perceive clearly	vb.	κατα-[√]-ω
≥10	ὅραμα ματος	vision, sight	neut.	[√]-μα
	ὅρασις εως	vision, appearance	fem.	[√]-σις
	ὁρατός ή όν	visible	adj.	[√]-τος
≥25	ὁράω	see, perceive	vb.	[√]-ω
	προοράω	see ahead of time	vb.	προ-[√]-ω
	συνοράω	realize, learn	vb.	συν-[√]-ω
	ὑπεροράω	overlook	vb.	ὑπερ-[√]-ω
	φρουρέω	guard	vb.	προ-[√]-εω

φαν φαιν φανερ   *147*
display / appear
Memory Aid: phenomenon, phantom, theophany, epiphany

	ἀναφαίνω	come into sight	vb.	ἀνα-[√]-ω
	ἀφανής ές	hidden	adj.	ἀ-[√]-ης
	ἀφανίζω	ruin	vb.	ἀ-[√]-ιζω
	ἀφανισμός οῦ	disappearance	masc.	ἀ-[√]-μος
	ἄφαντος ον	invisible	adj.	ἀ-[√]-τος
	ἐμφανής ές	visible, revealed	adj.	ἐν-[√]-ης
≥10	ἐμφανίζω	inform, reveal	vb.	ἐν-[√]-ιζω
	ἐπιφαίνω	appear, give light	vb.	ἐπι-[√]-ω
	ἐπιφάνεια ας	appearance, coming	fem.	ἐπι-[√]-εια
	ἐπιφανής ές	glorious	adj.	ἐπι-[√]-ης
	ὑπερηφανία ας	arrogance	fem.	ὑπερ-[√]-ια
	ὑπερήφανος ον	arrogant	adj.	ὑπερ-[√]-ος
≥25	φαίνω	shine, appear	vb.	[√]-ω
≥10	φανερός ά όν	known, visible, plain	adj.	[√]-ρος
≥25	φανερόω	make known, reveal	vb.	[√]-οω
	φανερῶς	openly, clearly	adv.	[√]-ως
	φανέρωσις εως	disclosure	fem.	[√]-σις
	φανός οῦ	lantern	masc.	[√]-ος
	φαντάζομαι	appear	vb.	[√]-αζω

| φαντασία ας | pomp | fem. | [√]-σια |
| φάντασμα ματος | phantom, ghost | neut. | [√]-μα |

σωμα   146
body / physical
Memory Aid: somatic

≥25	σύσσωμος ον	of same body	adj.	συν-[√]-ος
	σῶμα ματος	body, substance	neut.	[√]-μα
	σωματικός ή όν	physical	adj.	[√]-τικος
	σωματικῶς	in bodily (human) form	adv.	[√]-τικως

ἕως   145
until
Memory Aid:

| ≥25 | ἕως (*gen.*) | until | conj./prep. |

δε³   144
lack
Memory Aid: [*destitute*]

≥10	δέησις εως	prayer, request	fem.	[√]-σις
≥25	δεῖ	it is necessary	vb.	
≥10	δέομαι	ask, beg	vb.	[√]-ω
	ἐνδεής ές	needy (>in need)	adj.	ἐν-[√]-ης
	προσδέομαι	need	vb.	προς-[√]-ω

χωρ   142
place
Memory Aid: anchorite

≥10	ἀναχωρέω	withdraw, return	vb.	ἀνα-[√]-εω
	ἀποχωρέω	go away, leave	vb.	ἀπο-[√]-εω
	ἀποχωρίζομαι	separate	vb.	ἀπο-[√]-ιζω
	διαχωρίζομαι	leave	vb.	δια-[√]-ιζω
	ἐκχωρέω	leave	vb.	ἐκ-[√]-εω
	εὐρύχωρος ον	wide, spacious	adj.	(εὐρύς)-[√]-ος
	περίχωρος ου	neighborhood	fem.	περι-[√]-ος
	στενοχωρέομαι	be held in check	vb.	(στένος)-[√]-εω
	στενοχωρία ας	distress	fem.	(στένος)-[√]-ια
	ὑποχωρέω	withdraw, go away	vb.	ὑπο-[√]-εω
≥25	χώρα ας	country, land	fem.	[√]-α
≥10	χωρέω	make room for, accept	vb.	[√]-εω
≥10	χωρίζω	separate, leave	vb.	[√]-ιζω
≥10	χωρίον ου	field, piece of land	neut.	[√]-ιον
≥25	χωρίς	without, separately (*dat.*)	prep.	

λα   141
people
Memory Aid: laity

| ≥25 | λαός οῦ | people, nation | masc. | [√]-ος |

στρεφ στροφ 140
turn
Memory Aid: apostrophe, catastrophe

	ἀναστρέφω	return (pass. live)	vb.	ἀνα-[√]-ω
≥10	ἀναστροφή ῆς	manner of life	fem.	ἀνα-[√]-η
	ἀποστρέφω	turn away, remove	vb.	ἀπο-[√]-ω
	διαστρέφω	pervert, distort	vb.	δια-[√]-ω
	ἐκστρέφομαι	be perverted	vb.	ἐκ-[√]-ω
≥25	ἐπιστρέφω	turn back	vb.	ἐπι-[√]-ω
	ἐπιστροφή ῆς	conversion	fem.	ἐπι-[√]-η
	καταστρέφω	overturn	vb.	κατα-[√]-ω
	καταστροφή ῆς	ruin (>catastrophe)	fem.	κατα-[√]-η
	μεταστρέφω	change, alter	vb.	μετα-[√]-ω
	στρεβλόω	distort, twist	vb.	[√]-οω
≥10	στρέφω	turn	vb.	[√]-ω
≥25	ὑποστρέφω	return	vb.	ὑπο-[√]-ω

χαρ χαιρ 140
rejoice
Memory Aid:

	συγχαίρω	rejoice with	vb.	συν-[√]-ω
≥25	χαίρω	rejoice	vb.	[√]-ω
≥25	χαρά ᾶς	joy	fem.	[√]-α

νο 139
mind
Memory Aid: nous, paranoia

	ἀμετανόητος ον	unrepentant	adj.	ἀ-μετα-[√]-τος
	ἀνόητος ον	foolish, ignorant	adj.	ἀ-[√]-τος
	ἄνοια ας	stupidity, foolishness	fem.	ἀ-[√]-ια
	διανόημα ματος	thought	neut.	δια-[√]-μα
≥10	διάνοια ας	mind, understanding	fem.	δια-[√]-ια
	δυσνόητος ον	difficult to understand	adj.	δυσ-[√]-τος
	ἔννοια ας	attitude, thought	fem.	ἐν-[√]-ια
	ἐπίνοια ας	intent, purpose	fem.	ἐπι-[√]-ια
	εὐνοέω	make friends	vb.	εὐ-[√]-εω
	εὔνοια ας	good will, eagerness	fem.	εὐ-[√]-ια
≥10	κατανοέω	consider	vb.	κατα-[√]-εω
≥25	μετανοέω	repent	vb.	μετα-[√]-εω
≥10	μετάνοια ας	repentance	fem.	μετα-[√]-ια
	νοέω	understand	vb.	[√]-εω
	νόημα τος	mind, thought	neut.	[√]-μα
	νουθεσία ας	instruction	fem.	[√]-[τιθ]-σια
	νουθετέω	instruct (>place in mind)	vb.	[√]-[τιθ]-εω
	νουνεχῶς	wisely	adv.	[√]-[ἐχ]-ως
	προνοέω	plan	vb.	προ-[√]-εω

πρόνοια ας	provision	fem.	προ-[√]-ια
ὑπονοέω	suppose, suspect	vb.	ὑπο-[√]-εω
ὑπόνοια ας	suspicion	fem.	ὑπο-[√]-ια

παλ 139
again
Memory Aid: palindrome, palimpsest

≥25 πάλιν	again, once	adv.	

καλ¹ 137
good / proper
Memory Aid: calligraphy, calisthenics, kaleidoscope

	κάλλιον	very well	adv.	[√]-ων
	καλοποιέω	do what is good	vb.	[√]-[ποι]-εω
≥25	καλός ή όν	good, proper	adj.	[√]-ος
≥25	καλῶς	well	adv.	[√]-ως

αἰρ 136
take up / choose
Memory Aid: diaeresis

≥25	αἴρω	take	vb.	[√]-ω
	ἀπαίρω	take away	vb.	ἀπο-[√]-ω
	ἐξαίρω	remove, drive out	vb.	ἐκ-[√]-ω
≥10	ἐπαίρω	raise, lift up	vb.	ἐπι-[√]-ω
	μεταίρω	leave	vb.	μετα-[√]-ω
	προαιρέομαι	decide	vb.	προ-[√]-εω
	συναίρω	settle with	vb.	συν-[√]-ω
	ὑπεραίρομαι	be puffed up with pride	vb.	ὑπερ-[√]-ω

ὁδ 136
way / travel
Memory Aid: Exodus, odometer, synod

	ἄμφοδον ου	street	neut.	ἀμφι-[√]-ον
	διέξοδος ου	outlet, passage	fem.	δια-ἐκ-[√]-ος
	διοδεύω	go about	vb.	δια-[√]-ευω
	εἴσοδος ου	coming, entrance	fem.	εἰς-[√]-ος
	ἔξοδος ου	departure (>Exodus)	fem.	ἐκ-[√]-ος
	εὐοδόομαι	have things go well	vb.	εὐ-[√]-οω
	μεθοδεία ας	trickery	fem.	μετα-[√]-εια
	ὁδεύω	travel	vb.	[√]-ευω
	ὁδηγέω	lead, guide	vb.	[√]-[ἀγ]-εω
	ὁδηγός οῦ	guide, leader	masc.	[√]-[ἀγ]-ος
	ὁδοιπορέω	travel	vb.	[√]-[πορ]-εω
	ὁδοιπορία ας	journey	fem.	[√]-[πορ]-ια
≥25	ὁδός οῦ	way, journey	fem.	[√]-ος
	πάροδος ου	passage	fem.	παρα-[√]-ος

| συνοδεύω | travel with | vb. | συν-[√]-ευω |
| συνοδία ας | group (>synod) | fem. | συν-[√]-ια |

παι παιδ   134
child / education
Memory Aid: encyclopaedia, pedagogue, pedantic

	ἀπαίδευτος ον	ignorant (>not learned)	adj.	ἀ-[√]-τος
	ἐμπαιγμονή ῆς	mockery, ridicule	fem.	ἐν-[√]-η
	ἐμπαιγμός οῦ	public ridicule	masc.	ἐν-[√]-μος
≥10	ἐμπαίζω	ridicule	vb.	ἐν-[√]-ιζω
	ἐμπαίκτης ου	mocker	masc.	ἐν-[√]-της
	παιδαγωγός οῦ	instructor (>pedagogue)	masc.	[√]-[ἀγ]-ος
	παιδάριον ου	boy	neut.	[√]-αριον
	παιδεία ας	discipline, instruction	fem.	[√]-εια
	παιδευτής οῦ	teacher	masc.	[√]-της
≥10	παιδεύω	instruct, correct	vb.	[√]-ευω
	παιδιόθεν	from childhood	adv.	[√]-θεν
≥25	παιδίον ου	child, infant	neut.	[√]-ιον
≥10	παιδίσκη ης	maid, slave	fem.	[√]-η
	παίζω	play, dance	vb.	[√]-ιζω
≥10	παῖς παιδός	child, servant	masc./fem.	[√]-ς

νεκρ   133
death
Memory Aid: necropolis

≥25	νεκρός ά όν	dead	adj.	[√]-ος
	νεκρόω	put to death, make dead	vb.	[√]-οω
	νέκρωσις εως	death, barrenness	fem.	[√]-σις

τεκν τικ τοκ   133
child
Memory Aid: Theotokos [A *child* is a little *tike*.]

	ἄτεκνος ον	childless	adj.	ἀ-[√]-ος
	τεκνίον ου	little child	neut.	[√]-ιον
	τεκνογονέω	have children	vb.	[√]-[γεν]-εω
	τεκνογονία ας	childbirth	fem.	[√]-[γεν]-ια
≥25	τέκνον ου	child	neut.	[√]-ον
	τεκνοτροφέω	bring up children	vb.	[√]-[τρεφ]-εω
≥10	τίκτω	give birth to, yield	vb.	[√]-ω
	τόκος ου	interest (>child of money)	masc.	[√]-ος
	φιλότεκνος ον	child-loving	adj.	[φιλ]-[√]-ος

εὐχ   129
pray
Memory Aid:

| | εὐχή ῆς | prayer, vow | fem. | [√]-η |

εὔχομαι	pray	vb.	[√]-ω
≥25 προσευχή ῆς	prayer	fem.	προς-[√]-η
≥25 προσεύχομαι	pray	vb.	προς-[√]-ω

δεκα   128
ten

Memory Aid: decade, decalogue, decimate

ἀποδεκατόω	tithe, make one tithe	vb.	ἀπο-[√]-οω
≥25 δέκα	ten	adj.	
δέκα ὀκτώ	eighteen	adj.	(ὀκτώ)
δεκαπέντε	fifteen	adj.	[√]-[πεντ]
Δεκάπολις εως	Decapolis (ten city area)	fem.	[√]-[πολ]-ς
δεκάτη ης	tithe	fem.	[√]-η
δέκατος η ον	tenth	adj.	[√]-τος
δεκατόω	collect (pay) tithes	vb.	[√]-οω
≥25 δώδεκα	twelve	adj.	[δευ]-[√]
δωδέκατος η ον	twelfth	adj.	[δευ]-[√]-τος
ἕνδεκα	eleven	adj.	[ἑις]-[√]
ἑνδέκατος η ον	eleventh	adj.	[ἑις]-[√]-τος

ψυχ   128
self / soul / cold (unspiritual)

Memory Aid: psyche, psychology, psychiatry

ἀνάψυξις εως	refreshment	fem.	ἀνα-[√]-σις
ἀναψύχω	refresh (>cooled)	vb.	ἀνα-[√]-ω
ἀποψύχω	faint	vb.	ἀπο-[√]-ω
ἄψυχος ον	inanimate	adj.	ἀ-[√]-ος
δίψυχος ον	undecided (>two minds)	adj.	[δευ]-[√]-ος
ἐκψύχω	die	vb.	ἐκ-[√]-ω
εὐψυχέω	be encouraged	vb.	εὐ-[√]-εω
ἰσόψυχος ον	sharing same feelings	adj.	[ἰσ]-[√]-ος
καταψύχω	cool, refresh	vb.	κατα-[√]-ω
σύμψυχος ον	united	adj.	συν-[√]-ος
≥25 ψυχή ῆς	self, person	fem.	[√]-η
ψυχικός ή όν	unspiritual, material	adj.	[√]-ικος
ψύχομαι	grow cold	vb.	[√]-ω
ψῦχος ους	cold	neut.	[√]-ς
ψυχρός ά όν	cold	adj.	[√]-ρος

ἀμην   126
truly

Memory Aid: amen

≥25 ἀμήν	amen, truly	adv.	

μιμν μν μνη μνημ   123
remember

Memory Aid: mnemonic, amnesia, amnesty [*memory, memorial*]

ἀναμιμνήσκω	remind	vb.	ἀνα-[√]-σκω
ἀνάμνησις εως	reminder, remembrance	fem.	ἀνα-[√]-σις
ἐπαναμιμνήσκω	remind	vb.	ἐπι-ἀνα-[√]-σκω
≥10 μιμνήσκομαι	remember	vb.	[√]-σκω
μνεία ας	remembrance, mention	fem.	[√]-εια
≥10 μνῆμα ματος	grave, tomb (>memorial)	neut.	[√]-μα
≥25 μνημεῖον ου	grave, monument	neut.	[√]-ειον
μνήμη ης	remembrance, memory	fem.	[√]-η
≥10 μνημονεύω	remember	vb.	[√]-ευω
μνημόσυνον ου	memorial	neut.	[√]-συνη-ον
ὑπομιμνήσκω	remind	vb.	ὑπο-[√]-σκω
ὑπόμνησις εως	remembrance	fem.	ὑπο-[√]-σις

ἀγαθ
good
122

Memory Aid:

ἀγαθοεργέω	do good, be generous	vb.	[√]-[ἐργ]-εω
ἀγαθοποιέω	do good, be helpful	vb.	[√]-[ποι]-εω
ἀγαθοποιΐα ας	good-doing	fem.	[√]-[ποι]-ια
ἀγαθοποιός οῦ	good doer	masc.	[√]-[ποι]-ος
≥25 ἀγαθός ή όν	good, useful	adj.	[√]-ος
ἀγαθουργέω	do good, be kind	vb.	[√]-[ἐργ]-εω
ἀγαθωσύνη ης	goodness	fem.	[√]-συνη
ἀφιλάγαθος ον	not good-loving	adj.	ἀ-[φιλ]-[√]-ος
φιλάγαθος ον	good-loving	adj.	[φιλ]-[√]-ος

αἰτ
ask / reason / cause / accusation
122

Memory Aid: etiology

≥25 αἰτέω	ask, require	vb.	[√]-εω
αἴτημα ματος	request, demand	neut.	[√]-μα
≥10 αἰτία ας	reason, cause, charge	fem.	[√]-ια
αἴτιον ου	guilt, reason	neut.	[√]-ιον
αἴτιος ου	cause, source	masc.	[√]-ιος
αἰτίωμα ματος	charge, accusation	neut.	[√]-μα
ἀναίτιος ον	not guilty (>no charge)	adj.	ἀ-[√]-ιος
ἀπαιτέω	demand (in return)	vb.	ἀπο-[√]-εω
ἐξαιτέομαι	ask, demand	vb.	ἐκ-[√]-εω
ἐπαιτέω	beg	vb.	ἐπι-[√]-εω
≥10 παραιτέομαι	ask for, excuse	vb.	παρα-[√]-εω
προαιτιάομαι	accuse beforehand	vb.	προ-[√]-αω
προσαιτέω	beg	vb.	προς-[√]-εω
προσαίτης ου	beggar	masc.	προς-[√]-της

μονο
only
122

Memory Aid: monopoly, monologue, monotone, monarch

μονογενής ές	only begotten, unique	adj.	[√]-[γεν]-ης
≥25 μόνον	only, alone	adv.	[√]-ον
μονόομαι	be left alone	vb.	[√]-οω
≥25 μόνος η ον	only, alone	adj.	[√]-ος

ταγ ταк ταξ ταχ¹ τασσ   122
order

Memory Aid: tactic, syntax, paratactic, taxonomy

ἀνατάσσομαι	compile, draw up	vb.	ἀνα-[√]-σσω
ἀντιτάσσομαι	resist, oppose	vb.	ἀντι-[√]-σσω
ἀνυπότακτος	disorderly	adj.	ἀ-ὑπο-[√]-τος
ἀτακτέω	be lazy (>not ordered)	vb.	ἀ-[√]-εω
ἄτακτος ον	lazy (>not ordered)	adj.	ἀ-[√]-τος
ἀτάκτως	lazily	adv.	ἀ-[√]-τως
διαταγή ῆς	decree	fem.	δια-[√]-η
διάταγμα ματος	order, decree	neut.	δια-[√]-μα
≥10 διατάσσω	command	vb.	δια-[√]-σσω
ἐπιδιατάσσομαι	add to (a will)	vb.	ἐπι-δια-[√]-σσω
ἐπιταγή ῆς	command, authority	fem.	ἐπι-[√]-η
≥10 ἐπιτάσσω	order	vb.	ἐπι-[√]-σσω
προστάσσω	command	vb.	προς-[√]-σσω
συντάσσω	direct, instruct	vb.	συν-[√]-σσω
τάγμα ματος	proper order	neut.	[√]-μα
τακτός ή όν	appointed, fixed	adj.	[√]-τος
τάξις εως	order, division	fem.	[√]-σις
τάσσω	appoint	vb.	[√]-ω
ὑποταγή ῆς	obedience, submission	fem.	ὑπο-[√]-η
≥25 ὑποτάσσω	subject	vb.	ὑπο-[√]-σσω

λειπ λοιπ λειμ λιμ   121
leave / lack

Memory Aid: eclipse

ἀδιάλειπτος ον	endless, constant	adj.	ἀ-δια-[√]-τος
ἀδιαλείπτως	constantly, always	adv.	ἀ-δια-[√]-ως
ἀνέκλειπτος ον	never decreasing	adj.	ἀ-ἐκ-[√]-τος
ἀπολείπω	leave behind	vb.	ἀπο-[√]-ω
διαλείπω	cease, stop	vb.	δια-[√]-ω
διαλιμπάνω	stop, quit	vb.	δια-[√]-ανω
≥10 ἐγκαταλείπω	forsake, leave	vb.	ἐν-κατα-[√]-ω
ἐκλείπω	fail, cease, leave	vb.	ἐκ-[√]-ω
ἐπιλείπω	run short	vb.	ἐπι-[√]-ω
ἐπίλοιπος ον	remaining	adj.	ἐπι-[√]-ος
≥10 καταλείπω	leave, forsake	vb.	κατα-[√]-ω
κατάλοιπος ον	rest, remaining	adj.	κατα-[√]-ος
λεῖμμα ματος	remnant	neut.	[√]-μα

λείπω	lack, leave	vb.	[√]-ω
≥25 λοιπός ή όν	rest, remaining	adj.	[√]-ος
περιλείπομαι	remain	vb.	περι-[√]-ω
ὑπόλειμμα ματος	remnant	neut.	ὑπο-[√]-μα
ὑπολείπω	leave	vb.	ὑπο-[√]-ω
ὑπολιμπάνω	leave	vb.	ὑπο-[√]-ανω

ἐρωτ   120
ask
Memory Aid:

διερωτάω	learn	vb.	δια-[√]-αω
≥25 ἐπερωτάω	ask, ask for	vb.	ἐπι-[√]-αω
ἐπερώτημα ματος	promise, answer	neut.	ἐπι-[√]-μα
≥25 ἐρωτάω	ask	vb.	[√]-αω

βαπτ   119
baptize / dip
Memory Aid: baptize, baptism

≥25 βαπτίζω	baptize	vb.	[√]-ιζω
≥10 βάπτισμα ματος	baptism	neut.	[√]-μα
βαπτισμός οῦ	washing, baptism	masc.	[√]-ισμος
≥10 βαπτιστής οῦ	Baptist (Baptizer)	masc.	[√]-ιστης
βάπτω	dip	vb.	[√]-ω
ἐμβάπτω	dip	vb.	ἐν-[√]-ω
καταβαπτίζομαι	wash oneself	vb.	κατα-[√]-ιζω

ἰδι   118
own
Memory Aid: idiosyncratic, idiomatic

≥25 ἴδιος α ον	one's own, personal	adj.	[√]-ιος
ἰδιώτης ου	untrained person	masc.	[√]-της

ἰερ ἰερατ   117
priest
Memory Aid: hierarchy, hieroglyph

ἱερατεία ας	priestly office	fem.	[√]-εια
ἱεράτευμα ματος	priesthood	neut.	[√]-μα
ἱερατεύω	serve as a priest	vb.	[√]-ευω
≥25 ἱερεύς έως	priest	masc.	[√]-ευς
ἱερόθυτος ον	sacrificial	adj.	[√]-[θυ]-τος
≥25 ἱερόν οῦ	temple	neut.	[√]-ον
ἱεροπρεπής ές	reverent	adj.	[√]-(πρέπω)-ης
ἱερός ά όν	sacred	adj.	[√]-ος
ἱεροσυλέω	commit sacrilege	vb.	[√]-(συλάω)εω
ἱερόσυλος ου	sacrilegious person	masc.	[√]-(συλάω)-ος
ἱερουργέω	work as a priest	vb.	[√]-[ἐργ]-εω

ἱερωσύνη ης	priesthood	fem.	[√]-συνη

ὀπ ὀπτ ωπ 117
see
Memory Aid: optical

≥25 ἐνώπιον (gen.)	before (>in sight of)	prep.	ἐν-[√]-ιον
ἐποπτεύω	see, observe	vb.	ἐπι-[√]-ευω
ἐπότης ου	observer, eyewitness	masc.	ἐπι-[√]-της
ἔσοπτρον ου	mirror	neut.	εἰς-[√]-τρον
κατοπρίζω	behold	vb.	κατα-[√]-ιζω
μέτωπον ου	forehead	neut.	μετα-[√]-ον
μυωπάζω	be shortsighted	vb.	(μύω)-[√]-αζω
ὀπτάνομαι	appear (>gain sight of)	vb.	[√]-ανω
ὀπτασία ας	vision	fem.	[√]-σια
σκυθρωπός ή όν	sad	adj.	(σκυθρός)-[√]-ος
ὑπωπιάζω	control (>under the eye)	vb.	ὑπο-[√]-αζω

κακ 116
bad
Memory Aid: cacography, cacophony, kaka

ἄκακος ον	innocent	adj.	ἀ-[√]-ος
ἀνεξίκακος ον	tolerant	adj.	ἀνα-[ἐχ]-[√]-ος
ἐγκακέω	become discouraged	vb.	ἐν-[√]-εω
κακία ας	evil, trouble	fem.	[√]-ια
κακοήθεια ας	meanness	fem.	[√]-(>ἔθος)-εια
κακολογέω	speak evil of, curse	vb.	[√]-[λεγ]-εω
κακοπάθεια ας	suffering, endurance	fem.	[√]-[παθ]-εια
κακοπαθέω	suffer, endure	vb.	[√]-[παθ]-εω
κακοποιέω	do evil	vb.	[√]-[ποι]-εω
κακοποιός οῦ	criminal, wrong doer	masc.	[√]-[ποι]-ος
κακός ή όν	evil, bad	adj.	[√]-ος
κακοῦργος ου	criminal	masc.	[√]-[ἐργ]-ος
κακουχέομαι	be treated badly	vb.	[√]-[ἐχ]-εω
κακόω	treat badly, harm	vb.	[√]-οω
κακῶς	badly	adv.	[√]-ως
κάκωσις εως	oppression, suffering	fem.	[√]-σις
συγκακουχέομαι	suffer with	vb.	συν-[√]-[ἐχ]-εω

ὁμο ὁμοι 115
same / like
Memory Aid: homogeneous, homonym, homoousion, homoiousion

	ἀφομοιόω	be like	vb.	ἀπο-[√]-οω
	ὁμοιάζω	resemble	vb.	[√]-αζω
	ὁμοιοπαθής ές	similar (>same feelings)	adj.	[√]-[παθ]-ης
≥25	ὅμοιος α ον	like	adj.	[√]-ιος
	ὁμοιότης ητος	likeness	fem.	[√]-οτης

≥10	ὁμοιόω	make like, compare	vb.	[√]-οω
	ὁμοίωμα ματος	likeness	neut.	[√]-μα
≥25	ὁμοίως	too, in the same way	adv.	[√]-ως
	ὁμοίωσις εως	likeness	fem.	[√]-σις
	ὁμοῦ	together	adv.	[√]-ου
	ὅμως	even	adv.	[√]-ως
	παρομοιάζω	be like	vb.	παρα-[√]-αζω
	παρόμοιος ον	like, similar	adj.	παρα-[√]-ος

σῳζ   115
save
Memory Aid: creosote

	διασῴζω	rescue	vb.	δια-[√]-ω
	ἐκσῴζω	save, keep safe	vb.	ἐκ-[√]-ω
≥25	σῴζω	save, rescue, preserve	vb.	[√]-ω

θυμ   114
feelings (emotions)
Memory Aid:

	ἀθυμέω	become discouraged	vb.	ἀ-[√]-εω
	διενθυμέομαι	think over	vb.	δια-ἐν-[√]-εω
	ἐνθυμέομαι	think about, think	vb.	ἐν-[√]-εω
	ἐνθύμησις εως	thought, idea	fem.	ἐν-[√]-σις
≥10	ἐπιθυμέω	desire, covet, lust for	vb.	ἐπι-[√]-εω
	ἐπιθυμητής οῦ	one who desires	masc.	ἐπι-[√]-της
≥25	ἐπιθυμία ας	desire, lust	fem.	ἐπι-[√]-ια
	εὐθυμέω	take courage, be happy	vb.	εὐ-[√]-εω
	εὔθυμος ον	encouraged	adj.	εὐ-[√]-ος
	εὐθύμως	cheerfully	adv.	εὐ-[√]-ως
	θυμομαχέω	be very angry	vb.	[√]-[μαχ]-εω
	θυμόομαι	be furious	vb.	[√]-οω
≥10	θυμός οῦ	anger	masc.	[√]-ος
≥10	ὁμοθυμαδόν	with one mind	adv.	[ὁμο]-[√]-δον
	παραμυθέομαι	console	vb.	παρα-[√]-εω
	παραμυθία ας	comfort	fem.	παρα-[√]-ια
	παραμύθιον ου	comfort	neut.	παρα-[√]-ιον
	προθυμία ας	willingness, zeal	fem.	προ-[√]-ια
	πρόθυμος ον	willing	adj.	προ-[√]-ος
	προθύμως	willingly, eagerly	adv.	προ-[√]-ως

ὁλ   114
whole / all
Memory Aid: holocaust, catholic [Sounds like *whole.*]

	καθόλου	completely, altogether	adv.	[√]-κατα
≥25	ὅλος η ον	whole, all	adj.	[√]-ος

| ὁλοτελής ές | wholly | adj. | [√]-[τελ]-ης |
| ὅλως | at all, actually | adv. | [√]-ως |

φρ φρο φρον   *113*
think

Memory Aid: schizophrenia

	ἀφροσύνη ης	folly	fem.	ἀ-[√]-συνη
≥10	ἄφρων ον	foolish	adj.	[√]-ων
≥10	εὐφραίνω	make glad	vb.	εὐ-[√]-αινω
	εὐφροσύνη ης	gladness	fem.	εὐ-[√]-συνη
	καταφρονέω	despise	vb.	κατα-[√]-εω
	καταφρονητής οῦ	scoffer	masc.	κατα-[√]-της
	ὁμόφρων ον	of one mind	adj.	[ὁμο]-[√]-ων
	παραφρονέω	be insane	vb.	παρα-[√]-εω
	παραφρονία ας	insanity	fem.	παρα-[√]-ια
	περιφρονέω	esteem lightly, disregard	vb.	περι-[√]-εω
	σωφρονέω	be sane, sensible	vb.	[σῳζ]-[√]-εω
	σωφρονίζω	train, teach	vb.	[σῳζ]-[√]-ιζω
	σωφρονισμός οῦ	sound judgment	masc.	[σῳζ]-[√]-ισμος
	σωφρόνως	sensibly	adv.	[σῳζ]-[√]-ως
	σωφροσύνη ης	good sense	fem.	[σῳζ]-[√]-συνη
	σώφρων ον	sensible	adj.	[σῳζ]-[√]-ων
	ὑπερφρονέω	hold high opinion of	vb.	ὑπερ-[√]-εω
	φιλοφρόνως	kindly	adv.	[φιλ]-[√]-ως
	φρήν φρενός	thought, understanding	fem.	[√]-ην
≥25	φρονέω	think	vb.	[√]-εω
	φρόνημα ματος	way of thinking, mind	neut.	[√]-μα
	φρόνησις εως	insight, wisdom	fem.	[√]-σις
≥10	φρόνιμος ον	wise	adj.	[√]-μος
	φρονίμως	wisely	adv.	[√]-ως
	φροντίζω	concentrate upon	vb.	[√]-ιζω

σπερ σπειρ σπορ   *113*
scatter

Memory Aid: sperm, sporadic, diaspora

	διασπείρω	scatter	vb.	δια-[√]-ω
	διασπορά ᾶς	dispersion (>diaspora)	fem.	δια-[√]-α
	ἐπισπείρω	sow in addition	vb.	ἐπι-[√]-ω
≥25	σπείρω	sow	vb.	[√]-ω
≥25	σπέρμα ματος	seed, offspring	neut.	[√]-μα
	σπερμολόγος ου	gossiper (>word scatter)	masc.	[√]-[λεγ]-ος
	σπορά ᾶς	seed, origin	fem.	[√]-α
	σπόριμα ων (*pl.*)	grainfields	neut.	[√]-ον
	σπόρος ου	seed	masc.	[√]-ος

καθαρ καθαιρ 112
clean
Memory Aid: catharsis, Cathar

≥10 ἀκαθαρσία ας	impurity	fem.	ἀ-[√]-ια
≥25 ἀκάθαρτος ον	unclean	adj.	ἀ-[√]-τος
διακαθαίρω	clean out	vb.	δια-[√]-ω
διακαθαρίζω	clean out	vb.	δια-[√]-ιζω
ἐκκαθαίρω	clean out	vb.	ἐκ-[√]-ω
καθαίρω	clean, prune	vb.	[√]-ω
≥25 καθαρίζω	cleanse	vb.	[√]-ιζω
καθαρισμός οῦ	cleansing	masc.	[√]-ισμος
≥25 καθαρός ά όν	clean, pure	adj.	[√]-ρος
καθαρότης ητος	purification, purity	fem.	[√]-οτης
περικάθαρμα ματος	rubbish	neut.	περι-[√]-μα

ὠρ 112
time / hour
Memory Aid: horoscope, hour

ἡμίωρον ου	half an hour	neut.	ἡμι-[√]-ον
≥25 ὥρα ας	moment, time	fem.	[√]-α
ὡραῖος α ον	timely, welcome	adj.	[√]-ιος

μελλ 110
about
Memory Aid: Greek *about* is μελ, Greek *concerning* is μελλ.

≥25 μέλλω	be going, be about	vb.	[√]-ω

ὀλλ 109
destroy
Memory Aid: Apollyon

≥25 ἀπόλλυμι	destroy	vb.	ἀπο-[√]-μι
≥10 ἀπώλεια ας	destruction	fem.	ἀπο-[√]-εια
συναπόλλυμαι	perish with	vb.	συν-ἀπο-[√]-μι

ἐξουσ 108
authority
Memory Aid:

≥25 ἐξουσία ας	authority, official	fem.	[√]-ια
ἐξουσιάζω	have power over	vb.	[√]-αζω
ἐξουσιαστικός ή όν	authoritative	adj.	[√]-τικος
κατεξουσιάζω	rule over	vb.	κατα-[√]-αζω

πο[1] ποδ πεδ πεζ 108
foot
Memory Aid: podiatry, podium, tripod, pedestrian

ὀρθοποδέω	be consistent	vb.	(ὀρθός)-[√]-εω

πέδη ης	chain (for feet)	fem.	[√]-η
πεδινός ή όν	level (ground)	adj.	[√]-ινος
πεζεύω	travel by land	vb.	[√]-ευω
πεζῇ	on foot, by land	adv.	[√]-η
≥25 πούς ποδός	foot	masc.	[√]-ς
ὑποπόδιον ου	footstool	neut.	ὑπο-[√]-ιον

ἀκολουθ
follow
106

Memory Aid: acolyte

≥25 ἀκολουθέω	follow, be a disciple	vb.	[√]-εω
ἐξακολουθέω	follow, be obedient	vb.	ἐκ-[√]-εω
ἐπακολουθέω	follow	vb.	ἐπι-[√]-εω
κατακολουθέω	follow, accompany	vb.	κατα-[√]-εω
παρακολουθέω	follow closely	vb.	παρα-[√]-εω
συνακολουθέω	follow, accompany	vb.	συν-[√]-εω

πεμπ
send
106

Memory Aid:

ἀναπέμπω	send, send back / up	vb.	ἀνα-[√]-ω
ἐκπέμπω	send out / away	vb.	ἐκ-[√]-ω
μεταπέμπομαι	send for	vb.	μετα-[√]-ω
≥25 πέμπω	send	vb.	[√]-ω
προπέμπω	send on one's way, escort	vb.	προ-[√]-ω
συμπέμπω	send along with	vb.	συν-[√]-ω

τεσσαρ τεταρ τετρα
four
104

Memory Aid: tetrahedron, tetrarch

δεκατέσσαρες	fourteen	adj.	[δεκα]-[√]
≥10 τεσσαράκοντα	forty	adj.	[√]-κοντα
≥25 τέσσαρες α	four	adj.	[√]-ες
τεσσαρεσκαιδέκατος	fourteenth	adj.	[√]-και-[δεκα]-τος
τεταρταῖος α ον	on the fourth day	adj.	[√]-ιος
≥10 τέταρτος η ον	fourth	adj.	[√]-τος
τετρααρχέω	be tetrarch, be ruler	vb.	[√]-[ἀρχ]-εω
τετραάρχης ου	tetrarch (ruler)	masc.	[√]-[ἀρχ]-ης
τετράγωνος ον	squared (>four-angled)	adj.	[√]-(γωνία)-ος
τετράδιον ου	squad (of four men)	neut.	[√]-ιον
τετρακισχίλιοι αι α	four thousand	adj.	[√]-κις-χιλιοι
τετρακόσιοι αι α	four hundred	adj.	[√]-κοσιοι
τετράμηνος ου	period of four months	fem.	[√]-[μην]-ος
τετραπλοῦς ῆ οῦν	four times as much	adj.	[√]-[πλει]-ος
τετράπουν ποδος	animal (>four-footed)	neut.	[πο(1)]

ὀφθαλμ
eye *103*

Memory Aid: ophthalmology

ἀντοφθαλμέω	head into, face	vb.	ἀντι-[√]-εω
ὀφθαλμοδουλία ας	eye-service	fem.	[√]-[δουλ]-ια
≥25 ὀφθαλμός οῦ	eye	masc.	[√]-ος

εὐθ
immediate / straight *101*

Memory Aid:

≥25 εὐθέως	immediately, soon	adv.	[√]-ως
εὐθύνω	make straight	vb.	[√]-υνω
≥25 εὐθύς	immediately	adv.	
εὐθύς εῖα ύ	straight, (up)right	adj.	[√]-υς
εὐθύτης ητος	uprightness, justice	fem.	[√]-οτης
κατευθύνω	direct, guide	vb.	κατα-[√]-υνω

καιρ
time *100*

Memory Aid:

ἀκαιρέομαι	be without opportunity	vb.	ἀ-[√]-εω
ἀκαίρως	untimely	adv.	ἀ-[√]-ως
εὐκαιρέω	have time, spend time	vb.	εὐ-[√]-εω
εὐκαιρία ας	opportune moment	fem.	εὐ-[√]-ια
εὔκαιρος ον	suitable, timely	adj.	εὐ-[√]-ος
εὐκαίρως	when the time is right	adv.	εὐ-[√]-ως
≥25 καιρός οῦ	time, age	masc.	[√]-ος
πρόσκαιρος ον	temporary	adj.	προς-[√]-ος

τοπ
place *100*

Memory Aid: topography, Utopia, isotope

ἄτοπος ον	improper	adj.	ἀ-[√]-ος
ἐντόπιος α ον	local (*pl.* residents)	adj.	ἐν-[√]-ιος
≥25 τόπος ου	place	masc.	[√]-ος

αἱμ
blood *99*

Memory Aid: hemophilia, hemorrhage, anemia, hemoglobin

≥25 αἷμα τος	blood, death	neut.	[√]-α
αἱματεκχυσία ας	shedding of blood	fem.	[√]-ἐκ-[χε]-ια
αἱμορροέω	hemorrhage, bleed	vb.	[√]-[ρε]-εω

δοκ²
think / seem *99*

Memory Aid: Docetic

≥25	δοκέω	think, seem	vb.	[√]-εω
≥10	εὐδοκέω	be pleased, choose, will	vb.	εὐ-[√]-εω
	εὐδοκία ας	good will, pleasure	fem.	εὐ-[√]-ια
	παράδοξος ον	incredible (>paradox)	adj.	παρα-[√]-ος
	συνευδοκέω	approve of	vb.	συν-ευ-[√]-εω

εἰρην
peace
99
Memory Aid: irenic

	εἰρηνεύω	be at peace	vb.	[√]-ευω
≥25	εἰρήνη ης	peace	fem.	[√]-η
	εἰρηνικός ή όν	peaceful, irenic	adj.	[√]-ικος
	εἰρηνοποιέω	make peace	vb.	[√]-[ποι]-εω
	εἰρηνοποιός οῦ	peace-maker	masc.	[√]-[ποι]-ος

ἕτερ
other / different
99
Memory Aid: heterodox, heterosexual

≥25	ἕτερος α ον	other, different	adj.	[√]-ος
	ἑτέρως	otherwise, differently	adv.	[√]-ως

διακον
serve
98
Memory Aid: deacon

≥25	διακονέω	serve, care for	vb.	[√]-εω
≥25	διακονία ας	service, help	fem.	[√]-ια
≥25	διάκονος ου	servant, deacon	masc./fem.	[√]-ος

ἀρτ[1]
bread
97
Memory Aid:

≥25	ἄρτος ου	bread, food	masc.	[√]-ος

πυρ
fire
96
Memory Aid: pyre, Pyrex [Fire: *see Grimm's Law.*]

	ἀναζωπυρέω	stir into flame	vb.	ἀνα-[ζω]-[√]-εω
≥25	πῦρ ός	fire	neut.	[√]-ρ
	πυρά ᾶς	fire	fem.	[√]-α
	πυρέσσω	be sick with fever	vb.	[√]-σσω
	πυρετός οῦ	fever	masc.	[√]-ος
	πύρινος η ον	fiery red (color)	adj.	[√]-ινος
	πυρόομαι	burn	vb.	[√]-οω
	πυρράζω	be red (for sky)	vb.	[√]-αζω
	πυρρός ά όν	red (color)	adj.	[√]-ος
	πύρωσις εως	burning, ordeal	fem.	[√]-σις

φωσ φωτ
light
96

Memory Aid: photograph, photosynthesis, phosphorus

	ἐπιφώσκω	dawn, draw near	vb.	ἐπι-[√]-σκω
≥25	φῶς φωτός	light, fire	neut.	[√]-ς
	φωστήρ ῆρος	light, star	masc.	[√]-τηρ
	φωσφόρος ου	morning star	masc.	[√]-[φερ]-ος
	φωτεινός ή όν	full of light	adj.	[√]-ινος
≥10	φωτίζω	give light, shine on	vb.	[√]-ιζω
	φωτισμός οῦ	light, revelation	masc.	[√]-μος

ὁρ
boundary
94

Memory Aid: aphorism, horizon

	ἀποδιορίζω	cause divisions	vb.	ἀπο-δια-[√]-ιζω
≥10	ἀφορίζω	separate, exclude	vb.	ἀπο-[√]-ιζω
	ὁρίζω	decide, determine	vb.	[√]-ιζω
≥10	ὅριον ου	territory, vicinity	neut.	[√]-ιον
	ὁροθεσία ας	limit, boundary	fem.	[√]-[τιθ]-ια
≥25	ὅρος ου	limit, boundary	masc.	[√]-ος

χρη χρα χρει
need / use
94

Memory Aid:

	ἀπόχρησις εως	process of being used	fem.	ἀπο-[√]-σις
	ἀχρειόομαι	be worthless	vb.	ἀ-[√]-οω
	ἀχρεῖος ον	worthless, mere	adj.	ἀ-[√]-ιος
	ἄχρηστος ον	of little use, useless	adj.	ἀ-[√]-τος
	εὔχρηστος ον	useful	adj.	εὐ-[√]-τος
	καταχράομαι	use, use fully	vb.	κατα-[√]-ω
≥10	παραχρῆμα	immediately	adv.	παρα-[√]-μα
	συγχράομαι	associate with	vb.	συν-[√]-ω
	χράομαι	use	vb.	[√]-αω
≥25	χρεία ας	need	fem.	[√]-εια
	χρή	it ought	vb.	
	χρῄζω	need	vb.	[√]-ιζω
	χρῆμα ματος	possessions, wealth	neut.	[√]-μα
	χρήσιμον ου	good, value	neut.	[√]-ιμος
	χρῆσις εως	sexual intercourse	fem.	[√]-σις

ἀντι
oppose / replace
93

Memory Aid: Antichrist, anti-aircraft, antibiotic, Antarctic

≥10	ἀντί (gen.)	in place of, against	prep.
	ἄντικρυς (gen.)	opposite, off	prep.
	ἀντιπέρα (gen.)	opposite	prep.

ἀπάντησις εως	meeting	fem.	ἀπο-[√]-σις
ἀπέναντι (*gen.*)	opposite, before	prep.	ἀπο-ἐν-[√]
ἔναντι (*gen.*)	before (in judgment of)	prep.	ἐν-[√]
ἐναντίον (*gen.*)	before (in judgment of)	prep.	ἐν-[√]
ἐναντιόομαι	oppose, contradict	vb.	ἐν-[√]-οω
ἐναντίος α ον	against, hostile	adj.	ἐν-[√]-ιος
≥10 καταντάω	come, arrive	vb.	κατα-[√]-αω
κατέναντι (*gen.*)	opposite	prep./adv.	κατα-ἐν-[√]
συναντάω	meet, happen	vb.	συν-[√]-αω
τουναντίον	on the contrary	adv.	(τὸ ἐναντίον)
≥10 ὑπαντάω	meet, fight, oppose	vb.	ὑπο-[√]-αω
ὑπάντησις εως	meeting	fem.	ὑπο-[√]-σις
ὑπεναντίος α ον	against	adj.	ὑπο-ἐν-[√]-ιος

ἑπτ 93
seven
Memory Aid: Heptateuch

≥25 ἑπτά	seven	adj.	
ἑπτάκις	seven times	adv.	[√]-κις
ἑπτακισχίλιοι αι α	seven thousand	adj.	[√]-κις-χιλιοι
ἑπταπλασίων ον	seven times as much	adj.	[√]-ων (πλασίων)

θαλλασ 93
sea
Memory Aid:

διθάλασσος ον	between the seas	adj.	[δευ]-[√]-ος
≥25 θάλασσα ης	sea	fem.	[√]-α
παραθαλάσσιος α ον	by the sea or lake	adj.	παρα-[√]-ιος

πλε πλο 93
sail
Memory Aid: A boat *plies* the sea.

ἀποπλέω	set sail	vb.	ἀπο-[√]-ω
διαπλέω	sail across	vb.	δια-[√]-ω
ἐκπλέω	sail	vb.	ἐκ-[√]-ω
καταπλέω	sail	vb.	κατα-[√]-ω
παραπλέω	sail past	vb.	παρα-[√]-ω
πλέω	sail	vb.	[√]-ω
πλοιάριον ου	boat	neut.	[√]-αριον
≥25 πλοῖον ου	boat	neut.	[√]-ιον
πλοῦς πλοός	voyage	masc.	[√]-ς
ὑποπλέω	sail under the shelter of	vb.	ὑπο-[√]-ω

μαλ μαλλ 92
more
Memory Aid:

| ≥10 μάλιστα | most of all | adv. | [√]-ιστος |

≥25 μᾶλλον	more	adv.	[√]-ον

περισσ 91
abundance
Memory Aid:

ἐκπερισσῶς	emphatically	adv.	ἐκ-[√]-ως
περισσεία ας	abundance	fem.	[√]-εια
περίσσευμα ματος	abundance	neut.	[√]-μα
≥25 περισσεύω	be left over, abound	vb.	[√]-ευω
περισσός ή όν	more	adj.	[√]-ος
≥10 περισσότερος α ον	greater, more	adj.	[√]-τερος
≥10 περισσοτέρως	all the more	adv.	[√]-τερος-ως
περισσῶς	all the more	adv.	[√]-ως
ὑπερεκπερισσοῦ	with all earnestness	adv.	ὑπερ-ἐκ-[√]-ου
ὑπερπερισσεύω	increase abundantly	vb.	ὑπερ-[√]-ευω
ὑπερπερισσῶς	completely	adv.	ὑπερ-[√]-ως

κρατ 89
strong / power
Memory Aid: autocratic, democracy, democrat

ἀκρασία ας	lack of self control	fem.	ἀ-[√]-ια
ἀκρατής ές	uncontrolled, violent	adj.	ἀ-[√]-ης
ἐγκράτεια ας	self-control	fem.	ἐν-[√]-εια
ἐγκρατεύομαι	be self-controlled	vb.	ἐν-[√]-ευω
ἐγκρατής ές	self-controlled	adj.	ἐν-[√]-ης
κραταιόομαι	become strong	vb.	[√]-οω
κραταιός ά όν	strong	adj.	[√]-ιος
≥25 κρατέω	hold, seize	vb.	[√]-εω
κράτιστος η ον	most excellent	adj.	[√]-ιστος
≥10 κράτος ους	strength, power	neut.	[√]-ς
≥10 παντοκράτωρ ορος	the All-Powerful	masc.	[παν]-[√]-ρ
περικρατής ές	in control of	adj.	περι-[√]-ης

σημ 89
sign / indication
Memory Aid: semantics, semaphore

ἄσημος ον	insignificant	adj.	ἀ-[√]-ος
ἐπίσημος ον	well known	adj.	ἐπι-[√]-ος
εὔσημος ον	intelligible	adj.	εὐ-[√]-ος
παράσημος ον	marked by a figurehead	adj.	παρα-[√]-ος
σημαίνω	indicate	vb.	[√]-αινω
≥25 σημεῖον ου	sign, miracle	neut.	[√]-ιον
σημειόομαι	take / make note of	vb.	[√]-οω

θεα θεωρ 88
see
Memory Aid: theatre, theory

	ἀναθεωρέω	observe closely	vb.	ἀνα-[√]-εω
≥10	θεάομαι	see, observe	vb.	[√]-ω
	θεατρίζω	expose to public shame	vb.	[√]-ιζω
	θέατρον ου	theatre, spectacle	neut.	[√]-τρον
≥25	θεωρέω	see, observe	vb.	[√]-εω
	θεωρία ας	sight	fem.	[√]-ια
	παραθεωρέω	overlook	vb.	παρα-[√]-εω

κει 88
lie
Memory Aid: cemetery

≥10	ἀνάκειμαι	be seated (lie) at a table	vb.	ἀνα-[√]-μι
	ἀντίκειμαι	oppose	vb.	ἀντι-[√]-μι
	ἀπόκειμαι	be stored away	vb.	ἀπο-[√]-μι
	ἐπίκειμαι	lie on, crowd	vb.	ἐπι-[√]-μι
≥10	κατάκειμαι	lie, be sick	vb.	κατα-[√]-μι
≥10	κεῖμαι	lie, be laid, be	vb.	[√]-μι
	παράκειμαι	be present	vb.	παρα-[√]-μι
	περίκειμαι	be placed around	vb.	περι-[√]-μι
	πρόκειμαι	be set before, be present	vb.	προ-[√]-μι
	συνανάκειμαι	sit at table with	vb.	συν-ἀνα-[√]-μι

μητηρ μητρ 88
mother
Memory Aid: maternal, matron, matriarchy [Mother: *Grimm's Law.*]

	ἀμήτωρ ορος	without a mother	adj.	ἀ-[√]-ρ
≥25	μήτηρ τρός	mother	fem.	[√]-ρ
	μήτρα ας	womb	fem.	[√]-α
	μητρολῴας ου	mother-murderer	masc.	[√]-(ἀλοάω)-ας

πλει πλεον 88
more
Memory Aid: Pliocene [Sounds like *plenty.*]

	πλεῖστος η ον	most, large	adj.	[√]-ιστος
≥25	πλείων ον	more	adj.	[√]-ων
	πλεονάζω	increase, grow	vb.	[√]-αζω
	πλεονεκτέω	take advantage of	vb.	[√]-[ἐχ]-εω
	πλεονέκτης ου	one who is greedy	masc.	[√]-[ἐχ]-της
≥10	πλεονεξία ας	greed (>have more)	fem.	[√]-[ἐχ]-ια
	ὑπερπλεονάζω	overflow	vb.	ὑπερ-[√]-αζω

φυλακ φυλασσ 88
guard
Memory Aid: phylactery, prophylactic

	γαζοφυλάκιον ου	treasury, offering box	neut.	(γάζα)-[√]-ειον
	διαφυλάσσω	protect	vb.	δια-[√]-σσω

≥25 φυλακή ῆς	prison	fem.	[√]-η
φυλακίζω	imprison	vb.	[√]-ιζω
φυλακτήριον ου	phylactery	neut.	[√]-τηριον
φύλαξ ακος	guard	masc.	[√]-ξ
≥25 φυλάσσω	guard, keep, obey	vb.	[√]-σσω

ἀνοιγ 87
open / start
Memory Aid: *Opening* and closing doors *annoy* people.

≥25 ἀνοίγω	open	vb.	[√]-ω
ἄνοιξις εως	opening	fem.	[√]-σις
διανοίγω	open	vb.	δια-[√]-ω

κεφαλ 87
head / sum
Memory Aid: encephalitis [*cap, capital, captain*]

ἀνακεφαλαιόω	sum up, unite	vb.	ἀνα-[√]-οω
ἀποκεφαλίζω	behead	vb.	ἀπο-[√]-ιζω
κεφάλαιον ου	main point, summary	neut.	[√]-ιον
≥25 κεφαλή ῆς	head	fem.	[√]-η
κεφαλιόω	beat over the head	vb.	[√]-οω
περικεφαλαία ας	helmet	fem.	περι-[√]-ια
προσκεφάλαιον ου	pillow	neut.	προς-[√]-ιον

πειθ 87
persuade
Memory Aid:

ἀναπείθω	persuade, incite	vb.	ἀνα-[√]-ω
ἀπείθεια ας	disobedience	fem.	ἀ-[√]-εια
≥10 ἀπειθέω	disobey	vb.	ἀ-[√]-εω
ἀπειθής ές	disobedient	adj.	ἀ-[√]-ης
εὐπειθής ές	open to reason	adj.	εὐ-[√]-ης
πειθαρχέω	obey	vb.	[√]-[ἀρχ]-εω
πειθός ή όν	persuasive	adj.	[√]-ος
≥25 πείθω	persuade	vb.	[√]-ω
πειθώ οῦς	persuasiveness	fem.	ς
πεισμονή ῆς	persuasion	fem.	[√]-η

ἐλπ 86
hope
Memory Aid:

ἀπελπίζω	expect in return	vb.	ἀπο-[√]-ιζω
≥25 ἐλπίζω	hope	vb.	[√]-ιζω
≥25 ἐλπίς ίδος	hope	fem.	[√]-ς
προελπίζω	be the first to hope	vb.	προ-[√]-ιζω

ἐντολ ἐνταλ   85
commandment
Memory Aid: One must obey the *commandments in total.*

	ἔνταλμα ματος	commandment	neut.	[√]-μα
≥10	ἐντέλλομαι	command	vb.	[√]-ω
≥25	ἐντολή ῆς	commandment	fem.	[√]-η

τηρ   85
keep / observe
Memory Aid:

	διατηρέω	keep, treasure up	vb.	δια-[√]-εω
	παρατηρέω	keep, watch, observe	vb.	παρα-[√]-εω
	παρατήρησις εως	observation	fem.	παρα-[√]-σις
	συντηρέω	protect	vb.	συν-[√]-εω
≥25	τηρέω	keep, observe	vb.	[√]-εω
	τήρησις εως	custody, keeping	fem.	[√]-σις

ὑδρ   85
water
Memory Aid: hydrant, hydroplane, hydro-electric

	ἄνυδρος ον	waterless, desert	adj.	ἀ-[√]-ος
	ὑδρία ας	water jar	fem.	[√]-ια
	ὑδροποτέω	drink water	vb.	[√]-[πο²]-εω
	ὑδρωπικός ή όν	suffering from dropsy	adj.	[√]-ικος
≥25	ὕδωρ ὕδατος	water	neut.	[√]-ρ

σθεν   84
strong
Memory Aid: asthenia

≥10	ἀσθένεια ας	weakness	fem.	ἀ-[√]-εια
≥25	ἀσθενέω	be weak, be sick	vb.	ἀ-[√]-εω
	ἀσθένημα ματος	weakness	neut.	ἀ-[√]-μα
≥25	ἀσθενής ές	weak, sick	adj.	ἀ-[√]-ης
	σθενόω	strengthen	vb.	[√]-οω

ἑκασκ   82
each
Memory Aid:

≥25	ἕκαστος η ον	each, every	adj.	[√]-τος
	ἑκάστοτε	at all times	adv.	[√]-[οτε]

καρπ   82
fruit
Memory Aid: pericarp [Harvest: *see Grimm's Law.*]

	ἄκαρπος ον	barren, useless	adj.	ἀ-[√]-ος
≥25	καρπός οῦ	fruit	masc.	[√]-ος

| καρποφορέω | be fruitful / productive | vb. | [√]-[φερ]-εω |
| καρποφόρος ον | fruitful | adj. | [√]-[φερ]-ος |

πιν
drink
82

Memory Aid: symposium

	καταπίνω	swallow (>drink down)	vb.	κατα-[√]-ω
≥25	πίνω	drink	vb.	[√]-ω
	συμπίνω	drink with	vb.	συν-[√]-ω
	συμπόσιον ου	group (>symposium)	neut.	συν-[√]-ιον

στομ
mouth
80

Memory Aid: The *mouth* is the entrance to the *stomach*.

	ἀποστοματίζω	question (>from mouth)	vb.	ἀπο-[√]-ιζω
	ἐπιστομίζω	make silent	vb.	ἐπι-[√]-ιζω
≥25	στόμα ματος	mouth	neut.	[√]-μα

δεικ δειγ δειξ
show / example
79

Memory Aid: paradigm, paradigmatic, indicate

	ἀναδείκνυμι	show clearly, appoint	vb.	ἀνα-[√]-μι
	ἀνάδειξις εως	public appearance	fem.	ἀνα-[√]-σις
	ἀποδείκνυμι	attest, proclaim	vb.	ἀπο-[√]-μι
	ἀπόδειξις εως	proof, demonstration	fem.	ἀπο-[√]-σις
	δεῖγμα ματος	example, warning	neut.	[√]-μα
	δειγματίζω	disgrace, show publicly	vb.	μα-[√]-ιζω
≥25	δείκνυμι	show, explain	vb.	[√]-μι
	ἔνδειγμα ματος	evidence, proof	neut.	ἐν-[√]-μα
≥10	ἐνδείκνυμαι	show, give indication	vb.	ἐν-[√]-μι
	ἔνδειξις εως	evidence, indication	fem.	ἐν-[√]-σις
	ἐπιδείκνυμι	show	vb.	ἐπι-[√]-μι
	παραδειγματίζω	expose to ridicule	vb.	παρα-[√]-ιζω
	ὑπόδειγμα τος	example, copy	neut.	ὑπο-[√]-μα
	ὑποδείκνυμι	show, warn	vb.	ὑπο-[√]-μι

διο
therefore
79

Memory Aid:

≥25	διό	therefore	cj./pt.	
	διόπερ	therefore (emphatic)	cj./pt.	[√]-περ
≥10	διότι	because, for, therefore	cj./pt.	[√]-[ὅτι]

σταυρ
cross
79

Memory Aid: Sounds like *star—a cross*.

ἀνασταυρόω	crucify, crucify again	vb.	ἀνα-[√]-οω
≥25 σταυρός οῦ	cross	masc.	[√]-ος
≥25 σταυρόω	crucify	vb.	[√]-οω
συσταυρόομαι	be crucified together	vb.	συν-[√]-οω

δαιμ   78
demon

Memory Aid: demon

≥10 δαιμονίζομαι	be demon possessed	vb.	[√]-ιζω
≥25 δαιμόνιον ου	demon, spirit	neut.	[√]-ιον
δαιμονιώδης ες	demonic	adj.	[√]-ης
δαίμων ονος	demon	masc.	[√]-ων

ἐλε   78
mercy

Memory Aid:

ἀνελεήμων ον	unmerciful	adj.	ἀ-[√]-μων
ἀνέλεος ον	unmerciful	adj.	ἀ-[√]-ος
≥25 ἐλεάω (>ἐλεέω)	be merciful	vb.	[√]-αω-(εω)
ἐλεεινός ή όν	pitiable	adj.	[√]-ινος
≥10 ἐλεημοσύνη ης	charity	fem.	[√]-μων-συνη
ἐλεήμων ον	merciful	adj.	[√]-μων
≥25 ἔλεος ους	mercy	neut.	[√]-ος

λιθ   78
stone

Memory Aid: Paleolithic, lithograph, monolithic

καταλιθάζω	stone	vb.	κατα-[√]-αζω
λιθάζω	stone	vb.	[√]-αζω
λίθινος η ον	made of stones	adj.	[√]-ινος
λιθοβολέω	stone (>throw stones)	vb.	[√]-[βαλ]-εω
≥25 λίθος ου	stone	masc.	[√]-ος
λιθόστρωτον ου	pavement	neut.	[√]-(στορέννυμι)-ον

προσωπ   78
face

Memory Aid:

εὐπροσωπέω	make a good showing	vb.	εὐ-προς-[√]-εω
προσωπολημπτέω	show favoritism	vb.	[√]-[λαμβ]-εω
προσωπολήμπτης ου	shower of favoritism	masc.	[√]-[λαμβ]-της
προσωπολημψία ας	favoritism	fem.	[√]-[λαμβ]-σια
≥25 πρόσωπον	face		

ἐγγ   77
near

Memory Aid:

| ≥25 ἐγγίζω | approach | vb. | [√]-ιζω |

ἔγγυος ου	guarantor	masc.	[√]-ος
≥25 ἐγγύς	near	adv.	
ἐγγύτερον	nearer	adv.	[√]-τερον
προσεγγίζω	come near	vb.	προς-[√]-ιζω

μερ   77
part

Memory Aid: polymer [In a *merger*, different *parts* are brought together.]

≥10 διαμερίζω	divide	vb.	δια-[√]-ιζω
διαμερισμός οὖ	division	masc.	δια-[√]-ισμος
≥10 μερίζω	divide	vb.	[√]-ιζω
μερίς ίδος	part	fem.	[√]-ς
μερισμός οὖ	distribution, division	masc.	[√]-ισμος
μεριστής οὖ	one who divides	masc.	[√]-ιστης
≥25 μέρος ους	part, piece	neut.	[√]-ς
συμμερίζομαι	share with	vb.	συν-[√]-ιζω

σοφ   77
wisdom

Memory Aid: philosophy, Sophia

ἄσοφος ον	senseless, foolish	adj.	ἀ-[√]-ος
κατασοφίζομαι	take advantage of	vb.	κατα-[√]-ιζω
≥25 σοφία ας	wisdom	fem.	[√]-ια
σοφίζω	give wisdom	vb.	[√]-ιζω
≥10 σοφός ή όν	wise, experienced	adj.	[√]-ος
φιλοσοφία ας	philosophy	fem.	[φιλ]-[√]-ια
φιλόσοφος ου	philosopher, teacher	masc.	[φιλ]-[√]-ος

βουλ   76
plan

Memory Aid: boule [Plan: *see Grimm's Law.*]

βουλεύομαι	plan, consider	vb.	[√]-ευω
βουλευτής οὖ	councillor	masc.	[√]-της
≥10 βουλή ῆς	plan, intention	fem.	[√]-η
βούλημα ματος	plan, intention, desire	neut.	[√]-μα
≥25 βούλομαι	plan, want	vb.	[√]-ω
ἐπιβουλή ῆς	plot	fem.	ἐπι-[√]-η
συμβουλεύω	advise	vb.	συν-[√]-ευω
συμβούλιον ου	plan, plot	neut.	συν-[√]-ιον
σύμβουλος ου	counselor	masc.	συν-[√]-ος

ἐμ   76
my / mine

Memory Aid: Reverse of letters of English *me.*

≥25 ἐμός ή όν	my, mine	adj.	[√]-ος

ἐσθι   75
eat

Memory Aid:

≥25 ἐσθίω	eat	vb.	[√]-ω
κατεσθίω	eat up, devour	vb.	κατα-[√]-ω
συνεσθίω	eat with	vb.	συν-[√]-ω

ἰσχυ   75
strong

Memory Aid:

διϊσχυρίζομαι	insist	vb.	δια-[√]-ιζω
ἐνισχύω	strenghten	vb.	ἐν-[√]-ω
ἐξισχύω	be fully able	vb.	ἐκ-[√]-ω
ἐπισχύω	insist	vb.	ἐπι-[√]-ω
≥25 ἰσχυρός ά όν	strong	adj.	[√]-ρος
≥10 ἰσχύς ύος	strength	fem.	[√]-ς
≥25 ἰσχύω	be able	vb.	[√]-ω
κατισχύω	have strength, defeat	vb.	κατα-[√]-ω

κραζ κραυγ   75
shout

Memory Aid: Note shared letters c-r-y in word cry.

ἀνακράζω	cry out	vb.	ἀνα-[√]-ω
≥25 κράζω	shout, call out	vb.	[√]-ω
κραυγάζω	shout, call out	vb.	[√]-ω
κραυγή ῆς	shout	fem.	[√]-η

κτειν   74
kill

Memory Aid:

≥25 ἀποκτείνω	kill	vb.	ἀπο-[√]-ω

μεσο μεσι   74
middle

Memory Aid: Mesopotamia

μεσιτεύω	mediate	vb.	[√]-ευω
μεσίτης ου	mediator	masc.	[√]-της
μεσονύκτιον ου	midnight	neut.	[√]-[νυ]-ιον
Μεσοποταμία ας	Mesopotamia	fem.	[√]-[πο(1)]-ια
≥25 μέσος η ον	middle	adj.	[√]-ος
μεσότοιχον ου	dividing wall	neut.	[√]-(τεῖχος)-ον
μεσουράνημα τος	mid-heaven	neut.	[√]-[οὐραν]-μα
μεσόω	be in the middle	vb.	[√]-οω

σωτηρ   74
salvation

Memory Aid: soteriology, Soter

≥10	σωτήρ ἦρος	savior	masc.	[√]-ρ
≥25	σωτηρία ας	salvation, release	fem.	[√]-ια
	σωτήριον ου	salvation	neut.	[√]-ιον
	σωτήριος ον	saving	adj.	[√]-ιος

θυ θυσ   73
sacrifice
Memory Aid:

	εἰδωλόθυτον ου	meat offered to idols	neut.	[εἰδωλ]-[√]-ον
≥25	θυσία ας	sacrifice	fem.	[√]-ια
≥10	θυσιαστήριον ου	altar (>place of sacrifice)	neut.	[√]-τηριον
≥10	θύω	sacrifice, kill	vb.	[√]-ω

κηρυξ κηρυγ κηρυσσ   73
preach
Memory Aid: kerygma

	κήρυγμα ματος	message, kerygma	neut.	[√]-μα
	κῆρυξ υκος	preacher	masc.	[√]-ξ
≥25	κηρύσσω	preach, proclaim	vb.	[√]-σσω
	προκηρύσσω	preach beforehand	vb.	προ-[√]-σσω

κοιν κοινων   73
common
Memory Aid: koinonia, koine Greek [*common, community*]

≥10	κοινός ή όν	common, profane	adj.	[√]-ος
≥10	κοινόω	defile (>make common)	vb.	[√]-οω
	κοινωνέω	share, participate	vb.	[√]-εω
≥10	κοινωνία ας	fellowship	fem.	[√]-ια
	κοινωνικός ή όν	liberal, generous, sharing	adj.	[√]-ικος
≥10	κοινωνός οῦ	partner	masc./fem.	[√]-ος
	συγκοινωνέω	take part in	vb.	συν-[√]-εω
	συγκοινωνός οῦ	sharer	masc.	συν-[√]-ος

πρεσβυ   73
old / elderly
Memory Aid: presbyter

	πρεσβυτέριον ου	body of elders	neut.	[√]-τερος-ιον
≥25	πρεσβύτερος ου	elder, presbyter	masc.	[√]-τερος
	πρεσβύτης ου	old man	masc.	[√]-της
	πρεσβῦτις ιδος	old woman	fem.	[√]-ς
	συμπρεσβύτερος ου	fellow-elder	masc.	συν-[√]-τερος

φιλ   73
love
Memory Aid: philanthropy, philosophy, Philadelphia

	καταφιλέω	kiss	vb.	κατα-[√]-εω
	προσφιλής ές	pleasing	adj.	προς-[√]-ης

φίλαυτος ον	selfish	adj.	[√]-[αὐτο]-ος
≥25 φιλέω	love, like, kiss	vb.	[√]-εω
φίλημα ματος	kiss	neut.	[√]-μα
φιλία ας	love, friendship	fem.	[√]-ια
≥25 φίλος ου	friend	masc.	[√]-ος
φιλοτιμέομαι	aspire	vb.	[φιλ]-[√]εω

πασχ   72
suffer

Memory Aid: passion, compassion, Paschal lamb

≥25 πάσχα	Passover	neut.	
≥25 πάσχω	suffer	vb.	[√]-ω
προπάσχω	suffer previously	vb.	προ-[√]-ω
συμπάσχω	suffer together	vb.	συν-[√]-ω

σκ σκοτ   71
dark

Memory Aid: scotoma

ἀποσκίασμα ματος	shadow, darkness	neut.	ἀπο-[√]-μα
ἐπισκιάζω	overshadow	vb.	ἐπι-[√]-αζω
σκιά ᾶς	shadow, shade	fem.	[√]-α
σκοτεινός ή όν	dark	adj.	[√]-ινος
≥10 σκοτία ας	darkness	fem.	[√]-ια
σκοτίζομαι	become dark	vb.	[√]-ιζω
σκοτόομαι	become dark	vb.	[√]-οω
≥25 σκότος ους	darkness, sin	neut.	[√]-ς

καλυπτ καλυμ καλυψ   70
hide

Memory Aid: Apocalypse

ἀκατακάλυπτος ον	uncovered	adj.	ἀ-κατα-[√]-τος
ἀνακαλύπτω	uncover, unveil	vb.	ἀνα-[√]-ω
≥25 ἀποκαλύπτω	reveal	vb.	ἀπο-[√]-ω
≥10 ἀποκάλυψις εως	revelation, Apocalypse	fem.	ἀπο-[√]-σις
ἐπικάλυμμα ματος	covering, pretext	neut.	ἐπι-[√]-μα
ἐπικαλύπτω	cover (sin)	vb.	ἐπι-[√]-ω
κάλυμμα ματος	veil	neut.	[√]-μα
καλύπτω	cover, hide	vb.	[√]-ω
κατακαλύπτομαι	cover one's head	vb.	κατα-[√]-ω
παρακαλύπτομαι	be hidden	vb.	παρα-[√]-ω
περικαλύπτω	cover, conceal	vb.	περι-[√]-ω
συγκαλύπτω	cover up	vb.	συν-[√]-ω

ῥη² ῥητ   70
word

Memory Aid: orator, rhetoric

≥25 ῥῆμα ματος	word, thing, event	neut.	[√]-μα
ῥήτωρ ορος	lawyer, spokesperson	masc.	[√]-τωρ
ῥητῶς	expressly	adv.	[√]-ως

πλου
rich
69

Memory Aid: plutocracy [*plush, plumage*]

≥25 πλούσιος α ον	rich	adj.	[√]-ιος
πλουσίως	richly	adv.	[√]-ως
≥10 πλουτέω	be rich, prosper	vb.	[√]-εω
πλουτίζω	make rich	vb.	[√]-ιζω
≥10 πλοῦτος ου	wealth	masc.	[√]-ος

τεμν τομ
cut
69

Memory Aid: appendectomy, mastectomy, tome, atom

ἀπερίτμητος ον	uncircumcised	adj.	ἀ-περι-[√]-τος
ἀποτομία ας	severity	fem.	ἀπο-[√]-ια
ἀποτόμως	severely	adv.	ἀπο-[√]-ως
ἄτομος ον	indivisible	adj.	ἀ-[√]-ος
δίστομος ον	double-edged	adj.	[δευ]-[√]-ος
διχοτομέω	cut in pieces	vb.	[δευ]-[√]-εω
κατατομή ῆς	mutilation	fem.	κατα-[√]-η
λατομέω	cut, hew (of rock)	vb.	[λιθ]-[√]-εω
≥10 περιτέμνω	circumcise	vb.	περι-[√]-ω
≥25 περιτομή ῆς	circumcision	fem.	περι-[√]-η
συντέμνω	cut short	vb.	συν-[√]-ω
τομός ή όν	sharp, cutting	adj.	[√]-ος

πειρ
test
68

Memory Aid: pirate

ἀπείραστος ον	unable to be tempted	adj.	ἀ-[√]-τος
ἐκπειράζω	test, tempt	vb.	ἐκ-[√]-αζω
πεῖρα ας	attempt	fem.	[√]-α
≥25 πειράζω	test, tempt	vb.	[√]-αζω
πειράομαι	try, attempt	vb.	[√]-αω
≥10 πειρασμός οῦ	trial, period of testing	masc.	[√]-σμος
περιπείρω	pierce through	vb.	περι-[√]-ω

πο² ποτ ποταμ
drink / river (compare πιν)
68

Memory Aid: Mesopotamia, hippopotamus

πόσις εως	drink	fem.	[√]-σις
≥10 ποταμός οῦ	river	masc.	[√]-ος
ποταμοφόρητος ον	swept away	adj.	[√]-[φερ]-τος

≥25 ποτήριον ου	cup (>place for water)	neut.	[√]-τηριον
≥10 ποτίζω	give to drink, water	vb.	[√]-ιζω
πότος ου	drunken orgy	masc.	[√]-ος

ἱματ
clothe
Memory Aid:

ἱματίζω	clothe, dress	vb.	[√]-ιζω
≥25 ἱμάτιον ου	clothes, coat	neut.	[√]-ιον
ἱματισμός οῦ	clothing	masc.	[√]-ισμος

67

νυ νυκ νυχ νυσ
night
Memory Aid: Sounds like the first syllable in *nocturnal*.

διανυκτερεύω	spend the night	vb.	δια-[√]-ευω
ἔννυχα	in the night	adv.	ἐν-[√]-α
κατάνυξις εως	stupor, numbness	fem.	κατα-[√]-ς
≥25 νύξ νυκτός	night	fem.	[√]-ξ
νυστάζω	be asleep, drowsy, idle	vb.	[√]-αζω
νυχθήμερον ου	a night and a day	neut.	[√]-[ἡμερ]-ον

67

ἄχρι
until
Memory Aid:

| ≥25 ἄχρι *(gen.)* | until, to, as, when | cj./prep. | |
| ≥10 μέχρι *(gen.)* | until, to | cj./prep. | |

66

ἑτοιμ
ready / prepare
Memory Aid:

≥25 ἑτοιμάζω	prepare, make ready	vb.	[√]-αζω
ἑτοιμασία ας	readiness, equipment	fem.	[√]-ια
≥10 ἕτοιμος η ον	ready	adj.	[√]-ος
ἑτοίμως	readily	adv.	[√]-ως
προετοιμάζω	prepare beforehand	vb.	προ-[√]-αζω

64

καυχη καυχα
proud
Memory Aid: A *proud* person is often *cocky*.

ἐγκαυχάομαι	boast	vb.	ἐν-[√]-αω
κατακαυχάομαι	be proud, despise	vb.	κατα-[√]-αω
≥25 καυχάομαι	be proud, boast	vb.	[√]-αω
≥10 καύχημα ματος	pride, boasting	neut.	[√]-μα
≥10 καύχησις εως	pride, boasting	fem.	[√]-σις

64

κληρ
share / choose
Memory Aid: clergy

64

≥10	κληρονομέω	receive, share (in)	vb.	[√]-[νομ]-εω
≥10	κληρονομία ας	property	fem.	[√]-[νομ]-ια
≥10	κληρονόμος ου	heir	masc.	[√]-[νομ]-ος
≥10	κλῆρος ου	lot, share	masc.	[√]-ος
	κληρόω	choose	vb.	[√]-οω
	προσκληρόομαι	join	vb.	προσ-[√]-οω
	συγκληρονόμος ον	sharing	adj.	συν-[√]-[νομ]-ος

ὀρ   64
hill
Memory Aid:

	ὀρεινή ῆς	hill country	fem.	[√]-η
≥25	ὄρος ους	mountain, hill	neut.	[√]-ς

θρον   62
throne
Memory Aid: throne

≥25	θρόνος ου	throne	masc.	[√]-ος

στρατ   61
army
Memory Aid: strategy

	ἀντιστρατεύομαι	war against	vb.	ἀντι-[√]-ευω
	στρατεία ας	warfare, fight	fem.	[√]-εια
	στράτευμα ματος	troops, army	neut.	[√]-μα
	στρατεύομαι	serve as a soldier, battle	vb.	[√]-ευω
≥10	στρατηγός οῦ	chief officer	masc.	[√]-[ἀγ]-ος
	στρατιά ᾶς	army	fem.	[√]-ια
≥25	στρατιώτης ου	soldier	masc.	[√]-της
	στρατολογέω	enlist soldiers	vb.	[√]-[λεγ]-εω
	στρατοπεδάρχης ου	officer	masc.	[√]-[πο¹] [ἀρχ]-ης
	στρατόπεδον ου	army	neut.	[√]-[πο¹]-ον
	συστρατιώτης ου	fellow-soldier	masc.	συν-[√]-της

ὧδε   61
here
Memory Aid:

≥25	ὧδε	here	adv.	

δε²   60
bind
Memory Aid: diadem, syndetic

≥25	δέω	bind	vb.	[√]-ω
	διάδημα ματος	diadem	neut.	δια-[√]-μα
	καταδέω	bandage, bind up	vb.	κατα-[√]-ω
	περιδέω	wrap, bind	vb.	περι-[√]-ω
	συνδέομαι	be in prison with	vb.	συν-[√]-ω

	ὑποδέομαι	put on shoes	vb.	ὑπο-[√]-ω
≥10	ὑπόδημα ματος	sandal	neut.	ὑπο-[√]-μα

ἤδη 60
now / already
Memory Aid:

≥25 ἤδη	now, already	adv.	

προσκυν 60
worship
Memory Aid:

≥25 προσκυνέω	worship	vb.	[√]-εω
προσκυνητής οῦ	worshiper	masc.	[√]-της

τρεπ τροπ 60
turn
Memory Aid: tropic, trophy

	ἀνατρέπω	overturn	vb.	ἀνα-[√]-ω
	ἀποτρέπομαι	avoid (>turn from)	vb.	ἀπο-[√]-ω
	ἐκτρέπομαι	wander, go astray	vb.	ἐκ-[√]-ω
	ἐντρέπω	make ashamed	vb.	ἐν-[√]-ω
	ἐντροπή ῆς	shame	fem.	ἐν-[√]-η
≥10	ἐπιτρέπω	let, allow	vb.	ἐπι-[√]-ω
	ἐπιτροπή ῆς	commission	fem.	ἐπι-[√]-η
	ἐπίτροπος ου	steward, guardian	masc.	ἐπι-[√]-ος
	μετατρέπω	turn, change	vb.	μετα-[√]-ω
	περιτρέπω	drive insane	vb.	περι-[√]-ω
	προτρέπομαι	encourage	vb.	προ-[√]-ω
	τροπή ῆς	turning, change	fem.	[√]-η
≥10	τρόπος ου	way, manner	masc.	[√]-ος
	τροποφορέω	put up with	vb.	[√]-[φερ]-εω

χρον 60
time
Memory Aid: chronology, synchronize, chronicles, chronic

	χρονίζω	delay (>use time)	vb.	[√]-ιζω
≥25	χρόνος ου	time	masc.	[√]-ος
	χρονοτριβέω	spend time	vb.	[√]-(τρίβω)-εω

ἀξι 59
worthy
Memory Aid: axiom

	ἀνάξιος ον	unworthy	adj.	ἀ-[√]-ιος
	ἀναξίως	unworthily	adv.	ἀ-[√]-ως
≥25	ἄξιος α ον	worthy	adj.	[√]-ιος
	ἀξιόω	consider / make worthy	vb.	[√]-οω

| ἀξίως | worthily | adv. | [√]-ως |
| κατaξιόω | make / count worthy | vb. | κατα-[√]-οω |

ἐρημ
desert
Memory Aid: hermit, eremite

	ἐρημία ας	desert	fem.	[√]-ια
	ἐρημόομαι	to be made waste	vb.	[√]-οω
≥25	ἔρημος ον	lonely, desolate	adj.	[√]-ος
	ἐρήμωσις εως	desolation	fem.	[√]-σις

59

πρασ πραγ
matter / event / something done
Memory Aid: practice, pragmatic

	διαπραγματεύομαι	make a profit, earn	vb.	δια-[√]-ευω
≥10	πρᾶγμα ματος	matter, event	neut.	[√]-μα
	πραγματεῖαι ῶν (*pl.*)	affairs	fem.	[√]-εια
	πραγματεύομαι	trade, do business	vb.	[√]-ευω
	πρᾶξις εως	deed, practice	fem.	[√]-σις
≥25	πράσσω	do	vb.	[√]-σσω

59

συν
with
Memory Aid: synonym, sympathy, symphony, synthesis

| ≥25 | σύν (*dat.*) | with | prep. | |

59

θλιβ θλιψ
trouble / crowd
Memory Aid: thlipsis

	ἀποθλίβω	crowd in upon	vb.	ἀπο-[√]-ω
≥10	θλίβω	crush, press	vb.	[√]-ω
≥25	θλῖψις εως	trouble	fem.	[√]-ς
	συνθλίβω	crowd, press upon	vb.	συν-[√]-ω

58

διωκ διωγ
persecute
Memory Aid:

≥10	διωγμός οῦ	persecution	masc.	[√]-μος
	διώκτης ου	persecutor	masc.	[√]-της
≥25	διώκω	persecute, pursue	vb.	[√]-ω
	ἐκδιώκω	persecute harshly	vb.	ἐκ-[√]-ω
	καταδιώκω	pursue diligently	vb.	κατα-[√]-ω

57

πλαν
error / wandering
Memory Aid: planet

| | ἀποπλανάω | mislead, deceive | vb. | ἀπο-[√]-αω |

57

≥25 πλανάω	lead astray	vb.	[√]-αω
≥10 πλάνη ης	error, deceit	fem.	[√]-η
πλανήτης ου	wanderer	masc.	[√]-της
πλάνος ον	deceitful	adj.	[√]-ος

βλασφημ 56
blaspheme (compare φα)
Memory Aid: blaspheme

≥25 βλασφημέω	blaspheme, slander	vb.	[√]-εω
≥10 βλασφημία ας	blasphemy, slander	fem.	[√]-ια
βλάσφημος ον	blasphemous	adj.	[√]-ος

γαμ 56
marriage
Memory Aid: monogamy, bigamy, polygamy

	ἄγαμος ου	unmarried, single	masc./fem.	ἀ-[√]-ος
≥25	γαμέω	marry	vb.	[√]-εω
	γαμίζω	give in marriage	vb.	[√]-ιζω
	γαμίσκω	give in marriage	vb.	[√]-σκω
≥10	γάμος ου	marriage, wedding	masc.	[√]-ος
	ἐπιγαμβρεύω	marry	vb.	ἐπι-[√]-ευω

δοκιμ 56
examine
Memory Aid: One should *examine* legal *documents* closely.

	ἀδόκιμος ον	disqualified, worthless	adj.	ἀ-[√]-ος
	ἀποδοκιμάζω	reject (after testing)	vb.	ἀπο-[√]-αζω
≥10	δοκιμάζω	examine, discern	vb.	[√]-αζω
	δοκιμασία ας	examination, test	fem.	[√]-ια
	δοκιμή ῆς	character, evidence	fem.	[√]-η
	δοκίμιον ου	examination, testing	neut.	[√]-ιον
	δόκιμος ον	approved, examined	adj.	[√]-ος

μακαρ 55
blessed
Memory Aid: macarism

	μακαρίζω	consider blessed	vb.	[√]-ιζω
≥25	μακάριος α ον	blessed, happy	adj.	[√]-ιος
	μακαρισμός οῦ	blessing, happiness	masc.	[√]-ισμος

σεβ 55
worship / piety / religion
Memory Aid: Eusebius

	ἀσέβεια ας	godlessness	fem.	ἀ-[√]-εια
	ἀσεβέω	live in an impious way	vb.	ἀ-[√]-εω
	ἀσεβής ές	godless	adj.	ἀ-[√]-ης
≥10	εὐσέβεια ας	godliness, religion	fem.	εὐ-[√]-εια

εὐσεβέω	worship	vb.	εὐ-[√]-εω
εὐσεβής ές	godly, religious	adj.	εὐ-[√]-ης
εὐσεβῶς	in a godly manner	adv.	εὐ-[√]-ως
σεβάζομαι	worship, reverence	vb.	[√]-αζω
σέβασμα ματος	object / place of worship	neut.	[√]-μα
σεβαστός ή όν	imperial	adj.	[√]-τος
≥10 σέβομαι	worship	vb.	[√]-ω

δεξ
right
Memory Aid: dexterity

| ≥25 δεξιός ά όν | right | adj. | [√]-ιος |

54

ἐτ
year
Memory Aid:

διετής ές	two years old	adj.	[δευ]-[√]-ης
διετία ας	two-year period	fem.	[δευ]-[√]-ια
≥25 ἔτος ους	year	neut.	[√]-ς
τεσσαρακονταετής ές	forty years	adj.	[τεσσ]-κοντα-[√]-ης

54

μακρ μακρο
long
Memory Aid: macrocosm, macron

≥10 μακράν	far, at a distance	adv.	
≥10 μακρόθεν	far, at a distance	adv.	[√]-θεν
≥10 μακροθυμέω	be patient	vb.	[√]-[θυμ]-εω
≥10 μακροθυμία ας	patience	fem.	[√]-[θυμ]-ια
μακροθύμως	patiently	adv.	[√]-[θυμ]-ως
μακρός ά όν	long, distant	adj.	[√]-ρος
μακροχρόνιος ον	long-lived	adj.	[√]-[χρον]-ιος

54

ὑψ
high
Memory Aid: hypsography

ὑπερυψόω	raise to highest position	vb.	ὑπερ-[√]-οω
≥10 ὑψηλός ή όν	high	adj.	[√]-λος
ὑψηλοφρονέω	be proud	vb.	[√]-[φρ]-εω
≥10 ὕψιστος η ον	highest	adj.	[√]-ιστος
ὕψος ους	height, heaven	neut.	[√]-ος
≥10 ὑψόω	exalt (>make high)	vb.	[√]-οω
ὕψωμα ματος	height, stronghold	neut.	[√]-μα

54

ἐσχατ
last / final
Memory Aid: eschatology, eschaton

| ≥25 ἔσχατος η ον | last, final | adj. | [√]-τος |
| ἐσχάτως | finally | adv. | [√]-ως |

53

τυφλ
blind   *53*

Memory Aid: *Blindness* is a *tough (tuf) loss.*

≥25	τυφλός ή όν	blind	adj.	[√]-ος
	τυφλόω	make blind	vb.	[√]-οω

θαυμ
wonder   *52*

Memory Aid: thaumaturgy

	ἐκθαυμάζω	be completely amazed	vb.	ἐκ-[√]-αζω
	θαῦμα ματος	wonder, miracle	neut.	[√]-μα
≥25	θαυμάζω	marvel	vb.	[√]-αζω
	θαυμάσιος α ον	wonderful	adj.	[√]-ιος
	θαυμαστός ή όν	marvelous, astonishing	adj.	[√]-τος

γλωσσ
tongue   *51*

Memory Aid: glossary, glossalalia, gloss

≥25	γλῶσσα ης	tongue, language	fem.	[√]-α
	ἑτερόγλωσσος ον	with strange language	adj.	[ἑτερ]-[√]-ος

δεσμ
bind / imprison (compare δε²)

Memory Aid: *51*

	δεσμεύω	bind	vb.	[√]-ευω
	δέσμη ης	bundle	fem.	[√]-η
≥10	δέσμιος ου	prisoner	masc.	[√]-ιος
≥10	δεσμός οῦ	bond, chain, jail	masc.	[√]-ος
	δεσμοφύλαξ ακος	jailer	masc.	[√]-[φυλακ]
	δεσμωτήριον ου	jail, prison	neut.	[√]-τηριον
	δεσμώτης ου	prisoner	masc.	[√]-της
	σύνδεσμος ου	bond, chain	masc.	συν-[√]-ος

ἡγ ἡγεμ ἡγεμον
govern (compare with ἀγ)

Memory Aid: hegemony   *51*

	ἡγεμονεύω	be governor, rule	vb.	[√]-ευω
	ἡγεμονία ας	reign, rule	fem.	[√]-ια
≥10	ἡγεμών όνος	governor, ruler	masc.	[√]-ων
≥25	ἡγέομαι	lead, rule, consider	vb.	[√]-εω

καιν
new   *51*

Memory Aid: Cenozoic, Pliocene

	ἀνακαινίζω	renew	vb.	ἀνα-[√]-ιζω
	ἀνακαινόω	renew, remake	vb.	ἀνα-[√]-οω

ἀνακαίνωσις εως	renewal	fem.	ἀνα-[√]-σις
ἐγκαινίζω	inaugurate, open	vb.	ἐν-[√]-ιζω
≥25 καινός ή όν	new	adj.	[√]-ος
καινότης ητος	newness	fem.	[√]-οτης

οι   51
such / as
Memory Aid: See Chart A.

≥10 οἷος α ον	such, such as	adj.	[√]-ος
ὁποῖος α ον	as, such as	adj.	[√]-ος
≥25 ποῖος α ον	what, what kind of	pron.	[√]-ος

φθαρ φθειρ φθορ   51
decay
Memory Aid:

ἀφθαρσία ας	imperishability	fem.	ἀ-[√]-ια
ἄφθαρτος ον	imperishable	adj.	ἀ-[√]-τος
ἀφθορία ας	integrity	fem.	ἀ-[√]-ια
διαφθείρω	decay, destroy	vb.	δια-[√]-ω
διαφθορά ᾶς	decay	fem.	δια-[√]-α
καταφθείρω	corrupt, ruin	vb.	κατα-[√]-ω
φθαρτός ή όν	perishable, mortal	adj.	[√]-τος
φθείρω	corrupt, ruin	vb.	[√]-ω
φθινοπωρινός ή όν	of late autumn	adj.	[√]-(ὀπώρα)-ινος

ψευδ   51
false
Memory Aid: pseudonym, Pseudepigrapha

ἀψευδής ές	trustworthy, non-lying	adj.	ἀ-[√]-ης
ψευδάδελφος ου	false brother	masc.	[√]-[ἀδελφ]-ος
ψευδαπόστολος ου	false apostle	masc.	[√]-[στελ]-ος
ψευδής ές	false	adj.	[√]-ης
ψευδοδιδάσκαλος ου	false teacher	masc.	[√]-[διδασκ]-ος
ψευδολόγος ου	liar	masc.	[√]-[λεγ]-ος
≥10 ψεύδομαι	lie	vb.	[√]-ω
ψευδομαρτυρέω	give false witness	vb.	[√]-[μαρτυρ]-εω
ψευδομαρτυρία ας	false witness	fem.	[√]-[μαρτυρ]-ια
ψευδόμαρτυς υρος	false witness	masc.	[√]-[μαρτυρ]-ς
≥10 ψεῦδος ους	lie, imitation	neut.	[√]-ς
ψεῦσμα ματος	lie, untruthfulness	neut.	[√]-μα
≥10 ψεύστης ου	liar	masc.	[√]-της

ἀσχημ αἰσχ   50
shame
Memory Aid: Sounds something like *ashamed*.

| αἰσχροκερδής ές | greedy (>shameful gain) | adj. | [√]-[κερδ]-ης |

αἰσχροκερδῶς	greedily	adv.	[√]-[κερδ]-ως
αἰσχρολογία ας	obscene speech	fem.	[√]-[λεγ]-ια
αἰσχρός ά όν	disgraceful	adj.	[√]-ρος
αἰσχρότης ητος	shameful behavior	fem.	[√]-οτης
αἰσχύνη ης	shame, shameful thing	fem.	[√]-η
αἰσχύνομαι	be ashamed	vb.	[√]-υνω
ἀνεπαίσχυντος ον	unashamed	adj.	ἀ-ἐπι-[√]-τος
ἀσχημονέω	act improperly	vb.	[√]-εω
ἀσχημοσύνη ης	shameless act	fem.	[√]-συνη
ἀσχήμων ον	unpresentable, shameful	adj.	[√]-ων
≥10 ἐπαισχύνομαι	be ashamed	vb.	ἐπι-[√]-υνω
≥10 καταισχύνω	put to shame	vb.	κατα-[√]-υνω

δυ *50*
clothe
Memory Aid: endue

ἀπεκδύομαι	disarm, discard	vb.	ἀπο-ἐκ-[√]-ω
ἀπέκδυσις εως	putting off	fem.	ἀπο-ἐκ-[√]-σις
ἐκδύω	strip	vb.	ἐκ-[√]-ω
ἐνδιδύσκω	dress in	vb.	ἐν-[√]-σκω
ἔνδυμα ματος	clothing	neut.	ἐν-[√]-μα
ἔνδυσις εως	wearing	fem.	ἐν-[√]-σις
≥25 ἐνδύω	clothe, wear (>endue)	vb.	ἐν-[√]-ω
ἐπενδύομαι	put on	vb.	ἐπι-ἐν-[√]-ω
ἐπενδύτης ου	outer garment	masc.	ἐπι-ἐν-[√]-της

κοπ *50*
work
Memory Aid: Some people find it hard to *cope* with *work*.

εὐκοπώτερος α ον	easier	adj.	εὐ-[√]-τερος
κοπή ῆς	slaughter, defeat	fem.	[√]-η
≥10 κοπιάω	work, grow tired	vb.	[√]-αω
≥10 κόπος ου	work, trouble	masc.	[√]-ος
προκοπή ῆς	progress	fem.	προ-[√]-η
προκόπτω	advance, progress	vb.	προ-[√]-ω

ὀφειλ *50*
debt
Memory Aid:

ὀφειλέτης ου	debtor, offender	masc.	[√]-της
ὀφειλή ῆς	debt	fem.	[√]-η
ὀφείλημα ματος	debt	neut.	[√]-μα
≥25 ὀφείλω	owe, ought	vb.	[√]-ω
προσοφείλω	owe	vb.	προς-[√]-ω
χρεοφειλέτης ου	debtor	masc.	[χρ]-[√]-της

ἀγορ 49
market / place of business transactions
Memory Aid: agora

≥10 ἀγορά ᾶς	market place	fem.	[√]-α
≥25 ἀγοράζω	buy, redeem	vb.	[√]-αζω
ἀγοραῖος ου	loafer, court session	masc.	[√]-ιος
ἀλληγορέω	speak allegorically	vb.	[ἀλλ]-[√]-εω
δημηγορέω	make a speech	vb.	[δημ]-[√]-εω
ἐξαγοράζω	set free	vb.	ἐκ-[√]-αζω

αἱρ 49
take away / seize
Memory Aid: diaeresis

ἀναίρεσις εως	killing, murder	fem.	ἀνα-[√]-σις
≥10 ἀναιρέω	do away with, take life	vb.	ἀνα-[√]-εω
≥10 ἀφαιρέω	take away	vb.	ἀπο-[√]-εω
διαίρεσις εως	variety, difference	fem.	δια-[√]-σις
διαιρέω	divide, distribute	vb.	δια-[√]-εω
ἐξαιρέω	pull out, rescue	vb.	ἐκ-[√]-εω
καθαίρεσις εως	destruction	fem.	κατα-[√]-σις
καθαιρέω	take down, destroy	vb.	κατα-[√]-εω
περιαιρέω	take away, remove	vb.	περι-[√]-εω

κρυπτ κρυφ 49
hide
Memory Aid: crypt, cryptic, cryptography, Apocrypha

ἀποκρύπτω	hide, keep secret	vb.	ἀπο-[√]-ω
ἀπόκρυφος ον	hidden, secret	adj.	ἀπο-[√]-ος
ἐγκρύπτω	place / mix / hide in	vb.	ἐν-[√]-ω
κρύπτη ης	hidden place, cellar	fem.	[√]-η
≥10 κρυπτός ή όν	hidden, secret	adj.	[√]-ος
≥10 κρύπτω	hide, cover	vb.	[√]-ω
κρυφαῖος α ον	hidden, secret	adj.	[√]-ιος
κρυφῇ	secretly	adv.	[√]-η
περικρύβω	keep in seclusion	vb.	περι-[√]-ω

παυ 49
stop
Memory Aid: pause, menopause, pose, repose

ἀκατάπαυστος ον	unceasing	adj.	ἀ-κατα-[√]-τος
ἀνάπαυσις εως	relief, rest	fem.	ἀνα-[√]-σις
≥10 ἀναπαύω	relieve, rest, refresh	vb.	ἀνα-[√]-ω
ἐπαναπαύομαι	rest / rely upon	vb.	ἐπι-ἀνα-[√]-ω
κατάπαυσις εως	place of rest, rest	fem.	κατα-[√]-σις
καταπαύω	cause to rest, prevent	vb.	κατα-[√]-ω

≥10	παύω	stop	vb.	[√]-ω
	συναναπαύομαι	have a time of rest with	vb.	συν-ἀνα-[√]-ω

θηρ
wild animal   48
Memory Aid:

	θήρα ας	trap	fem.	[√]-α
	θηρεύω	catch	vb.	[√]-ευω
	θηριομαχέω	fight wild beasts	vb.	[√]-[μαχ]-εω
≥25	θηρίον ου	animal	neut.	[√]-ιον

μειζ
greater   48
Memory Aid:

≥25	μείζων ον	greater	adj.	[√]-ων

ὀργ
anger   48
Memory Aid: *Ogres* are usually *angry*.

≥25	ὀργή ῆς	anger, punishment	fem.	[√]-η
	ὀργίζομαι	be angry	vb.	[√]-ιζω
	ὀργίλος η ον	quick-tempered	adj.	[√]-λος
	παροργίζω	make angry	vb.	παρα-[√]-ιζω
	παροργισμός οῦ	anger	masc.	παρα-[√]-μος

πεντ
five   48
Memory Aid: Pentecost, Pentagon

	πεντάκις	five times	adv.	[√]-κις
	πεντακισχίλιοι	five thousand	adj.	[√]-κις-χιλιοι
	πεντακόσιοι αι α	five hundred	adj.	[√]-κοσιοι
≥25	πέντε	five	adj.	
	πεντεκαιδέκατος	fifteenth	adj.	[√]-[και]-[δεκ]-τος
	πεντήκοντα	fifty		[√]-κοντα

ῥε ῥη[1] ῥυ
flow   48
Memory Aid: diarrhea, rheumatic, rheostat

	ἀναντίρρητος ον	undeniable	adj.	ἀ-ἀντι-[√]-τος
	ἀναντιρρήτως	without objection	adv.	ἀ-ἀντι-[√]-ως
	ἄρρητος ον	unutterable (>unflowing)	adj.	ἀ-[√]-τος
	παραρρέω	drift away	vb.	παρα-[√]-ω
≥25	παρρησία ας	openness (>all flowing)	fem.	[παρ]-[√]-ια
	παρρησιάζομαι	speak boldly	vb.	[παρ]-[√]-αζω
	ῥέω	flow	vb.	[√]-ω
	ῥύσις εως	flow, hemorrhage	fem.	[√]-σις

βιβλ
book

47

Memory Aid: Bible, bibliography, bibliotheca

	βιβλαρίδιον ου	little book	neut.	[√]-αριον
≥25	βιβλίον ου	book, scroll	neut.	[√]-ιον
≥10	βίβλος ου	book, record	fem.	[√]-ος

θεραπ
healing / service

47

Memory Aid: therapeutic, therapy, chemotherapy

	θεραπεία ας	healing, house servants	fem.	[√]-εια
≥25	θεραπεύω	heal, serve	vb.	[√]-ευω
	θεράπων οντος	servant	masc.	[√]-ων

κλαι κλαυ
weep

47

Memory Aid:

	κλαίω	weep	vb.	[√]-ω
≥25				
	κλαυθμός οῦ	bitter crying	masc.	[√]-μος

λυπ
pain

47

Memory Aid: lupus

	ἀλυπότερος α ον	freed from pain / sorrow	adj.	ἀ-[√]-τερος
≥25	λυπέω	pain, grieve, be sad	vb.	[√]-εω
≥10	λύπη ης	pain, grief	fem.	[√]-η
	περίλυπος ον	very sad	adj.	περι-[√]-ος
	συλλυπέομαι	feel sorry for	vb.	συν-[√]-εω

θερ θερμ
warm / harvest

46

Memory Aid: thermal, thermometer, thermos, hypothermia

	θερίζω	harvest, gather	vb.	[√]-ιζω
≥10	θερισμός οῦ	harvest, crop	masc.	[√]-μος
≥10	θεριστής οῦ	reaper	masc.	[√]-ιστης
	θερμαίνομαι	warm oneself	vb.	[√]-αινω
	θέρμη ης	heat	fem.	[√]-η
	θέρος ους	summer	neut.	[√]-ς

μικρ
small

46

Memory Aid: microscope, microfilm, micrometer

	μικρόν	a little while	adv.	[√]-ον
≥10				
≥25	μικρός ά όν	small, insignificant	adj.	[√]-ρος

θυρ
door

45

Memory Aid: Door: *see Grimm's Law.*

≥25	θύρα ας	door	fem.	[√]-α
	θυρίς ίδος	window	fem.	[√]-ς
	θυρωρός οῦ	doorkeeper	masc./fem.	[√]-[ὠρ]-ος

κλα   45
break
Memory Aid: iconoclastic

	ἐκκλάω	break off	vb.	ἐκ-[√]-ω
	κατακλάω	break in pieces	vb.	κατα-[√]-ω
≥10	κλάδος ου	branch	masc.	[√]-ος
	κλάσις εως	breaking (of bread)	fem.	[√]-σις
	κλάσμα ματος	fragment, piece	neut.	[√]-μα
≥10	κλάω	break	vb.	[√]-ω
	κλῆμα ματος	branch	neut.	[√]-μα

να   45
temple
Memory Aid:

| ≥25 | ναός οῦ | temple | masc. | [√]-ος |

νε νεο νεω νεα   45
new
Memory Aid: neophyte, new [French: *nouveau*]

	ἀνανεόω	renew, make new	vb.	ἀνα-[√]-οω
	νεανίας ου	young man	masc.	[√]-ας
≥10	νεανίσκος ου	young man	masc.	[√]-ος
	νεομηνία ας	new moon	fem.	[√]-[μην]-ια
≥10	νέος α ον	new, young	adj.	[√]-ος
	νεότης ητος	youth	fem.	[√]-οτης
	νεόφυτος ον	new convert (>neophyte)	masc.	[√]-[φυσ]-τος
	νεωτερικός ή όν	youthful	adj.	[√]-τερος-ικος

οὐαι   45
woe
Memory Aid:

| ≥25 | οὐαί | woe | interj. | |

φυ φυσ φυτ   45
natural / growth / planted
Memory Aid: physical, physics, physiology, neophyte

	ἐκφύω	sprout	vb.	ἐκ-[√]-ω
	ἐμφυσάω	breathe on (>infuse)	vb.	ἐν-[√]-αω
	ἔμφυτος ον	implanted, planted	adj.	ἐν-[√]-τος
	συμφύομαι	grow up with	vb.	συν-[√]-ω
	σύμφυτος ον	sharing in	adj.	συν-[√]-τος
	φυσικός ή όν	natural	adj.	[√]-ικος
	φυσικῶς	naturally	adv.	[√]-ικως

φυσιόω	make conceited	vb.	[√]-οω
≥10 φύσις εως	nature	fem.	[√]-σις
φυσίωσις εως	conceit	fem.	[√]-σις
φυτεία ας	plant	fem.	[√]-εια
≥10 φυτεύω	plant	vb.	[√]-ευω
φύω	grow	vb.	[√]-ω

χρυσ
gold
45

Memory Aid: chrysanthemum

≥10 χρυσίον ου	gold	neut.	[√]-ιον
χρυσοδακτύλιος ον	wearing a gold ring	adj.	[√]-(δάκτυλος)-ιος
χρυσόλιθος ου	chrysolite	masc.	[√]-[λιθ]-ος
χρυσόπρασος ου	chrysoprase (gem)	masc.	[√]-ος
χρυσός οῦ	gold	masc.	[√]-ος
≥10 χρυσοῦς ῆ οῦν	golden	adj.	[√]-ος
χρυσόω	make golden	vb.	[√]-οω

κλιν
recline / incline / turn
44

Memory Aid: incline, recline (as at dinner)

ἀκλινής ές	firm (not turned)	adj.	ἀ-[√]-ης
ἀνακλίνω	seat at table, put to bed	vb.	ἀνα-[√]-ω
ἀρχιτρίκλινος ου	head steward	masc.	[ἀρχ]-[τρι]-[√]-ος
ἐκκλίνω	turn out / away	vb.	ἐκ-[√]-ω
κατακλίνω	cause to recline, dine	vb.	κατα-[√]-ω
κλινάριον ου	small bed	neut.	[√]-αριον
κλίνη ης	bed	fem.	[√]-η
κλινίδιον ου	bed	neut.	[√]-ιον
κλίνω	lay, put to flight	vb.	[√]-ω
κλισία ας	group	fem.	[√]-ια
προσκλίνομαι	join	vb.	προς-[√]-ω
πρόσκλισις εως	favoritism	fem.	προς-[√]-σις
πρωτοκλισία ας	place of honor	fem.	[προ]-[√]-ια

σκανδαλ
scandal
44

Memory Aid: scandal

≥25 σκανδαλίζω	scandalize	vb.	[√]-ιζω
≥10 σκάνδαλον ου	scandal	neut.	[√]-ον

φευγ φυγ
flee
44

Memory Aid: fugitive

ἀποφεύγω	escape	vb.	ἀπο-[√]-ω
διαφεύγω	escape	vb.	δια-[√]-ω

ἐκφεύγω	escape, flee	vb.	ἐκ-[√]-ω
καταφεύγω	flee	vb.	κατα-[√]-ω
≥25 φεύγω	flee	vb.	[√]-ω
φυγή ῆς	flight	fem.	[√]-η

ἁπτ   43
light / touch
Memory Aid:

ἀνάπτω	kindle	vb.	ἀνα-[√]-ω
≥25 ἅπτω	kindle, ignite	vb.	[√]-ω
καθάπτω	fasten on	vb.	κατα-[√]-ω
περιάπτω	kindle	vb.	περι-[√]-ω

ἀστρ ἀστηρ ἀστερ   43
star
Memory Aid: star, astronomy, asterisk

≥10 ἀστήρ έρος	star	masc.	[√]-ρ
ἀστήρικτος ον	unsteady	adj.	[√]-τος
ἀστραπή ῆς	lightning, ray	fem.	[√]-η
ἀστράπτω	flash, dazzle	vb.	[√]-ω
ἄστρον ου	star, constellation	neut.	[√]-ον
ἐξαστράπτω	flash (like lightning)	vb.	ἐκ-[√]-ω
περιαστράπτω	flash around	vb.	περι-[√]-ω

δωρ   43
gift
Memory Aid: Dorothy

≥10 δωρεά ᾶς	gift	fem.	[√]-α
δωρεάν	without cost	adv.	
δωρέομαι	give	vb.	[√]-εω
δώρημα ματος	gift	neut.	[√]-μα
≥10 δῶρον ου	gift, offering	neut.	[√]-ον

ἱκαν   43
able
Memory Aid: Sounds like *"I can"* (i.e., I am *able).*

≥25 ἱκανός ή όν	able, worthy	adj.	[√]-ος
ἱκανότης ητος	capability, capacity	fem.	[√]-οτης
ἱκανόω	make able, make fit	vb.	[√]-οω

κοπτ   43
cut
Memory Aid: comma

ἀποκόπτω	cut off (mid. castrate)	vb.	ἀπο-[√]-ω
ἀπρόσκοπος ον	blameless	adj.	ἀ-προς-[√]-ος
ἐγκοπή ῆς	obstacle (>cutting in)	fem.	ἐν-[√]-η
ἐγκόπτω	prevent (>cut in)	vb.	ἐν-[√]-ω
≥10 ἐκκόπτω	cut off, remove	vb.	ἐκ-[√]-ω

κατακόπτω	cut badly, beat	vb.	κατα-[√]-ω
κόπτω	cut (mid. mourn)	vb.	[√]-ω
προσκοπή ῆς	obstacle, offense	fem.	προς-[√]-η
προσκόπτω	stumble, be offended	vb.	προς-[√]-ω

μισθ 43
pay
Memory Aid:

ἀντιμισθία ας	recompense, punishment	fem.	ἀντι-[√]-ια
μισθαποδοσία ας	reward, punishment	fem.	[√]-[πο(1)]-ια
μισθαποδότης ου	rewarder	masc.	[√]-[πο(1)]-της
μίσθιος ου	hired man, laborer	masc.	[√]-ιος
μισθόομαι	hire (>make a payee)	vb.	[√]-οω
≥25 μισθός οῦ	pay	masc.	[√]-ος
μίσθωμα ματος	expense, rent	neut.	[√]-μα
μισθωτός οῦ	hired man, laborer	masc.	[√]-ος

ὀλιγ 43
little / few
Memory Aid: oligarchy

≥25 ὀλίγος η ον	little, few	adj.	[√]-ος
ὀλιγόψυχος ον	faint-hearted	adj.	[√]-[ψυχ]-ος
ὀλιγωρέω	think lightly of	vb.	[√]-[ὠρ]-εω
ὀλίγως	barely, just	adv.	[√]-ως

ἀγρ 42
field / wild
Memory Aid: agriculture

ἀγραυλέω	be out of doors	vb.	[√]-[αὐλ]-εω
ἀγρεύω	trap	vb.	[√]-ευω
ἀγριέλαιος ου	wild olive tree	fem.	[√]-[ἐλαι]-ος
ἄγριος α ον	wild	adj.	[√]-ιος
≥25 ἀγρός οῦ	field, farm	masc.	[√]-ος

ἐλευθερ 42
free
Memory Aid:

ἀπελεύθερος ου	freedman	masc.	ἀπο-[√]-ος
≥10 ἐλευθερία ας	freedom	fem.	[√]-ια
≥10 ἐλεύθερος α ον	free	adj.	[√]-ος
ἐλευθερόω	set / make free	vb.	[√]-οω

ὀπισ 42
behind / after
Memory Aid:

ὄπισθεν	behind	cj./pt.	[√]-θεν
≥25 ὀπίσω	behind, after	cj./pt.	[√]-ω

ζηλ
zealous / jealous
41

Memory Aid: zeal, zealous

	ζηλεύω	be zealous	vb.	[√]-ευω
≥10	ζῆλος ου	zeal, jealousy	masc.	[√]-ος
≥10	ζηλόω	be jealous	vb.	[√]-οω
	ζηλωτής οῦ	someone zealous	masc.	[√]-της
	παραζηλόω	make jealous	vb.	παρα-[√]-οω

ἡλι
sun
41

Memory Aid: heliocentric, helium

	ἡλικία ας	age, years	fem.	[√]-ια
≥25	ἥλιος ου	sun	masc.	[√]-ος
	συνηλικιώτης ου	contemporary	masc.	συν-[√]-ικος-της

μαχ
fight
40

Memory Aid: Sounds like *match*, as in *boxing match*.

	ἄμαχος ον	peaceable	adj.	ἀ-[√]-ος
	διαμάχομαι	protest violently	vb.	δια-[√]-ω
≥25	μάχαιρα ης	sword	fem.	[√]-α
	μάχη ης	fight	fem.	[√]-η
	μάχομαι	fight	vb.	[√]-ω

προβατ
sheep
40

Memory Aid:

	προβατικός ή όν	pertaining to sheep	adj.	[√]-ικος
	προβάτιον ου	lamb, sheep	neut.	[√]-ιον
≥25	πρόβατον ου	sheep	neut.	[√]-ον

ὑσ
last / lack
40

Memory Aid: hysteria

≥10	ὑστερέω	lack, need	vb.	[√]-τερος-εω
	ὑστέρημα ματος	what is lacking	neut.	[√]-τερος-μα
	ὑστέρησις εως	lack, need	fem.	[√]-τερος-σις
≥10	ὕστερον	later, afterwards, then	adv.	[√]-τερον
	ὕστερος α ον	later, last	adj.	[√]-τερος

κτ κτισ
create (Two of the consonant sounds [k and t] are shared.)
39

Memory Aid:

≥10	κτίζω	create, make	vb.	[√]-ω
≥10	κτίσις εως	creation	fem.	[√]-σις

| κτίσμα ματος | creation | neut. | [√]-μα |
| κτίστης ου | creator | masc. | [√]-της |

μισ 39
hate
Memory Aid: misanthropy

| ≥25 μισέω | hate, be indifferent to | vb. | [√]-εω |

οἰν 39
wine
Memory Aid: sounds something like *wine*

	οἰνοπότης ου	drinker, drunkard	masc.	[√]-[πο²]-της
≥25	οἶνος ου	wine	masc.	[√]-ος
	οἰνοφλυγία ας	drunkenness	fem.	[√]-(φλέω)-ια
	πάροινος ου	drunkard	masc.	παρα-[√]-ος

παθ ποθ 39
feel / desire
Memory Aid: pathology, sympathy, pathetic, psychopath, pathos

	ἐπιποθέω	desire	vb.	ἐπι-[√]-εω
	ἐπιπόθησις εως	longing	fem.	ἐπι-[√]-σις
	ἐπιπόθητος ον	longed for	adj.	ἐπι-[√]-τος
	ἐπιποθία ας	desire	fem.	ἐπι-[√]-ια
	μετριοπαθέω	be gentle with	vb.	[μετρ]-[√]-εω
≥10	πάθημα ματος	suffering, passion	neut.	[√]-μα
	παθητός ή όν	subject to suffering	adj.	[√]-τος
	πάθος ους	lust, passion	neut.	[√]-ς
	συγκακοπαθέω	share in hardship	vb.	συν-[κακ]-[√]-εω
	συμπαθέω	sympathize	vb.	συν-[√]-εω
	συμπαθής ές	sympathetic	adj.	συν-[√]-ης

ποιμ ποιμν 39
sheep
Memory Aid: David wrote *poems* while tending *sheep*.

≥10	ποιμαίνω	tend, rule	vb.	[√]-αινω
≥10	ποιμήν ένος	shepherd	masc.	[√]-ην
	ποίμνη ης	flock	fem.	[√]-η
	ποίμνιον ου	flock	neut.	[√]-ιον

σκην 39
tent
Memory Aid: scene, scenario

	ἐπισκηνόω	rest upon, live in	vb.	ἐπι-[√]-οω
	κατασκηνόω	nest, live, dwell	vb.	κατα-[√]-οω
	κατασκήνωσις εως	nest	fem.	κατα-[√]-σις
≥10	σκηνή ῆς	tent	fem.	[√]-η

σκηνοπηγία ας	Feast of Tabernacles	fem.	[√]-(πήγνυμι)-ια
σκηνοποιός οῦ	tent-maker	masc.	[√]-[ποι]-ος
σκῆνος ους	tent	neut.	[√]-ς
σκηνόω	live, dwell	vb.	[√]-οω
σκήνωμα ματος	body, dwelling place	neut.	[√]-μα

ἀν² 38
up / again
Memory Aid: Anabaptist, anatomy, analysis

≥10	ἀνά (>acc.)	up, each	prep.	[√]-ἀνα
	ἄνω	above, up	adv.	[√]-ω
≥10	ἄνωθεν	from above, again	adv.	ἀνα-[√]-θεν
	ἀνωτερικός ή όν	upper, inland	adj.	[√]-τερος-ικος
	ἀνώτερον	first, above	adv.	[√]-τερον

ἐχθρ 38
enemy
Memory Aid:

| | ἔχθρα ας | hostility, hatred | fem. | [√]-α |
| ≥25 | ἐχθρός ά όν | hated (*as noun*: enemy) | adj. | [√]-ος |

ἰα ἰατρ 38
heal
Memory Aid: psychiatric, psychiatry

	ἴαμα ματος	healing	neut.	[√]-μα
≥25	ἰάομαι	heal	vb.	[√]-ω
	ἴασις εως	healing	fem.	[√]-σις
	ἰατρός οῦ	physician, healer	masc.	[√]-ος

πτωχ 38
poor
Memory Aid:

	πτωχεία ας	poverty	fem.	[√]-εια
	πτωχεύω	become poor	vb.	[√]-ευω
≥25	πτωχός ή όν	poor	adj.	[√]-ος

σκευ 38
prepare
Memory Aid:

	ἀνασκευάζω	disturb	vb.	ανά-[√]-αζω
	ἀπαρασκεύαστος ον	unprepared	adj.	ἀ-παρα-[√]-τος
	ἐπισκευάζομαι	prepare, make ready	vb.	ἐπι-[√]-αζω
	κατασκευάζω	prepare, make ready	vb.	κατα-[√]-αζω
	παρασκευάζω	prepare, make ready	vb.	παρα-[√]-αζω
	παρασκευή ῆς	day of preparation	fem.	παρα-[√]-η
	σκευή ῆς	gear	fem.	[√]-η
≥10	σκεῦος ους	thing, container	neut.	[√]-ς

ταχ² 38
quick
Memory Aid: tachometer

≥10	ταχέως	quickly	adv.	[√]-ως
	ταχινός ή όν	soon, swift	adj.	[√]-ινος
	τάχιον	quickly	adv.	[√]-ον
	τάχιστα	as soon as possible	adv.	[√]-ιστος
	τάχος ους	speed	neut.	[√]-ς
≥10	ταχύ	quickly	adv.	
	ταχύς εῖα ύ	quick	adj.	[√]-ς

φον 38
murder
Memory Aid: phoenix

	φονεύς έως	murderer	masc.	[√]-ευς
≥10	φονεύω	murder, put to death	vb.	[√]-ευω
≥10	φόνος ου	murder, killing	masc.	[√]-ος

ἐπει 37
since
Memory Aid:

≥25	ἐπεί	since, because, as	cj./pt.	
≥10	ἐπειδή	since, because, for, when	cj./pt.	
	ἐπειδήπερ	inasmuch as, since	cj./pt.	[√]-περ

λατρ 37
worship
Memory Aid: idolatry, bibliolatry, mariolatry

	εἰδωλολάτρης ου	idol worshipper	masc.	[εἰδωλ]-[√]-ης
	εἰδωλολατρία ας	idolatry	fem.	[εἰδωλ]-[√]-ια
	λατρεία ας	worship, service	fem.	[√]-εια
≥10	λατρεύω	worship, serve	vb.	[√]-ευω

σπευδ σπουδ 37
speed / eagerness
Memory Aid: Sounds something like *speed*.

	σπεύδω	hurry	vb.	[√]-ω
≥10	σπουδάζω	do one's best, work hard	vb.	[√]-αζω
	σπουδαῖος α ον	earnest	adj.	[√]-ιος
	σπουδαίως	eagerly	adv.	[√]-ως
≥10	σπουδή ῆς	earnestness, zeal	fem.	[√]-η

ἀναγκ 36
necessity
Memory Aid:

	ἀναγκάζω	force (>make necessary)	vb.	[√]-αζω
	ἀναγκαῖος α ον	necessary, forced	adj.	[√]-ιος
	ἀναγκαστῶς	under compulsion	adv.	[√]-ως

| ≥10 | ἀνάγκη ης | necessity, distress | fem. | [√]-η |
| | ἐπάναγκες | necessarily | adv. | ἐπι-[√] |

ἀρτι   36
now
Memory Aid:

| ≥25 | ἄρτι | now, at once | adv. | |

οὖς ὦτ   36
ear
Memory Aid: otology

| ≥25 | οὖς ὠτός | ear | neut. | [√]-ς |

περα   35
far / end
Memory Aid: far (see Grimm's Law)

	ἀπέραντος ον	endless	adj.	ἀ-[√]-τος
	διαπεράω	cross, cross over	vb.	δια-[√]-αω
	περαιτέρω	further	adv.	[√]-τερος-ω
≥10	πέραν	beyond, across	prep.	
	πέρας ατος	end, boundary	neut.	[√]-ς

τρεφ τροφ   35
feed / support
Memory Aid: atrophy: Sounds like _trough_—where animals _feed_.

	ἀνατρέφω	bring up, train	vb.	ἀνα-[√]-ω
	διατροφή ῆς	food	fem.	δια-[√]-η
	ἐκτρέφω	feed, raise	vb.	ἐκ-[√]-ω
	ἐντρέφομαι	live on, feed oneself on	vb.	ἐν-[√]-ω
	σύντροφος ου	close friend	masc.	συν-[√]-ος
	τρέφω	feed, support	vb.	[√]-ω
≥10	τροφή ῆς	food, keep	fem.	[√]-η
	τροφός οῦ	nurse	fem.	[√]-ος
	τροφοφορέω	care for	vb.	[√]-[φερ]-εω

ἀργυρ   34
money / silver
Memory Aid: Couples sometimes _argue_ over _money_.

≥10	ἀργύριον ου	silver coin, money	neut.	[√]-ιον
	ἀργυροκόπος ου	silversmith	masc.	[√]-[κοπ]-ος
	ἄργυρος ου	silver, coin	masc.	[√]-ος
	ἀργυροῦς ᾶ οῦν	made of silver	adj.	[√]-ους
	ἀφιλάργυρος ον	not money-loving	adj.	ἀ-[φιλ]-[√]-ος
	φιλαργυρία ας	love of money	fem.	[φιλ]-[√]-ια
	φιλάργυρος ον	money-loving	adj.	[φιλ]-[√]-ος

Ἑλλα Ἑλλην   34
Greek
Memory Aid: hellenistic

Ἑλλάς άδος | Greece | fem. | [√]-ς
≥25 Ἕλλην ηνος | Greek person, non-Jew | masc. | [√]-ην
Ἑλληνικός ή όν | hellenistic, Greek | adj. | [√]-ικος
Ἑλληνίς ίδος | Greek / Gentile woman | fem. | [√]-ς
Ἑλληνιστής οῦ | Hellenist | masc. | [√]-της
Ἑλληνιστί | in the Greek language | adv. |

μελ² — 34
part
Memory Aid: melody [*melee:* confused mixture of *parts*]
≥25 μέλος ους | part, member | neut. | [√]-ς

ναι — 34
yes
Memory Aid:
≥25 ναί | yes | cj./pt.

νικ — 34
victory
Memory Aid: Nike
≥25 νικάω | conquer | vb. | [√]-αω
νίκη ης | victory | fem. | [√]-η
νῖκος ους | victory | neut. | [√]-ς
ὑπερνικάω | be completely victorious | vb. | ὑπερ-[√]-αω

ταπειν — 34
humble (compare πειν)
Memory Aid:
ταπεινός ή όν | humble, poor | adj. | [√]-ινος
ταπεινοφροσύνη ης | (false) humility | fem. | [√]-[φρ]-συνη
ταπεινόφρων ον | humble | adj. | [√]-[φρ]-ων
≥10 ταπεινόω | make humble | vb. | [√]-οω
ταπείνωσις εως | humble state | fem. | [√]-σις

φυλ — 34
tribe
Memory Aid: phylogeny, phylum [file]
ἀλλόφυλος ον | foreign | adj. | [ἀλλ]-[√]-ος
δωδεκάφυλον ου | the Twelve Tribes | neut. | [δεκ]-[√]-ον
συμφυλέτης ου | fellow countryman | masc. | συν-[√]-της
≥25 φυλή ῆς | tribe, nation | fem. | [√]-η

χιλι — 34
thousand
Memory Aid: chiliasm
≥10 χιλιάς άδος | a thousand | fem. | [√]-ς
≥10 χίλιοι αι α | thousand | adj. | [√]-οι

ἀμπελ   *33*

grapevine

Memory Aid: Jesus made *ample wine* for the wedding.

ἄμπελος ου	grapevine	fem.	[√]-ος
ἀμπελουργός οῦ	vinedresser, gardener	masc.	[√]-[ἐργ]-ος
≥25 ἀμπελών ῶνος	vineyard	masc.	[√]-ων

εἰδωλ   *33*

image / idol

Memory Aid: idol, idolatry

εἰδωλεῖον ου	idol's temple	neut.	[√]-ειον
εἰδωλόθυτον ου	idol-meat	neut.	[√]-[θυ]-τον
εἰδωλολάτρης ου	idolater	masc.	[√]-[λατρ]-ης
εἰδωλολατρία ας	idolatry	fem.	[√]-[λατρ]-ια
≥10 εἴδωλον ου	idol, image	neut.	[√]-ον
κατείδωλος ον	full of idols	adj.	κατα-[√]-λος

παλαι   *33*

old

Memory Aid: paleontology, paleolithic

ἔκπαλαι	for a long time	adv.	ἐκ-[√]
πάλαι	long ago, formerly	adv.	
≥10 παλαιός ά όν	old, former	adj.	[√]-ιος
παλαιότης ητος	age	fem.	[√]-οτης
παλαιόω	make old	vb.	[√]-οω

τρεχ τροχ   *33*

run

Memory Aid: track, trek

εἰστρέχω	run in	vb.	εἰς-[√]-ω
ἐπισυντρέχω	gather rapidly, close in	vb.	ἐπι-συν-[√]-ω
κατατρέχω	run down	vb.	κατα-[√]-ω
περιτρέχω	run about	vb.	περι-[√]-ω
προστρέχω	run up (to someone)	vb.	προς-[√]-ω
προτρέχω	run on ahead	vb.	προ-[√]-ω
συντρέχω	run together, join with	vb.	συν-[√]-ω
≥10 τρέχω	run	vb.	[√]-ω
τροχιά ᾶς	path	fem.	[√]-ια
τροχός οῦ	wheel, cycle	masc.	[√]-ος
ὑποτρέχω	run under the shelter of	vb.	ὑπο-[√]-ω

ἀνεμ   *32*

wind

Memory Aid: anemometer, animate

ἀνεμίζομαι	be driven by wind	vb.	[√]-ιζω
≥25 ἄνεμος ου	wind	masc.	[√]-ος

κλεπτ κλοπ κλεμ 32
steal
Memory Aid: kleptomaniac

	κλέμμα ματος	theft	neut.	[√]-μα
≥10	κλέπτης ου	thief	masc.	[√]-της
≥10	κλέπτω	steal	vb.	[√]-ω
	κλοπή ῆς	theft	fem.	[√]-η

ξεν 32
strange / guest
Memory Aid: xenophobia

	ξενία ας	place of lodging, room	fem.	[√]-ια
≥10	ξενίζω	entertain strangers	vb.	[√]-ιζω
	ξενοδοχέω	be hospitable	vb.	[√]-[δεχ]-εω
≥10	ξένος η ον	strange, foreign	adj.	[√]-ος
	φιλοξενία ας	hospitality	fem.	[φιλ]-[√]-ια
	φιλόξενος ον	hospitable	adj.	[φιλ]-[√]-ος

σφραγι 32
seal
Memory Aid:

	κατασφραγίζω	seal	vb.	κατα-[√]-ιζω
≥10	σφραγίζω	seal, acknowledge	vb.	[√]-ιζω
≥10	σφραγίς ῖδος	seal, evidence	fem.	[√]-ς

αὐρ 31
tomorrow
Memory Aid:

≥10	αὔριον	tomorrow, soon	adv.	[√]-ιον
≥10	ἐπαύριον	next day	adv.	ἐπι-[√]-ιον

γε² 31
particle adding emphasis
Memory Aid: Slang *gee!* is used to add emphasis in English.

≥25	γέ	(used to add emphasis)	cj./pt.	

κλει 31
lock / close
Memory Aid: Note *cl* in words *close* and *exclude.*

	ἀποκλείω	lock, close	vb.	ἀπο-[√]-ω
	ἐκκλείω	exclude (>lock out)	vb.	ἐκ-[√]-ω
	κατακλείω	lock up (in prison)	vb.	κατα-[√]-ω
	κλείς κλειδός	key	fem.	[√]-ς
≥10	κλείω	lock, shut, close	vb.	[√]-ω
	συγκλείω	make / keep a prisoner	vb.	συν-[√]-ω

πλην　　　　　　　　　　　　　　　　　　　　　　　　　　　　　*31*
but
Memory Aid:
≥25　πλήν　　　　　　　　but, nevertheless　　　　cj./pt.

σκοπ σκεπ　　　　　　　　　　　　　　　　　　　　　　　　　*31*
view
Memory Aid: scope, stethoscope, periscope, skeptic

ἀλλοτριεπίσκοπος	busybody	masc.	[ἀλλ]-ἐπι-[√]-ος
≥10 ἐπισκέπτομαι	visit, care for	vb.	ἐπι-[√]-ω
ἐπισκοπέω	see to it, take care	vb.	ἐπι-[√]-εω
ἐπισκοπή ῆς	visitation, episcopate	fem.	ἐπι-[√]-η
ἐπίσκοπος ου	overseer, bishop	masc.	ἐπι-[√]-ος
κατασκοπέω	spy on	vb.	κατα-[√]-εω
κατάσκοπος ου	spy	masc.	κατα-[√]-ος
σκοπέω	pay attention to	vb.	[√]-εω
σκοπός οῦ	goal	masc.	[√]-ος

στερε στηρε　　　　　　　　　　　　　　　　　　　　　　　*31*
firm / solid
Memory Aid: stereotype, cholesterol, steroids

ἀποστερέω	defraud, deny	vb.	ἀπο-[√]-εω
ἐπιστηρίζω	strengthen	vb.	ἐπι-[√]-ιζω
στερεός ά όν	firm, solid	adj.	[√]-ος
στερεόω	make strong	vb.	[√]-οω
στερέωμα ματος	firmness	neut.	[√]-μα
στηριγμός οῦ	firm footing	masc.	[√]-μος
≥10 στηρίζω	strengthen	vb.	[√]-ιζω

τεν τειν τιν[1] τον　　　　　　　　　　　　　　　　　　　*31*
extend / stretch
Memory Aid: extend, tension, tone, intonation, catatonic, intense

≥10 ἐκτείνω	stretch out, extend	vb.	ἐκ-[√]-ω
ἐκτένεια ας	earnestness	fem.	ἐκ-[√]-εια
ἐκτενέστερον	more earnestly	adv.	ἐκ-[√]-τερον
ἐκτενής ές	constant, unfailing	adj.	ἐκ-[√]-ης
ἐκτενῶς	earnestly, constantly	adv.	ἐκ-[√]-ως
ἐκτινάσσω	shake off	vb.	ἐκ-[√]-σσω
ἐπεκτείνομαι	stretch toward	vb.	ἐπι-ἐκ-[√]-ω
παρατείνω	prolong	vb.	παρα-[√]-ω
προτείνω	tie up	vb.	προ-[√]-ω
ὑπερεκτείνω	go beyond	vb.	ὑπερ-ἐκ-[√]-ω
χειροτονέω	appoint, choose	vb.	[χειρ]-[√]-εω

χορτ
food   *31*

Memory Aid:

≥10 χορτάζω	feed, satisfy	vb.	[√]-αζω
χόρτασμα ματος	food	neut.	[√]-μα
≥10 χόρτος ου	grass, vegetation	masc.	[√]-ος

αἰν
praise   *30*

Memory Aid: paean

αἴνεσις εως	praise	fem.	[√]-σις
αἰνέω	praise	vb.	[√]-εω
αἶνος ου	praise	masc.	[√]-ος
ἐπαινέω	praise, commend	vb.	ἐπι-[√]-εω
≥10 ἔπαινος ου	praise, approval	masc.	ἐπι-[√]-ος
παραινέω	advise	vb.	παρα-[√]-εω

ἁρπ ἁρπαγ
seize   *30*

Memory Aid: [harpoon]

ἁρπαγή ῆς	greed, seizure	fem.	[√]-η
ἁρπαγμός οῦ	booty, prize	masc.	[√]-μος
≥10 ἁρπάζω	seize	vb.	[√]-αζω
ἅρπαξ αγος	robber (one who seizes)	masc.	[√]-ξ
διαρπάζω	plunder	vb.	δια-[√]-αζω
συναρπάζω	seize, drag	vb.	συν-[√]-αζω

θυγατηρ θυηατρ
daughter   *30*

Memory Aid: Daughter: *see Grimm's Law.*

≥25 θυγάτηρ τρός	daughter, woman	fem.	[√]-ρ
θυγάτριον ου	little daughter	neut.	[√]-ιον

λαμπ
lamp   *30*

Memory Aid: lamp

ἐκλάμπω	shine (out)	vb.	ἐκ-[√]-ω
λαμπάς άδος	lamp	fem.	[√]-ς
λαμπρός ά όν	bright, fine	adj.	[√]-ρος
λαμπρότης ητος	brightness	fem.	[√]-οτης
λαμπρῶς	splendidly	adv.	[√]-ως
λάμπω	shine	vb.	[√]-ω
περιλάμπω	shine around	vb.	περι-[√]-ω

μετρ   **30**
measure

Memory Aid: meter, odometer

ἄμετρος ον	immeasurable	adj.	ἀ-[√]-ος
ἀντιμετρέω	measure out in return	vb.	ἀντι-[√]-εω
≥10 μετρέω	measure, give	vb.	[√]-εω
μετρητής οῦ	measure	masc.	[√]-της
μετρίως	greatly	adv.	[√]-ως
≥10 μέτρον ου	measure, quantity	neut.	[√]-ον

πω   **30**
yet

Memory Aid:

οὐδέπω	not yet	adv.	[οὐ]-[√]
≥25 οὔπω	not yet	adv.	[οὐ]-[√]

συνειδη   **30**
conscience

Memory Aid:

≥25 συνείδησις εως	conscience	fem.	[√]-σις

βαστ   **29**
carry / bear

Memory Aid: Note common letters in *basket*: b-a-s-(k-e)-t

ἀδυσβάστακτος ον	not difficult to bear	adj.	ἀ-δυσ-[√]-τος
≥25 βαστάζω	carry, bear	vb.	[√]-αζω
δυσβάστακτος ον	difficult to bear	adj.	δυσ-[√]-τος

βρω   **29**
food

Memory Aid: ambrosia [German: *brot,* meaning *bread* or *food.*]

≥10 βρῶμα ματος	food	neut.	[√]-μα
βρώσιμος ον	eatable	adj.	[√]-ιμος
≥10 βρῶσις εως	food, eating	fem.	[√]-σις

δημ δομ   **29**
people / home

Memory Aid: demographics, democracy, epidemic

ἀποδημέω	leave home, go away	vb.	ἀπο-[√]-εω
ἀπόδημος ον	away from home	adj.	ἀπο-[√]-ος
δῆμος ου	people, crowd	masc.	[√]-ος
δημόσιος α ον	public	adj.	[√]-ιος
ἐκδημέω	leave home	vb.	ἐκ-[√]-εω
ἐνδημέω	be at home, be present	vb.	ἐν-[√]-εω
ἐπιδημέω	visit, live	vb.	ἐπι-[√]-εω
παρεπίδημος ου	refugee	masc.	παρα-ἐπι-[√]-ος

| συνέκδημος ου | travelling companion | masc. | συν-ἐκ-[√]-ος |
| συνοικοδομέω | build together | vb. | συν-ὀικ-[√]-ες |

μοιχ 29
adultery
Memory Aid:

μοιχαλίς ίδος	adulteress	fem.	[√]-ς
μοιχάομαι	commit adultery	vb.	[√]-αω
μοιχεία ας	adultery	fem.	[√]-εια
≥10 μοιχεύω	commit adultery	vb.	[√]-ευω
μοιχός οῦ	adulterer	masc.	[√]-ος

ἧκ 28
be present
Memory Aid:

| ἀνήκει | it is proper | vb. | ἀνα-[√]-ω |
| ≥25 ἥκω | have come, be present | vb. | [√]-ω |

κωμ 28
town
Memory Aid: community, common, commerce, communal

| ≥25 κώμη ης | small town | fem. | [√]-η |
| κωμόπολις εως | town | fem. | [√]-[πολ]-ς |

μελ[1] 28
concern / care
Memory Aid: melancholy, melodramatic

ἀμελέω	disregard, neglect	vb.	ἀ-[√]-εω
ἀμεταμέλητος ον	free from care	adj.	ἀ-μετα-[√]-τος
ἐπιμέλεια ας	care, attention	fem.	ἐπι-[√]-εια
ἐπιμελέομαι	take care of	vb.	ἐπι-[√]-εω
ἐπιμελῶς	carefully	adv.	ἐπι-[√]-ως
≥10 μέλει	it concerns (imper.)	vb.	[√]-ω
μεταμέλομαι	regret	vb.	μετα-[√]-ω
προμελετάω	prepare ahead of time	vb.	προ-[√]-αω

μεριμν 28
worry
Memory Aid:

ἀμέριμνος ον	free from worry	adj.	ἀ-[√]-ος
μέριμνα ης	worry, care	fem.	[√]-α
≥10 μεριμνάω	worry	vb.	[√]-αω
προμεριμνάω	worry beforehand	vb.	προ-[√]-αω

νυμφ 28
bride
Memory Aid: nymph, nuptial

	νύμφη ης	bride, daughter-in-law	fem.	[√]-η
≥10	νυμφίος ου	groom	masc.	[√]-ιος
	νυμφών ῶνος	wedding hall	neut.	[√]-ων

πυλ 28
gate / door
Memory Aid: One *pulls* a *gate* or *door*.

≥10	πύλη ης	gate, door	fem.	[√]-η
≥10	πυλών ῶνος	gate, entrance, porch	masc.	[√]-ων

ἐλαι 27
olive / oil
Memory Aid: oil, petroleum, linoleum

≥10	ἐλαία ας	olive, olive tree	fem.	[√]-α
≥10	ἔλαιον ου	olive oil, oil	neut.	[√]-ον
	ἐλαιών ῶνος	olive orchard	masc.	[√]-ων
	καλλιέλαιος ου	cultivated olive tree	fem.	[καλ¹]-[√]-ος

μυστηρ 27
mystery
Memory Aid: mystery

≥25	μυστήριον ου	secret, mystery	neut.	[√]-ιον

νηστ 27
hunger
Memory Aid: sounds something like *waste,* a cause of *hunger.*

	νηστεία ας	hunger, fasting	fem.	[√]-εια
≥10	νηστεύω	fast	vb.	[√]-ευω
	νῆστις ιδος	hungry	masc./fem.	[√]-ς

σει 27
quake
Memory Aid: seismic, seismograph

	ἀνασείω	incite, stir up	vb.	ἀνα-[√]-ω
	διασείω	take money by force	vb.	δια-[√]-ω
	ἐπισείω	urge on, stir up	vb.	ἐπι-[√]-ω
	κατασείω	move, make a sign	vb.	κατα-[√]-ω
≥10	σεισμός οῦ	earthquake, storm	masc.	[√]-μος
	σείω	shake, excite	vb.	[√]-ω

αὐξ 26
grow
Memory Aid: auction

≥10	αὐξάνω	grow / increase	vb.	[√]-ανω
	αὔξησις εως	growth	fem.	[√]-σις
	συναυξάνομαι	grow together	vb.	συν-[√]-ανω
	ὑπεραυξάνω	grow abundantly	vb.	ὑπερ-[√]-ανω

βαρ
burden / weight
26

Memory Aid: baritone, barium, barometer, burden

ἀβαρής ές	burdenless	adj.	ἀ-[√]-ης
βαρέω	burden, overcome	vb.	[√]-εω
βαρέως	with difficulty	adv.	[√]-ως
βάρος ους	burden, weight	neut.	[√]-ς
βαρύς εῖα ύ	heavy, weighty, hard	adj.	[√]-υς
ἐπιβαρέω	be a burden	vb.	ἐπι-[√]-εω
καταβαρέω	be a burden to	vb.	κατα-[√]-εω
καταβαρύνομαι	be very heavy	vb.	κατα-[√]-υνω

ἑνεκ
because of
26

Memory Aid:

≥25 ἕνεκα (*gen.*)	because of	prep.	

ἑορτ
feast
26

Memory Aid:

ἑορτάζω	observe a festival	vb.	[√]-αζω
≥25 ἑορτή ῆς	festival, feast	fem.	[√]-η

ζυμ
yeast
26

Memory Aid: enzyme, zymogenic

ἄζυμος ον	without yeast	adj.	ἀ-[√]-ος
≥10 ζύμη ης	yeast	fem.	[√]-η
ζυμόω	make / cause to rise	vb.	[√]-οω

θησαυρ
treasure
26

Memory Aid: treasure, thesaurus

ἀποθησαυρίζω	acquire as a treasure	vb.	ἀπο-[√]-ιζω
θησαυρίζω	save, store up	vb.	[√]-ιζω
≥10 θησαυρός οῦ	treasure, storeroom	masc.	[√]-ος

κελευ
command
26

Memory Aid:

κέλευσμα ματος	command	neut.	[√]-μα
≥25 κελεύω	command	vb.	[√]-ω

λευκ
white
26

Memory Aid: leukemia

λευκαίνω	make white	vb.	[√]-αινω
≥10 λευκός ή όν	white, shining	adj.	[√]-ος

λυχν
lamp
Memory Aid: lux, [*lucent*]

≥10 λυχνία ας	lampstand	fem.	[√]-ια
≥10 λύχνος ου	lamp	masc.	[√]-ος

26

νεφ
cloud
Memory Aid:

≥25 νεφέλη ης	cloud	fem.	[√]-η
νέφος ους	cloud	neut.	[√]-ς

26

ὀμ ὀμν
swear
Memory Aid:

≥25 ὀμνύω	swear, vow	vb.	[√]-ω

26

πληγ πλασσ πλησσ
plague / strike
Memory Aid: plague, paraplegic, apoplexy

ἐπιπλήσσω	reprimand	vb.	ἐπι-[√]-σσω
≥10 πληγή ῆς	plague, blow	fem.	[√]-η
πλήκτης ου	violent person	masc.	[√]-της
πλήσσω	strike	vb.	[√]-σσω

26

χηρ
widow
Memory Aid: *Widows* often need *charity*.

≥25 χήρα ας	widow	fem.	[√]-α

26

ὠφελ
gain
Memory Aid:

ἀνωφελής ές	useless	adj.	ἀ-[√]-ης
ὄφελος ους	gain, benefit	neut.	[√]-ς
ὠφέλεια ας	advantage, benefit	fem.	[√]-εια
≥10 ὠφελέω	gain, help	vb.	[√]-εω
ὠφέλιμος ον	valuable, beneficial	adj.	[√]-ιμος

26

βο βοηθ
shout
Memory Aid: A person sometimes *shouts boo!*

ἀναβοάω	cry out	vb.	ἀνα-[√]-αω
≥10 βοάω	call, shout	vb.	[√]-αω
βοή ής	shout, outcry	fem.	[√]-η
βοήθεια ας	help, aid	fem.	[√]-εια
βοηθέω	help	vb.	[√]-εω
βοηθός οῦ	helper	masc.	[√]-ος

25

δενδρ 25
tree
Memory Aid: Rhododendron

≥25 δένδρον ου	tree	neut.	[√]-ον

κωλυ 25
hinder
Memory Aid:

ἀκωλύτως	unhindered	adv.	ἀ-[√]-ως
διακωλύω	prevent	vb.	δια-[√]-ω
≥10 κωλύω	hinder	vb.	[√]-ω

πολεμ 25
war
Memory Aid: polemic

πολεμέω	fight, be at war	vb.	[√]-εω
≥10 πόλεμος ου	war, conflict, polemic	masc.	[√]-ος

σπλαγχν 25
pity
Memory Aid:

εὔσπλαγχνος ον	kind	adj.	εὐ-[√]-ος
≥10 σπλαγχνίζομαι	have pity	vb.	[√]-ιζω
≥10 σπλάγχνον ου	compassion, feeling	neut.	[√]-ον

τελων 25
tax
Memory Aid: toll

ἀρχιτελώνης ου	tax superintendent	masc.	[ἀρχ]-[√]-ης
≥10 τελώνης ου	tax-collector	masc.	[√]-ης
τελώνιον ου	tax (office)	neut.	[√]-ιον

γυμν 24
exercise / naked (sports were done in the nude by the Greeks)
Memory Aid: gymnastics, gym

γυμνάζω	train, discipline, exercise	vb.	[√]-αζω
γυμνασία ας	training	fem.	[√]-ια
γυμνιτεύω	be dressed in rags	vb.	[√]-ευω
≥10 γυμνός ή όν	naked	adj.	[√]-ος
γυμνότης ητος	nakedness, poverty	fem.	[√]-οτης

ἐξ 24
six
Memory Aid: hexameter, hex key, screwdriver

≥10 ἐξ	six	adj.	
ἑξακόσιοι αι α	six hundred	adj.	[√]-κοσοι
ἑξήκοντα	sixty	adj.	[√]-κοντα

κεν   24
empty
Memory Aid: cenotaph, kenosis

≥10	κενός ή όν	empty, senseless	adj.	[√]-ος
	κενόω	make empty / powerless	vb.	[√]-οω
	κενῶς	in vain	adv.	[√]-ως

πειν   24
hunger (compare ταπειν)
Memory Aid: Hunger *pains*

≥10	πεινάω	be hungry	vb.	[√]-αω
	πρόσπεινος ον	hungry	adj.	προς-[√]-ος

σαλπ   24
trumpet
Memory Aid:

≥10	σάλπιγξ ιγγος	trumpet	fem.	[√]-ξ
≥10	σαλπίζω	sound a trumpet	vb.	[√]-ιζω
	σαλπιστής οῦ	trumpeter	masc.	[√]-ιστης

τυγχ τυχ   24
obtain
Memory Aid: A groom must *obtain* a *tux* for his wedding.

	ἐντυγχάνω	intercede, plead, appeal	vb.	ἐν-[√]-ανω
	ἐπιτυγχάνω	obtain	vb.	ἐπι-[√]-ανω
	παρατυγχάνω	happen to be present	vb.	παρα-[√]-ανω
	συντυγχάνω	reach	vb.	συν-[√]-ανω
≥10	τυγχάνω	obtain	vb.	[√]-ανω
	ὑπερεντυγχάνω	intercede	vb.	ὑπερ-ἐν-[√]-ανω

ἀριθμ   23
number
Memory Aid: arithmetic

	ἀναρίθμητος ον	innumerable	adj.	ἀ-[√]-τος
	ἀριθμέω	number, count	vb.	[√]-εω
≥10	ἀριθμός οῦ	number, total	masc.	[√]-ος
	καταριθμέω	number	vb.	κατα-[√]-εω

γεμ γομ   23
full
Memory Aid:

	γεμίζω	fill	vb.	[√]-ιζω
≥10	γέμω	be full	vb.	[√]-ω
	γόμος ου	cargo	masc.	[√]-ος

κοιλ
stomach
Memory Aid:

≥10 κοιλία ας	stomach, appetite	fem.	[√]-ια

23

ξηρ
dry
Memory Aid: xerox

≥10 ξηραίνω	dry up	vb.	[√]-αινω
ξηρός ά όν	dry, withered	adj.	[√]-ος

23

ὀψ
late
Memory Aid: [Letters "P.S." —used to add ideas too *late* for main text.]

ὀψέ	late in the day, after	adv./prep.	
≥10 ὀψία ας	evening	fem.	[√]-ια
ὄψιμος ου	late rain, spring rain	masc.	[√]-ος
ὀψώνιον ου	pay (>given late in day)	neut.	[√]-ιον

23

σιτ
food / fat
Memory Aid: parasite

ἀσιτία ας	lack of appetite	fem.	ἀ-[√]-ια
ἄσιτος ον	without food	adj.	ἀ-[√]-ος
ἐπισιτισμός οῦ	food	masc.	ἐπι-[√]-μος
σιτευτός ή όν	fattened	adj.	[√]-τος
σιτίον ου	grain / food (*pl.*)	neut.	[√]-ιον
σιτιστός ή όν	fattened	adj.	[√]-ιστος
σιτομέτριον ου	ration	neut.	[√]-[μετρ]-ιον
≥10 σῖτος ου	grain	masc.	[√]-ος

23

ὑγι
health
Memory Aid: hygiene

≥10 ὑγιαίνω	be healthy, be sound	vb.	[√]-αινω
≥10 ὑγιής ές	healthy, whole	adj.	[√]-ης

23

ὑπηρετ
serve
Memory Aid: Sounds something like *helper*.

ὑπηρετέω	serve	vb.	ὑπο-[√]-εω
≥10 ὑπηρέτης ου	attendant, helper	masc.	ὑπο-[√]-της

23

χε χυ
pour
Memory Aid:

ἀνάχυσις εως	flood, excess	fem.	ἀνα-[√]-σις

23

≥10	ἐκχέω	pour out, shed	vb.	ἐκ-[√]-ω
	ἐπιχέω	pour on	vb.	ἐπι-[√]-ω
	καταχέω	pour over	vb.	κατα-[√]-ω
	συγχέω	confound	vb.	συν-[√]-ω
	σύγχυσις εως	confusion	fem.	συν-[√]-σις
	ὑπερεκχύννομαι	run over	vb.	ὑπερ-ἐκ-[√]-υνω

αὐλ 22
flute / courtyard
Memory Aid:

	αὐλέω	play a flute	vb.	[√]-εω
≥10	αὐλή ῆς	courtyard, house	fem.	[√]-η
	αὐλητής οῦ	flute player	masc.	[√]-της
	αὐλίζομαι	spend the night	vb.	[√]-ιζω
	αὐλός οῦ	flute	masc.	[√]-ος
	ἔπαυλις εως	house (>on the court)	fem.	ἐπι-[√]-ς
	προαύλιον ου	gateway, forecourt	neut.	προ-[√]-ιον

εὐδ 22
sleep
Memory Aid: People sometimes *sleep* in church (*cathedral*).

| ≥10 | καθεύδω | sleep | vb. | κατα-[√]-ω |

ζων 22
fasten / bind
Memory Aid: zone

	ἀναζώννυμι	bind up	vb.	ἀνα-[√]-μι
	διαζώννυμι	wrap around	vb.	δια-[√]-μι
	ζώνη ης	belt	fem.	[√]-η
	ζώννυμι	fasten	vb.	[√]-μι
	περιζώννυμι	wrap around	vb.	περι-[√]-μι
	ὑποζώννυμι	strengthen, brace	vb.	ὑπο-[√]-μι

θεμελι 22
foundation
Memory Aid: theme

	θεμέλιον ου	foundation	neut.	[√]-ον
≥10	θεμέλιος ου	foundation	masc.	[√]-ος
	θεμελιόω	establish (>make firm)	vb.	[√]-οω

ἰχθυ 22
fish
Memory Aid: ΙΧΘΥΣ (early Christian acronym for Jesus)

| | ἰχθύδιον ου | small fish, fish | neut. | [√]-ιον |
| ≥10 | ἰχθύς ύος | fish | masc. | [√]-ς |

μωρ
foolish
22

Memory Aid: moron

μωραίνω	make foolish	vb.	[√]-αινω
μωρία ας	foolishness	fem.	[√]-ια
μωρολογία ας	foolish talk	fem.	[√]-[λεγ]-ια
≥10 μωρός ά όν	foolish	adj.	[√]-ρος

ξυλ
wood
22

Memory Aid: xylophone

ξύλινος η ον	wooden	adj.	[√]-ινος
≥10 ξύλον ου	wood, tree, club	neut.	[√]-ον

πωλ
sell
22

Memory Aid: monopoly

≥10 πωλέω	sell	vb.	[√]-εω

ῥιζ
root
22

Memory Aid: licorice

ἐκριζόω	uproot (>make rootless)	vb.	ἐκ-[√]-οω
≥10 ῥίζα ης	root, descendant, source	fem.	[√]-α
ῥιζόομαι	be firmly rooted	vb.	[√]-οω

σι σιγ
silence
22

Memory Aid: Same initial syllable: *si.*

≥10 σιγάω	keep silent	vb.	[√]-αω
σιγή ῆς	silence	fem.	[√]-η
≥10 σιωπάω	be silent	vb.	[√]-αω

συκ
fig
22

Memory Aid: sycamore

συκάμινος ου	mulberry tree	fem.	[√]-ος
≥10 συκῆ ῆς	fig tree	fem.	[√]-η
συκομορέα ας	sycamore tree	fem.	[√]-(μόρον)α
σῦκον ου	fig	neut.	[√]-ον

ταρασσ ταραχ
trouble
22

Memory Aid: Sounds something like harass (i.e., *trouble*).

διαταράσσομαι	be deeply troubled	vb.	δια-[√]-σσω
ἐκταράσσω	stir up trouble	vb.	ἐκ-[√]-σσω
≥10 ταράσσω	trouble, disturb	vb.	[√]-σσω

| ταραχή ῆς | disturbance, trouble | fem. | [√]-η |
| τάραχος ου | confusion | masc. | [√]-ος |

ἁλ ἁλι
salt / fish
Memory Aid: halite, halibut

ἅλας ατος	salt	neut.	[√]-ς	21
ἁλιεύς έως	fisherman	masc.	[√]-ευς
ἁλιεύω	fish	vb.	[√]-ευω
ἁλίζω	salt	vb.	[√]-ιζω
ἅλς ἁλός	salt	neut.	[√]-ς
ἁλυκός ή όν	salty	adj.	[√]-ος
ἄναλος ον	without salt	adj.	ἀ-[√]-ος
ἐνάλιον ου	sea creature	neut.	ἐν-[√]-ιον
παράλιος ου	coastal district	fem.	παρα-[√]-ιος

ἀρεσκ ἀρεστ
please
Memory Aid: Most people are *pleased* to take *a rest*.

ἀνθρωπάρεσκος ον	people-pleasing	adj.	[√]-ος	21
ἀρεσκεία ας	desire to please	fem.	[√]-εια
ἀρέσκω	(try to) please	vb.	[√]-σκω
ἀρεστός ή όν	pleasing	adj.	[√]-τος
εὐαρεστέω	please, be pleasing to	vb.	εὐ-[√]-εω
εὐάρεστος ον	pleasing	adj.	εὐ-[√]-τος
εὐαρέστως	pleasingly	adv.	εὐ-[√]-ως

βασαν
torture
Memory Aid:

≥10 βασανίζω	torment, disturb	vb.	[√]-ιζω	21
βασανισμός οῦ	torture	masc.	[√]-ισμος
βασανιστής οῦ	torturer, jailer	masc.	[√]-ιστης
βάσανος ου	torment, pain	fem.	[√]-ος

βεβαι βεβαιο
reliable / firm
Memory Aid:

βέβαιος α ον	reliable, firm	adj.	[√]-ιος	21
βεβαιόω	confirm (>make firm)	vb.	[√]-οω
βεβαίωσις εως	confirmation	fem.	[√]-σις
διαβεβαιόομαι	speak confidently	vb.	δια-[√]-οω

δευ
place to / hither
Memory Aid:

| δεῦρο | hither (place to) | adv. | | 21 |
| ≥10 δεῦτε | come hither (place to) | vb. | |

νιπτ
wash
Memory Aid:

ἄνιπτος ον	not (ritually) washed	adj.	ἀ-[√]-ος
ἀπονίπτω	wash	vb.	ἀπο-[√]-ω
νιπτήρ ῆρος	washbasin	masc.	[√]-ρ
≥10 νίπτω	wash	vb.	[√]-ω

ὀρκ
oath
Memory Aid: exorcism

ἐνορκίζω	place under oath	vb.	ἐν-[√]-ιζω
ἐξορκίζω	place under oath	vb.	ἐκ-[√]-ιζω
ἐξορκιστής ου	exorcist	masc.	ἐκ-[√]-της
ἐπιορκέω	break an oath	vb.	ἐπι-[√]-εω
ἐπίορκος ου	oath-breaker, perjurer	masc.	ἐπι-[√]-ος
ὀρκίζω	place under oath	vb.	[√]-ιζω
≥10 ὅρκος ου	oath	masc.	[√]-ος
ὀρκωμοσία ας	oath	fem.	[√]-ια (ὄμνυμι)

στεφαν
crowd / reward
Memory Aid: Stephen

≥10 στέφανος ου	crown	masc.	[√]-ος
στεφανόω	crown, reward	vb.	[√]-οω

ἀρτ²
qualified / complete
Memory Aid: An *artist* is a *qualified* performer.

ἀπαρτισμός ού	completion	masc.	ἀπο-[√]-ισμος
ἄρτιος α ον	fully qualified	adj.	[√]-ιος
ἐξαρτίζω	be completed	vb.	ἐκ-[√]-ιζω
καταρτίζω	mend, make adequate	vb.	κατα-[√]-ιζω
κατάρτισις εως	adequacy	fem.	κατα-[√]-σις
καταρτισμός οῦ	adequacy	masc.	κατα-[√]-ισμος
προκαταρτίζω	prepare in advance	vb.	προ-κατα-[√]-ιζω

δειπν
dine
Memory Aid: [Except for *p*, sounds something like *dine* and *dinner*.]

δειπνέω	eat, dine	vb.	[√]-εω
≥10 δεῖπνον ου	feast, supper	neut.	[√]-ον

ἱππ
horse
Memory Aid: hippodrome, hippopotamus

ἱππεύς έως	horseman	masc.	[√]-ευς

| | ἱππικόν οῦ | cavalry | neut. | [√]-ικος |
| ≥10 | ἵππος ου | horse | masc. | [√]-ος |

κερδ 20
gain
Memory Aid: One *gains* access with a membership *card*.

≥10	κερδαίνω	gain, profit	vb.	[√]-αινω
	κέρδος ους	gain	neut.	[√]-ς

λανθαν λαθ 20
forget
Memory Aid:

ἐκλανθάνομαι	forget completely	vb.	ἐκ-[√]-ανω
ἐπιλανθάνομαι	forget, overlook	vb.	ἐπι-[√]-ανω
λανθάνω	be hidden, ignore	vb.	[√]-ανω
λάθρᾳ	secretly, quietly	adv.	[√]-ᾳ
λήθη ης	forgetfulness	fem.	[√]-η

λειτουργ 20
serve / worship (compare with ἐργ)
Memory Aid: liturgy

λειτουργέω	serve, worship	vb.	[√]-[ἐργ]-εω
λειτουργία ας	service, worship	fem.	[√]-[ἐργ]-ια
λειτουργικός ή όν	serving, ministering	adj.	[√]-[ἐργ]-ικος
λειτουργός οῦ	servant, minister	masc.	[√]-[ἐργ]-ος

τυπ 20
type / example
Memory Aid: type, typical, typify

	ἀντίτυπος ον	corresponding (copy)	adj.	ἀντι-[√]-ος
	ἐντυπόω	engrave, carve	vb.	ἐν-[√]-οω
	τυπικῶς	by way of example	adv.	[√]-ικως
≥10	τύπος ου	example, pattern	masc.	[√]-ος
	ὑποτύπωσις εως	example	fem.	ὑπο-[√]-σις

3

Derived English Words

Most of the words offered as examples in the Memory Aid section of the main lists are included here. Some words do not appear, however. Exceptions were made wherever a word matched closely the spelling and meaning of the root. For example, the memory aid "lamp" is given for the cognate λαμπ, but is not included in this section. The connection is obvious; no explanation is necessary.

Primarily, it is compound words that are included here, and for these the Greek roots are given. If the word is already a compound in ancient Greek, the word is marked with the symbol ♦. (But note: the meaning of the Greek compound is often not the same as that of the modern English compound.) Roots are generally given in the form they appear in the first line of the Cognate Group in the main section of this work. One can then refer to the Cognate Group section to examine how the particular root is employed in other words. If a variant form of the root better illustrates the basis of the English derivative, that form will be given, followed (in square brackets) by the primary form under which that root is listed in the Cognate Groups section. This allows for a clearer presentation of the English Memory Aids, yet affords an easy reference back to the Cognate Groups section. The one exception (which occurs often) is that λογ is given as the root of English words with the suffix -logy. This root is listed in the Cognate Groups section under the root λεγ.

Rare technical vocabulary has generally been avoided as being of little help as a memory aid. The exception is technical *theological* vocabulary. It is more likely that students of Greek will have a larger vocabulary in this area. One should note that certain prefixes have several meanings. The entries below suggest the most likely meaning for the word in question. The user should refer to the section on prefixes and suffixes for a more full presentation of these elements.

acolyte: one who assists (follows) a priest, performing minor parts of the ritual.
acoustic: anything having to do with sound or hearing; suffix -*ic* is the same as the Greek adjective suffix ικος.

acrobat: ♦ (top + walk—ἀκρ + βατ [βαιν]) one who walks a tight rope or high wire.

agape: one of several words for love used in the early church as the technical term for a common meal, which was misunderstood by outsiders as something immoral (from the idea of a love-feast).

agent: from root to lead or drive, thus *agent* for something capable of bringing about an effect: e.g., "an agent of change."

agnostic: ♦ (not + knowing—ἀ + γνο) one who believes that it is not possible to know whether God exists.

agora: term used widely in the ancient world for the local marketplace; often used in compounds with the sense of speak (e.g., *allegory*) because public discussion and town meetings were usually carried out in the market.

agriculture: (field + culture) English word comes from the Latin, but the first word of the compound is from Greek ἀγρ; *acre* comes from Greek too (see Grimm's Law).

allegory: ♦ (other + speak—ἀλλ + ἀγορ) *speak* is from the word for *marketplace*, where the local assembly met to discuss and make decisions; thus *allegory* for something spoken about one thing but meant for some other thing (see *agora* above).

allotrope: ♦ (other + turn—ἀλλ + τροπ [τρεπ]) general meaning: strangeness, variety; in chemistry: different forms of elements or compounds without a change in the chemical composition.

ambrosia: food of the gods.

amnesia: ♦ (no + memory—ἀ + μνη [μιμν]) the condition of having lost one's memory; suffix *-ia* is common Greek suffix.

amnesty: ♦ (not + remember—ἀ + μνη [μιμν]) the granting of a pardon by forgetting acts that had brought condemnation. Compare with *amnesia* above.

Anabaptist: (re + baptize—ἀνα + βαπτ) polemical term given to a group in the Protestant Reformation who held to "believer's baptism," and who required rebaptism of those who had been baptized as children; suffix *-ist* is from Greek suffix ιστος.

Anabasis: ♦ (up + go—ἀνα + βασ [βαιν]) from the title of Greek work by Xenophon about the retreat of a Greek army back up to the Black Sea; σις is common Greek suffix.

analysis: ♦ (up + loose—ἀνα + λυ) studying the whole by considering its individual parts; *-sis* is from the suffix σις.

anarchy: ♦ (no + rule—ἀ + ἀρχ) a breakdown of normal structures of authority. [Note: ν (English *n*) is usual between ἀ and a word that begins with a vowel.]

Anatolia: ♦ (up + far—ἀνα + τολ) the land of Turkey, which from the perspective of the Greeks was the distant land where the sun came up.

anatomy: ♦ (up + cut—ἀνα + τομ [τεμν]) a view of the body cut up into distinctive parts.

anchorite: ♦ (back + place—ἀνα + χωρ) meaning *withdraw* or *retire;* term for the form of monasticism that is solitary, in contrast to communal (or cenobite) monasticism.

androgynous: ♦ (male + female—ἀνδρ [ἀνηρ] + γυνη) something with both male and female characteristics.

android: ♦ (man + form—ἀνδρ [ἀνηρ] + οἰδ) an automaton with human form.

anemia: ♦ (no + blood—ἀ + αἱμ) deficiency in the red blood corpuscles. [Note: ν (English *n*) is usual between ἀ and a word that begins with a vowel.]

anemometer: (wind + measure—ἀνεμ + μετρ) instrument for measuring the velocity of the wind.

angel: *angel* is simply a transliteration of the Greek word ἄγγελος, meaning messenger. A divine messenger came to be called an *angel*.

antarctic: the land mass that is opposite to the Arctic.

anthropology: (man + study—ἀνθρωπ + λογ) the broad study of human culture and society.

anthropomorphic: (man + form—ἀνθρωπ + μορφ) often used for a description of God in terms of human attributes; *-ic* is from Greek suffix ικος.

antibiotic: (against + life—ἀντι + βι) against the life of a virus, which is really in aid of human life; *-tic* is from Greek suffix τικος.

Antichrist: ♦ word used in the Johannine letters to describe the chief source of opposition to the Christian church.

antidote: ♦ (against + give—ἀντι + δο [διδ]) something given against the effects of a poison; a remedy.

antinomian: ♦ (against + law—ἀντι + νομ) used for theological positions similar to Paul's, in which the Law is depreciated.

aphorism: ♦ (from + limit—ἀπο + ὀρ) brief statement of truth; a short definition; suffix *-ism* is from Greek ισμος.

Apocalypse: ♦ (from + cover—ἀπο + καλυψ [καλυπτ]) thus something revealed, as in the last book of the Bible — the Apocalypse or the Revelation.

Apocrypha: (from + hide—ἀπο + κρυφ [κρυπτ]) used for those books that church leaders believed should be hidden from the faithful (i.e., non-canonical).

Apollyon: destroying angel of the bottomless pit.

apoplexy: ♦ (utterly + strike—ἀπο + πλησσ [πλαγ]) ἀπο here has a sense of intensifier; thus, a crippling stroke.

apostle: ♦ (from + send—ἀπο + στελ) one sent from another to serve as representative of the sender.

apostrophe: ♦ (from + turn—ἀπο + στροφ [στρεφ]) sign that shows where some letters have been "turned away from" their place in a word.

appendectomy: (appendix + out + cut—appendix + ἐκ + τομ [τεμν]) *appendix* is from Latin base; the suffix is ἐκ + word for cut (i.e., cut out), thus to remove the appendix. Suffix *-ectomy* is often used in medical terminology for *removal by surgery.*

archaeology: ♦ (old + study—ἀρχ + λογ) a study of ancient things.

archangel: ♦ (chief + messenger—ἀρχ + ἀγγελ) an angel of the highest rank.

archbishop: (chief + bishop—ἀρχ + bishop) chief bishop of a province; *bishop* is Old English.

archetype: ♦ (beginning + example—ἀρχ + τυπ) an original model; a prototype.

arithmetic: the science of numbers.

asterisk: a little star; *-isk* is from Greek suffix ισκος.

asthenia: ♦ (no + strength—ἀ + σθεν) medical term for *weakness;* ια is a common Greek suffix.

astronomy: ♦ (star + law—ἀστρ + νομ) study of the laws by which the regular courses of astral bodies may be determined.

atheist: ♦ (no + god—ἀ + θε) one who does not believe in God; *-ist* is from the Greek suffix ιστος.

atom: (not + cut—ἀ + τομ [τεμν]) named for the part of matter that could not be divided — until our century showed otherwise.

atrophy: (not + support—ἀ + τροφ [τρεφ]) medical condition in which the body wastes away.

auction: a method of sale in which the price increases through bidding; more directly from the Latin.

autistic: condition of being completely withdrawn from all others but oneself; *-tic* is from Greek suffix τικος.

autobiography: (self + life + writing—αὐτο + βι + γραφ) a biography written by the subject.

autocratic: ♦ (self + power—αὐτο + κρατ) not "self-rule" in the sense of national independence, but the opposite — rule by one individual; others have no voice.

autograph: ♦ (self + writing—αὐτο + γραφ) technical term for the manuscript penned by the author personally, in contrast to all manuscripts copied from the original copy by scribes.

automatic: on one's own power.

axiom: established principle; something worthy of universal acceptance.

ballistic: of anything *thrown;* suffix *-ic* comes from the Greek suffix ικος.

baritone: ♦ (heavy + tone—βαρ + τον [τεν]) male singing voice between base and tenor; base is used for the lowest voice, since the lowest part of anything is its base (from βασις).

barium: element found primarily in heavy spar.

barometer: (heavy + measure—βαρ + μετρ) instrument for measuring the atmospheric pressure.

basilica: originally meant a royal hall.

Bible: plural of βιβλιον, meaning *book,* thus *Bible* for a collection of books.

bibliography: ♦ (book + writing—βιβλ + γραφ) a list of books.

bibliolatry: (book + worship—βιβλ + λατρ) used to describe attitude of various religious groups to their Scriptures (as with Muslims and fundamentalist Christians).

bibliotheca: (book + place—βιβλιο + θη [τιθ]) a place for books; a library.

bigamy: (two + marriage) prefix *bi-* is Latin prefix; for state in which one person is married while legally married to another.

boule: technical term widely used for the town council in Greek society.

cacography: (bad + writing—κακ + γραφ) bad writing; (cf. *calligraphy*).

cacaphony: ♦ (bad + sound—κακ + φων) discordant sound.

calisthenics: (beautiful + strength—καλ + σθεν) gymnastics to promote grace and strength.

calligraphy: ♦ (beautiful + writing—καλ + γραφ) the art of writing, for which medieval monks and Muslims are famous.

cardiac: pertaining to the heart.

cataclysm: ♦ (down + wash—κατα + κλυσμ) κατα often has a negative sense in a compound, thus the sense here of destruction.

catacomb: underground cemetery; the first part, κατα, is Greek; the second part, comb, is from Latin root, and the compound itself is late Latin.

catapult: ♦ (against + hurl—κατα + παλλ) instrument designed to hurl heavy stones at fortified walls.

cataract: ♦ (down + dash—κατα + ἀρα) waterfall.

catastrophe: ♦ (down + turn—κατα + στροφ [στρεφ) an overturning.

catatonic: ♦ (down + stretch—κατα + τον [τεν]) stretching down, as in a depression.

Cathar: medieval Christian group who judged material to be evil, and who, by asceticism, hoped to purify themselves.

catharsis: cleansing; *sis* is common noun ending.

cathedral: from Greek for *seat;* means the *seat* of the bishop.

catholic: (according to + the whole—κατα + ὁλ) the belief that is held by all the churches (i.e., universal).

cemetery: a place where the dead lie; more directly from Latin.

cenotaph: ♦ (empty + tomb—κεν + ταφ) monument to dead who are buried elsewhere.

Cenozoic: (recent + life) term for present geological system.

charismatic: gifted; suffix *-tic* is from Greek τικος.

charity: gift.

chemotherapy: (chemical + healing — chemical + θεραπ) a process of attempted healing by the use of chemicals; *chemical* is from the word *alchemy,* derived from Latin.

chiliasm: the theological position that focuses on a thousand-year golden age at the end of world history; from Greek for *thousand.*

chiropractic: (hand + practice — χειρ + πρασ) a method of curing that depends primarily on the use of the physician's hands.

cholesterol: (gall + solid — χολη + στερε) fatty substance, so-called because it was originally found in gall stones.

chronology: (time + study — χρον + λογ) the part of any study that deals with the time (sequence) of events.

chrysanthemum: ♦ (gold + flower — χρυσ + ἀνθ) a flower.

clergy: apparently so named from the Greek word for portion, because God was their portion.

comma: a mark that cuts into the flow of a sentence.

cosmetic: ordered; suffix *-tic* is from Greek suffix τικος.

cosmopolitan: ♦ (world + citizen — κοσμ + πολ) citizen of the world.

cosmos: the world as ordered.

creosote: a wood preservative.

crime: from the Latin, though sharing elements with Greek root κρι.

crisis: a time of decision or judgment.

critic: one who judges.

critique: judgment.

crypt: vault for burial or hiding.

cryptic: secret; hidden; *-ic* is from Greek suffix ικος.

cryptography: (hide + write — κρυπτ + γραφ) secret writing.

deacon: lower church office, for which the common term for servant was used.

decade: ten-year period.

decalogue: ♦ (ten + word — δεκ + λογ) the "Ten Words," another name for the Ten Commandments.

decimate: more directly from the Latin, meaning to kill off a large number (lit. to kill a tenth).

demagogue: ♦ (people + leader — δημ + ἀγ) a leader whose power is based on popular support among the people.

democracy: ♦ (people + power — δημ + κρατ) a system of government in which the government is in the hands of the people, often through elected representatives.

demographics: (people + writing — δημ + γραφ) statistics of births, deaths, diseases of human populations.

Deuteronomy: ♦ (second + law — δευ + νομ) name for the fifth book of the Pentateuch, in which the Law is repeated (see suffix τερος).

dexterity: skilful; originally associated with right-handedness; more directly from Latin.

diabolical: ♦ (across + throw — δια + βολ [βαλ]) from Greek word διάβολος, meaning devil or slanderer.

diadem: ♦ (through + bind — δια + δε) δια here intensifies the binding, thus the sense of to bind fully (as in a circle), thus diadem or crown.

diaeresis: ♦ (through + take—δια + αἱρ) δια is used here in the sense of division. Two vowels standing together in Greek are usually pronounced together (called a diphthong). If they are pronounced separately, two dots (¨) are placed over the second vowel, and the vowels are pronounced separately. The mark to indicate this separation is called a diaeresis.

diagnostic: ♦ (through + know—δια + γνο) δια here is an intensifier, as in a thorough examination.

diagonal: ♦ (through + angle—δια + γων) a line that cuts through the corner angles.

dialect: ♦ (through + say—δια + λεκτ [λεγ]) a variety of speech distinguished by particular idioms, pronunciation, etc., but which is understood by persons who speak another form of the primary language; δια may have a sense of division here.

diarrhea: ♦ (through + flow—δια + ῥη) no other term so adequately describes this disorder.

Didache: a translation of the Greek word for *teaching;* the term is used as a shortened title for one of the works of the Apostolic Fathers, called *The Teaching of the Twelve.*

didactic: transliteration of the Greek word διδακτικος; suffix *-tic* is the same as Greek τικος. Greek, of course, reflects a case ending too.

dilemma: ♦ (two + receive—δι + λημ [λαμβ]) a choice between two equally undesirable alternatives.

diocese: (through + dwell—δια + οἰκ) the churches under a bishop; δια here is used in the sense of "complete."

Docetic: a heretical group in the early second century distinguished by the belief that Jesus only *seemed* to have human form.

Dorothy: ♦ (gift + God—δωρ + θε) this personal name means "a gift of God."

doxology: ♦ (glory + word—δοξ + λογ) a hymn (*word*) of *praise.*

dynamic: characterized by energy or power; suffix *-ic* is from the Greek suffix ικος.

dynamo: see *dynamic* above.

dynamite: see *dynamic* above.

dynasty: from δυναστεια, which has the same root as *dynamic* above.

ecclesiastical: ♦ (out + call—ἐκ + κλη [καλ]) ἐκκλησία was the technical name chosen by the early Christians to describe their assemblies.

eclipse: ♦ (out + leave—ἐκ + λειπ) as when the sun is *eclipsed* by the moon.

ecology: (house + study—οἰκ + λογ) study of the environment (i.e., living space; house) of plants and animals.

economy: ♦ (house + law—οἰκ + νομ) related to the management of a household, or some larger household; the Greek root νομ (mainly pertaining to law in the New Testament) is related to the root νεμ, which means to deal out or distribute; the νεμ / νομ complex in Greek has a wide variety of meanings.

ecosystem: see *ecology* and *system.*

ecstasy: ♦ (out + stand—ἐκ + στα [ἰστη]) a behaviour that stands outside of the normal.

ecumenical: ♦ a movement including all inhabitants.

eisegesis: ♦ (into + lead—εἰς + ἠγε) theological term for bad exegesis; exegesis is reading (*leading*) "out of" the text what is in the text; eisegesis is reading "into" the text what is not intended by the text.

emporium: ♦ (in + journey—ἐν + πορ) a market; the word for *commerce* is ἐμπορία, reflecting the fact that travel was regularly involved in commerce.

encephalitis: (in + head—ἐν + κεφαλ) inflammation of the brain; Greek had already created the compound ἐγκέφαλος (in the head) to indicate the *brain.*

enchiridion: ♦ (in + hand—ἐν + χειρ) a handbook or manual (i.e., something *in the hand*).

encyclopaedia: ♦ (in + circle + training—ἐν + κυκλο + παιδεια) lit. *training in a circle* (i.e., general education).

energy: ♦ (in + work—ἐν + ἐργ) something that is present in work.

enzyme: (in + leaven—ἐν + ζυμ) a chemical ferment.

ephemeral: ♦ (on + day—ἐπι + ἡμερ) short-lived (lit. *on a day*).

epicentre: ♦ (on + centre—ἐπι + κεντρ) the point at which an earthquake is the strongest.

epidemic: ♦ (on + people—ἐπι + δημ) disease that has spread widely on a population.

epidermis: ♦ (on + skin—ἐπι + δερμ) the outer skin (lit. *on the skin*).

epiphany: ♦ (on + appear—ἐπι + φαν) appearance of a god.

epistemic: ♦ (on + stand—ἐπι + στη [ἰστη]) pertaining to knowledge; suffix *-ic* is from Greek suffix ικος.

epistemology: see *epistemic* above.

epitaph: ♦ (on + tomb—ἐπι + ταφ) what is written on a tomb.

epithet: ♦ (on + place—ἐπι + θη [τιθ]) a descriptive word used in place of the usual name.

eremite: hermit; more directly from the Latin, but related to Greek root ἐρημ, meaning desert.

eschatology: (last + study—ἐσκατ + λογ) a study of final things.

eschaton: the last days.

esophagus: ♦ (inside + eat—ἐσω [εἰς] + φαγ) a tube that carries eaten food inside the body.

esoteric: for the initiated only; for those on the inside (see suffix τερος).

essence: the real nature or being.

ethnarch: ♦ (nation + rule—ἐθν + ἀρχ) a ruler of a nation.

etiology (aetiology): ♦ (cause + study—αἰτ + λογ) the science of causes or reasons.

eucharist: ♦ (good + gift—εὐ + χαρι) as a compound, means *thanks* or *thanksgiving;* used as a technical term for a primary Christian sacrament.

eulogy: ♦ (good + word—εὐ + λογ) praise.

euphemistic: ♦ (good + say—εὐ + φη) pertaining to the use of a mild word in place of a harsh word.

euphony: ♦ (good + sound—εὐ + φων) a pleasing sound.

euphoria: ♦ (well + bear—εὐ + φορ [φερ]) sense of well-being (lit. a bearing well).

eureka: this word was supposedly shouted by Archimedes on his discovery of a method for determining the purity of gold; it means *I have found it!*

euthanasia: (good + death—εὐ + θαν) death that is not the result of a disease, but is done intentionally to avoid death by disease or old age; *-ia* is from Greek suffix ια.

evangelist: ♦ (good + messenger—εὐ + ἀγγελ) one who announces the good news.

ex cathedra: (from + chair—ἐκ + καθεδρ [καθ]) for those proclamations by the pope when he speaks from his position as bishop of Rome.

excommunicate: from the Latin, which Latin shares with Greek *ex-* (ἐκ [ἐξ]) to mean *out*.

exegesis: ♦ (out + lead—ἐξ [ἐκ] + ἠγε) theological term for good interpretation (a reading or *leading out of* the text what is in the text; cf. *eisegesis* above).

exile: from the Latin, but shares with the Greek the sense of *ex* (ἐκ [ἐξ]) as *out*.

Exodus: ♦ (out + way—ἐξ [ἐξ] + ὁδ) the way out.

exorcize: ♦ (out + oath—ἐκ + ὁρκ) to cast out by incantations and prayer. In the New Testament, ἐκβάλλω is more commonly used for "exorcize."

extend: ♦ (out + stretch—ἐκ + τεν) more directly from the Latin.

fugitive: one who is fleeing.

genealogy: ♦ (family + study—γεν + λογ) a study of family roots.

generation: more directly from Latin, but *gen-* is shared with Greek (see *genealogy* above).

genesis: a beginning; *-sis* is a common Greek suffix.

genetic: related to origin and development; *-tic* is from the Greek suffix τικος.

genocide: from the Latin, but Latin shares the meaning of the root *gen-* with Greek; means the killing (Latin: *cidere*) of a race.

genre: kind; family; more directly from Latin (see *generation* above).

geography: ♦ (earth + write—γη + γραφ) description of the earth.

George: (earth + worker—γη + ουργ [ἐργ]) the personal name George means *farmer.*

gloss: from Greek γλωσσα, meaning language or tongue; this comes to mean any marginal or explanatory notes in a text.

glossalalia: (tongues + speak—γλωσσ + λαλ) term for religious phenomenon in which a person speaks a language—normally unintelligible—by divine inspiration. If the unlearned language sopken were identifiable, it would be an instance of xenolalia.

glossary: a collection of glosses; dictionary of foreign words (see *gloss* above).

gnosis: transliterated directly from Greek; means knowledge.

gnosticism: see *gnosis* above; *-ism* is from Greek suffix ισμος.

grammar: the art of writing.

graphite: the material used in pencils.

gym — gymnastics: exercise; since exercise was done in the nude, both meanings can be conveyed by γυμν.

gynecology: (woman + study—γυνη + λογ) field of medicine that deals with problems associated with women.

Hagia Sophia: name of a church built by Justinian in the sixth century in Istanbul; means *Holy Wisdom.*

hagiology: (holy + study—ἁγι + λογ) literature dealing with the lives of saints.

halibut: a saltwater fish.

halite: rock salt.

hamartiology: the part of theology that deals with sin.

hegemony: leadership.

heliocentric: (sun + centre—ἑλι + κεντρ) any view having the sun as center; suffix *-ic* is from suffix ικος.

helium: name of gaseous element, so called because this element was first observed during an eclipse of the sun in 1868.

hellenistic: from Greek word for *Greek;* *-ic* is from Greek suffix ικος.

hemoglobin: the pigment in the red blood cells; *hemo-* is from the Greek word for blood; *globin* is from the Latin for ball or mass.

hemophilia: (blood + love—αἱμ + φιλ) used to describe the condition of excessive bleeding.

hemorrhage: ♦ (blood + flow —αἱμ + ῥη) discharge of blood from ruptured blood vessel.

henotheism: (one + god—ἑν + θε) a kind of polytheism in which one god has priority.

Heptateuch: ♦ (seven + book—ἑπτ + τευχ) τευχ can mean *book,* thus *Heptateuch:* the first seven books of the Old Testament.

hermit: from Greek word meaning *desert,* a place where monastic hermits generally lived.

heterodox: (different + belief—ἑτερ + δοξ) different belief, usually used with negative overtones similar to the word *heresy.*

heterosexual: (different + sex—ἑτερ + Latin *sex*) having the desire for the opposite sex.

heuristic: related to discovering or finding out; suffix *-ic* is from the Greek suffix ικος.

hex key: also called Allen wrench; it has six sides.

hexameter: ♦ (six + measure—ἐξ + μετρ) a verse of six metrical feet.

hierarchy: ♦ (priest + rule—ἱερ + ἀρχ) a graded system of officials, especially of sacred persons.

hieroglyph: ♦ (priest + carve—ἱερ + γλυφ) picture writing used by the ancient Egyptians and done by the priestly class.

hippodrome: ♦ (horse + run—ἱππ + δρομ) place where horses are raced.

hippopotamus: ♦ (horse + river—ἱππ + ποταμ [πο²]) an animal that spends much of its time in the water.

Holocaust: ♦ (whole + burnt—ὀλ + καυστ) whole burnt offering; primarily used since World War II for the wide-scale destruction of Jews.

homogeneous: (same + kind—ὁμο + γεν) for material that is the same throughout.

homogenize: (same + kind) as above, but with suffix *-ize* meaning, as in Greek, "to do—to make."

homonym: ♦ (same + name—ὁμο + ὀνομ) but not really meaning same name, rather it is term for a word that sounds the same as another word, though it has a different meaning, thus *same sound* is the real meaning of *homonym*.

homoiousion: ♦ (similar + substance—ὁμοι [ὁμο] + ουσ [εἰμι]), used in the Arian debate to distinguish between the view that the Son was of *similar* substance with the Father or whether the Son was of the *same* substance (*homoousion*) as the Father.

horizon: the *bounds* or *limits* of vision.

horoscope: ♦ (hour + watch—ὡρ + σκοπ) a chart of the zodiac, which people use to have insight into the future on the basis of a scheme related to the time of one's birth.

hydrant: device for the delivery of water; suffix *-ant* is from the Latin.

hydro-electric: use of water to produce electricity.

hydroplane: vehicle used to travel over the water.

hygiene: the science of health.

hyperactive: excessively active.

hyperbole: ♦ (excessive + throw—ὑπερ + βολ [βαλ]) an overstatement.

hypersensitive: *hyper* is from Greek ὑπερ; *sensitive* from Latin.

hypodermic: (under + skin—ὑπο + δερμ) anything pertaining to the area under the skin.

hypothermia: (under + heat—ὑπο + θερμ) the abnormal lowering of body temperature.

hypsography: (high + write—ὑψ + γραφ) a description (graphing) of the earth's surface.

hysteria: from the word for *womb;* it was originally thought that hysteria in a woman was caused by some disorder of the womb.

iconoclastic: ♦ (image + break—ἰκον + κλασ) term applied to the smashing of images, especially in the controversies in the eastern church during the eighth and ninth centuries.

idiomatic: of language: expressions peculiar to a particular language or group of languages (e.g., a *Semitic* idiom).

idiosyncratic: ♦ (own + with + mix—ἰδι + συν + κρασ) of mannerisms peculiar to an individual; similar to *syncretism,* which means a mixing together, but in this case, only of one individual.

idolatry: ♦ (idol + worship—εἰδωλ + λατρ) worship of idols.

intonation: more directly from the Latin *intonatus,* but related to Greek τειν / τον.

irenic: peaceful.

isotope: (equal + place—ἰσο + τοπ) two or more forms of an element having the same atomic number but different atomic weights.

kenosis: a term to express the *emptying* of divinity in the incarnation; from Philippians 2:5–11.

kerygma: preaching (merely transliterated as a technical term for the gospel).

kleptomaniac: (steal + maniac—κλεπτ + μαν) one who is controlled by the urge to steal.

koine Greek: common or vernacular Greek.

koinonia: merely transliterated from the Greek; often used in Christian circles today in place of the word *fellowship.*

kyrios: term for Lord, in theological works, often transliterated.

laity: the *people* (Greek λαός) contrasted to the *clergy.*

lexicon: dictionary.

leukemia: (white + blood—λευκ + αἱμ) a disease characterized by a marked increase in the number of white blood corpuscles.

licorice: ♦ (sweet + root—γλυκ + ῥιζ) note that the initial γ is dropped in the English transliteration.

lithograph: (stone + write—λιθ + γραφ) a method of printing from stone or metal plates.

liturgy: ♦ (public + work—λειτ + οὐργ [ἐργ]) originally used for any public service; now with religious sense.

lupus: painful disease of the skin.

lux: in physics, a unit of light.

macarcism: beatitude; blessing (the more common *beatitude* is from the Latin).

macrocosm: (far + world—μακρ + κοσμ) the universe (lit. the long or large world).

macron: an accent that indicates a long vowel, indicated by a short horizontal line placed over the vowel.

mariolatry: (Mary + worship—Μαρι + λατρ) an elevation of Mary, the mother of Jesus, to a position of worship and devotion.

martyr: originally meant *witness,* but came to mean *martyr,* as one who has witnessed to the death.

mastectomy: (breast + out + cut—μαστ + ἐκ + τομ [τεμν]) see *appendectomy* above.

maternal: from the Latin *maternus,* meaning *pertaining to a mother,* but related to Greek word for mother: μήτηρ.

math: originally meant learning generally.

matriarchy: (mother + rule—μητρ [μητηρ] + ἀρχ) term for a society in which the women hold the chief power.

matron: more directly from the Latin *matrona,* meaning *a married woman,* but related to the Greek word for mother: μήτηρ.

megalomania: (great + madness—μεγαλ [μεγ] + μαν) delusion of greatness.

megaphone: (great + sound—μεγ + φων) an instrument that magnifies (makes greater) the voice.

megaton: explosive power of a million tons of T.N.T.; the prefix *mega-* is used in the metric system for one million.

menopause: (month + stop—μην + παυσ) the period in life during which the monthly menstrual cycle stops.

Mesopotamia: ♦ (middle + river—μεσο + ποταμ [πο²]) land that lies between the Tigris and Euphrates Rivers.

metamorphosis: ♦ (change + form—μετα + μορφη) change of form; transformation.

metaphysics: ♦ (after + physics—μετα + φυσ) the section of Aristotle's writings that followed his section on physics.

metropolis: ♦ (mother + city—μητρ [μητηρ] + πολ) a capital city or a large urban area.

microfilm: greatly reduced photographic reproduction on film; *film* is from Old English.

micrometer: (small + measure—μικρ + μετρ) instrument used to measure small units.

microscope: (small + look—μικρ + σκοπ) an instrument used to look at small things.

misanthropy: ♦ (hate + man—μισ + ἀνθρωπ) a hatred of humans.

mnemonic: pertaining to the memory; suffix *-ic* is from the Greek suffix ικος.

monarch: ♦ (one + rule—μον + ἀρχ) one who is sole ruler.

monogamy: ♦ (one + marriage—μον + γαμ) being married to one wife or one husband at any one time.

monolithic: ♦ (one + stone—μον + λιθ) any large object viewed as being made of one mass.

monologue: ♦ (alone + speak—μον + λογ) a speech by a single person.

monopoly: ♦ (alone + sell—μονο + πωλ) exclusive right to sell a commodity.

monothelite: (one + will—μον + θελ) a christological controversy arising out of the monophysite debate; the monothelite position was orthodox in that it spoke of two natures but heretical in that it spoke of only one will.

monotone: ♦ (one + tone—μον + τον [τεν]) unvarying tone, either of sound or colour.

mystery: lit. place where one closes the eyes (i.e., secret); from suffix for place (τηριον).

necropolis: ♦ (dead + city—νεκρ + πολ) synonym for cemetery.

neophyte: ♦ (new + plant—νεο + φυτ [φυσ]) used of a recent convert to a religion or a beginner in an activity.

Nike: Greek goddess of victory; identified in Roman mythology with the goddess Victoria.

nominal: existing in name only, as a nominal ruler.

nomos: Law; often not translated in theological writings; words in English that end with the suffix *-onomy* or *-nomy* come from this root.

nous: the intellect.

nuptial: pertaining to marriage; more directly from the Latin *nuptialis*, but clearly related to the Greek νυμφη (directly below).

nymph: bride, maiden; from the Greek word for a class of minor female deities inhabiting the sea, wells, woods, etc.

odometer: ♦ (way + measure—ὁδ + μετρ) an instrument for measuring distance travelled.

oligarchy: ♦ (few + rule—ὀλιγ + ἀρχ) rule by a small group.

ochlocracy: (crowd + power—ὀχλο + κρατ) mob rule.

onomatopoeia: ♦ (name + make—ὀνομ + ποι) a literary term for a word that is pronounced like the natural sound it represents.

ontological: (being + study—ὀντ [εἰμι] + λογ) of things pertaining to the branch of metaphysics dealing with reality or *being*.

ophthalmology: (eye + study—ὀφθαλμ + λογ) the branch of medicine that deals with the eye.

orator: more directly from the Latin *oratio*, but related to the Greek ῥήτωρ, from which comes the closer English cognate *rhetoric*.

organ: instrument; an object that *works*.

otology: (ear + study—ὠτ [οὐς] + λογ) the branch of medicine that deals with the ear.

paleolithic: (old + stone—παλαι + λιθ) a period of human culture characterized by the use of flaked stone implements.

paleontology: (old + being + study—παλαι + οντ [εἰμι] + λογ) science that deals with ancient forms of life.

palimpsest: (again + rub—παλ + ψα) the paper or parchment of a manuscript that has been reused by rubbing out the old letters and writing the new text over it.

palindrome: (again + run—παλ + δρομ) a word or sentence that reads the same backwards as forward (e.g., *Madam, I'm Adam.*).

Pan America: any organization represented throughout the Americas.

panacea: (all + cure—παν + ἀκ) a cure-all.

panorama: (all + sight—παν + ὁρα) a complete view in all directions.

pantheon: ♦ (all + god—παν + θε) all the gods of a particular religion (e.g., the Olympic Pantheon), or a temple dedicated to all the gods.

Paraclete: ♦ (beside + call—παρα + κλη [καλ]) a synonym for the Holy Spirit, who is called along side to serve as a comforter.

paradigm: ♦ (beside + show—παρα + δειγ [δεικ]) pattern.

parallel: ♦ (beside + one another—παρα + ἀλλ) pertaining to two things that run beside each other.

paralysis: ♦ (beside + loose—παρα + λυ) a loss of motor function; here the negative side of the suffix παρα appears.

paramedic: one who works along side of a doctor; prefix *para-* is from Greek, *med* is a Latin root for healing.

paranoia: ♦ (beside + mind—παρα + νο) a mental disorder; here the negative side of the suffix παρα appears.

paraphernalia: ♦ (beside + carry—παρα + φερ) personal effects; more directly from the Latin.

paraplegic: ♦ (beside + strike—παρα + πληγ) here the negative side of the suffix παρα appears.

parasite:♦ (beside + food—παρα + σιτ) an organism that lives off another animal.

paratactic: (beside + arrange—παρα + τακ [ταγ]) grammatical term for a sentence in which clauses are attached by the word και, contrasted to *hypertactic* arrangement, where clauses are subordinated.

parousia:♦ (beside + being—παρα + οὐσ) an appearing; becomes a technical term in Christianity for the Second Coming of Christ.

paternity: more directly from the Latin *paternite,* but clearly related to the Greek πατήρ.

pathetic: something that arouses pity.

pathology: (suffer + study—παθ + λογ) the branch of medicine that deals with the origin and treatment of diseases (or *suffering*).

pathos: the quality that arouses feelings of pity or sorrow.

patriarch: ♦ (family + rule—πατρι + ἀρχ) a leader (ruler) of a family; one might also connect the ending -*arch* to the other meaning of the Greek word ἀρχή (old), thus *patriarch* as one of the old persons in a family.

patristics: pertaining to the Fathers of the early church; suffix -*ic* is from Greek compound suffix ικος.

pause: to stop.

pedagogy: ♦ (child + lead—παιδ + ἀγωγ [ἀγ]) education.

pedantic: one who makes needless display of learning.

pedestrian: more directly from the Latin, but related to the Greek word ποδ, for *foot.*

pediatrics: (child + heal—παιδ + ἰατρ) the branch of medicine that treats children.

Pentagon: ♦ (five + angle—πεντ + γων) a five-sided (or five-angled) figure, as is the shape of the building that houses the U.S. Department of Defense.

Pentecost: ♦ five + suffix κοστ, used to indicate *ten times,* thus 5x10 or 50; for a Jewish festival that was to follow an earlier festival by fifty days.

pericarp: ♦ (around + fruit—περι + καρπ) the wall of fruit.

perimeter: ♦ (around + measure—περι + μετρ) the distance around an object; a border.

Peripatetic: ♦ (about + walk—περι + πατ) applied to the philosophy of Aristotle, who lectured while walking around.

peripheral: ♦ (around + carry—περι + φερ) that which is related to the edge (perimeter) rather than the center.

periscope: (around + see—περι + σκοπ) an instrument (as on a submarine) that rotates and extends so that one can see around the ocean surface.

phantom: an apparition.

phenomenon: neuter passive participle (ομενον) of *show,* thus "something that is shown or seen."

Philadelphia: (love + brother—φιλ + ἀδελφ) new world Quaker city founded by William Penn where religious toleration was practised, thus its name "City of Brotherly Love."

philanthropy: ♦ (love + man—πιλ + ἀνθρωπ) a love of people (cf. *misanthropy*).

philosophy: (love + wisdom—φιλ + σοφ) the literal meaning of *philosophy* is the "love of wisdom."

phoneme: a sound in human speech.

phonetics: branch of linguistics dealing with sounds.

phosphorus: ♦ (light + bear—φως + φορ [φερ]) an element that is luminous in the dark.

photogenic: (light + generating—φωτ [φως] + γεν) here *photo* refers primarily to *photograph,* thus *photogenic* for what produces good photographs.

photograph: (light + writing —φωτ [φως] + γραφ) an image made by light being reflected onto a negative.

photosynthesis: the process by which plants combine elements into food by means of sunlight; *photo* is from Greek work for *light;* for the other part of the compound, see *synthesis* below.

phylactery: ♦ in Judaism, leather case in which Scripture verses are kept; from the word *guard* and the Greek suffix τηριον, used to indicate place where something is done.

phylogeny: (tribe + generation—φυλ + γεν) the history of a tribe.

phylum: a biological division.

physics: the branch of science that deals with features of the natural world.

physiology: ♦ (nature + study—φυσ + λογ) the branch of science that deals with the function of living organisms.

pirate: roughly from the word meaning "attempt"; perhaps to attempt an attack on a ship.

plague: calamity; something that attacks or strikes.

planet: From the perspective of ancient astronomers, planets appeared in the heavens like stars, yet they did not follow the expected courses of the stars, thus the use of the Greek word for *wandering* for these astral bodies.

plenary: full; complete.

Pleroma: gnostic word for the primary realm, the *Fullness.*

plethora: excessive fullness; superfluity.

Pliocene: examine a Geological Time Scale; a few of the names derived from the Greek are: Archeozoic, Proterozoic, Paleozoic, Mesozoic, Cenozoic, Pliestocene, Pliocene, Oligocene.

plutocracy: ♦ (wealth + rule—πλου + κρατ) rule by the wealthy.

pneumatic: related to air, as a pneumatic tool.

pneumonia: ♦ inflammation of the lungs.

podiatry: (foot + heal—ποδ [πο¹] + ἰατρ) the branch of medicine that deals with feet.

podium: a stand with legs or feet.

poem: something made or constructed.

polemic: war.

polis: suffix *-polis* indicates *city*.

political: pertaining to the activities of citizens.

polygamy: ♦ (many + marriage—πολυ [πολλ] + γαμ) the practice of one individual being legally married to more than one person at a time.

polygyny: ♦ (many + women—πολυ [πολλ] + γυν) the practice of one man having more than one wife at one time.

polymer: ♦ (many + part—πολ + μερ) compound of many parts.

polytheistic: ♦ (many + god—πολυ [πολλ] + θε) religion that worships more than one divine being.

pore: a small passage through the skin.

pornographic: (evil + writing—πορν + γραφ) related to the portrayal of sexually explicit scenes.

practice: to do again and again.

pragmatic: practical (see *practice* above).

presbyter: at first simply meant older man, but came to be employed for a specific office in the church in which age was probably a criterion.

progeny: more directly from the Latin; *gen* is common to Latin and Greek.

prognosis: ♦ (before + knowledge—προ + γνο) foreknowledge.

program: ♦ (before + writing—προ + γραφ) something written before the performance that it describes.

prologue: (before + word) the part of a book included before the main body of the text, as a brief introduction to the work.

prophecy: ♦ (before + say—προ + φη) something spoken about an event before it happens.

prophet: ♦ see *prophecy* above.

prophylactic: ♦ (before + guard—προ + φυλακ) something to guard against (i.e., to take precautions before the danger).

prosthesis: ♦ (to + place—προς + θη [τιθ]) an artificial limb attached to the body.

prototype: ♦ (first + type—πρωτ [προ] + τυπ) the first draft or sample.

protozoa: ♦ (first + life—πρωτ [προ] + ζω) name for the simplest organisms of the animal kingdom.

prow: fore of a ship.

Pseudepigrapha: ♦ (false + upon + writing—ψευδ + ἐπι + γραφ) collective name for Jewish writings with authors falsely attributed.

pseudonym: ♦ (false + name—ψευδ + ὀνομ) pen name (i.e., not one's real name).

psyche: soul.

psychiatric: see *psychiatry* below.

psychiatry: (psyche + heal—ψυχ + ἰατρ) the branch of medicine that deals with the treatment of the psyche.

psychology: ♦ (psyche + study—ψυχ + λογ) the study of the psyche.

psychopath: (psyche + suffer—ψυχ + παθ) one suffering from a mental disease.

pyre: pile of combustible material.

Pyrex: a trade name for a glass that is heat-resistant.

recline: more directly from the Latin, but related to Greek root κλιν.

rheostat: (flow + stand—ῥη + στα [ἰστη]) a device used to control the current (flow) of a circuit; in other words, it causes the flow to stand.

rheumatism: medical condition; as a memory aid, note that rheumatism prevents the flowing movement of joints and muscles.

Rhododendron: (rose + tree—ῥοδ + δενδρ) lit. rose-tree.

sarcastic: to tear flesh like a dog or to bite one's lips in rage; used for bitter or harsh speaking.

sarcophagus: ♦ (flesh + eat—σαρχ + φαγ) a coffin (lit. an eater of flesh).

scenario: an outline of a dramatic work.

scene: tent from where actors prepared; later applied to where they performed.

schizophrenia: (divide + mind—σχιζ + φρεν) a disease characterized by a split in the personality.

scotoma: dimness of vision.

seismic: related to earthquakes.

seismograph: (shake + write—σει + γραφ) instrument used to measure the movement of the earth during an earthquake (i.e., something that records [writes] movement).

semaphore: (sign + bear—σημ + φορ [φερ]) an apparatus used for signalling.

semantics: serving as a sign or warning; suffix *-ic* is from the Greek suffix ικος.

somatic: related to the body.

Sophia: in Gnosticism, Wisdom.

Soter: saviour; an epithet for Zeus, and later used by Christians for Jesus.

soteriology: (saviour + study—σωτηρ + λογ) branch of theology that deals with salvation.

sperm: seed.

sporadic: scattered.

static: stationary.

status: standing; position (more directly from the Latin).

Stephen: personal name, means *crown*.

stereotype: (firm + type—στερε + τυπ) a pattern.

steroids: as a memory aid, note that steroids are used to make a person firm or solid.

stethoscope: (breast + see—στηθο + σκοπ) instrument for hearing (note: not *seeing*) the breast.

strategy: ♦ (army + lead—στρατ + ἀγ) to *lead* an *army*, though used more widely without a military sense.

surgery: ♦ (hand + word—χειρ + ἐργ) the word for *hand* has become very abbreviated; the root *urg* for word remains unaffected.

sycamore: a fig tree.

syllable: ♦ (together + take—συν + λαβ [λαμβ]) letters taken together to produce one sound.

sympathy: ♦ (with + suffer—συν + παθ) the sharing in the suffering of others.

symphony: ♦ (together + sound—συν + φων) agreeable mixing of sounds.

symposium: ♦ (together + drink—συν + πoσ [πο²]) a meeting to discuss a particular topic; originally associated with a meal.

symptom: ♦ (with + fall—συν + πτομ [πιπτ]) any condition that occurs (falls) with a disease, and thus can be used to indicate the presence of the disease.

synagogue: ♦ (together + lead—συν + ἀγ) place where Jews were led together by a common interest.

synchronize: ♦ (with + time—συν + χρον) to set watches so that everyone is with the same time; *-ize* is like the Greek suffix ιζω; originally: to be contemporary with.

syndetic: ♦ (together + bind—συν + δε) uniting.

syndicate: ♦ (with + judge—συν + δικ) a group that decides (judges) together what course of action should be taken.

synod: ♦ (together + way—συν + ὁδ) an ecclesiastical council.

synonym: ♦ (with + name—συν + ὀνομ) does not really mean "with the same name" but "with the same (similar) meaning."

synoptic: ♦ (together + see—συν + ὀπτ) as the Synoptic Gospels, which are viewed together, thus giving a full view.

syntax: ♦ (together + arrange—συν + ταξ [ταγ]) the branch of linguistics dealing with the relationships among parts of a sentence.

synthesis: ♦ (together + place—συν + θη [τιθ]) act of placing together things once apart; *-sis* is Greek suffix.

synthetic: see *synthesis* above; *-ic* is from the Greek ending ικος.

system: ♦ (together + stand—συν + θη [τιθ]) something that *stands together*.

tachometer: (speed + measure—ταχ + μετρ) instrument for measuring speed.

tactics: (arrange + adjective ending—ταξ [ταγ] + ικος) science of troop arrangement. [Note: English word *tactics* (a noun) is simply a transliteration of a Greek adjective].

tautology: (same + word—ταυτ + λογ) unnecessary repetition of the same idea in different words.

taxidermy: (order + skin—ταξ [ταγ] + δερμ) bringing order to the skin of an animal, so that the original shape is restored.

taxonomy: (arrangement + law—ταξ [ταγ] + νομ) systematic arrangement according to established criteria.

teleology: (end + study—τελ + λογ) the branch of cosmology that deals with final causes.

telephone: (far + voice—τελ + φων) an instrument that carries the voice over a distance.

telescope: (far + sight—τελ + σκοπ) an instrument that permits one to *see* things that are far away.

television: from the Latin (far + see), though the first part of the compound is shared with Greek.

tension: more directly from the Latin, meaning the condition of being stretched tight; but see τειν.

tetrahedron: ♦ (four + base—τετρα + ἑδρον) a four-sided object.

tetrarch: ♦ (four + rule—τετρ + ἀρχ) ruler of small territory (a fourth part); title given to one of Herod the Great's sons after his kingdom was divided.

thaumaturgy: ♦ (wonder + work—θαυμ + ὑργ [ἐργ]) magic; the *working* of *wonders* or miracles.

theatre: ♦ place for seeing performances, from the word *sight* (θεα) and the suffix τηριον, used to indicate place where something is done.

theme: from τιθημι, for thing placed.

theology: ♦ (god + study—θε + λογ) study of divine matters.

theophany: ♦ (god + appear—θε + φαν [φαιν]) a term used for various appearances by gods, often in human form.

theory: something viewed (or speculated) about a phenomena.

Theotokos: (God + bear—θε + τοκ [τεκν]) means the *bearer of God,* and used of Mary in in the Nestorian debate.

therapeutic: transliterated from Greek for healing; the ending *-ic* is from the Greek ικος.

therapy: simply transliterated from the Greek; any practice or service directed toward the process of healing.

thermal: from Greek word for *warm;* the ending *-al* is the same as the Greek suffix αλος.

thermometer: (hot + measure—θερμ + μετρ) an instrument that measures the temperature.

thermos: a container used to keep liquids warm.

thesaurus: store house; treasure.

thesis: something put forward as an explanation; a proposition.

thlipsis: pressure on blood vessels.

tome: one of a series of volumes (i.e., something cut from a larger series to form a distinctive volume).

tone: a sound that changes depending on tension.

topography: ♦ (place + write—τοπ + γραφ) the representing (graphing) on a map of the physical features of a place.

track: more directly from Old French, but with close similarity to Greek τρεχ.

trek: more directly from culture of South Africa, meaning to *travel* by wagon.

triangle: ♦ (three + angle—τρι + γων): the form is more directly Latin, but is also close to the Greek.

trilogy: ♦ (three + word—τρι + λογ) any three-part production considered together.

trinity: (three + one) the form is Latin, as is the root *one,* but *tri-* is common to Greek and Latin.

triumvirate: from the Latin meaning ruling body of three people; τρι is both Greek and Latin.

tripod: ♦ (three + foot—τρι + ποδ [πο[1]]) device with three feet or legs.

trophy: originally, a memorial erected by the victorious army at the place of battle where they routed (turned) the enemy.

tropic: lines between the poles and the equator, at which point the sun turns back towards the equator.

Uranus: the sky god in Greek mythology.

Utopia: (no + place—οὐ + τοπ) coined in 1516 by Thomas More to describe a ideal country; prefix is from οὐ, not from the normal negating prefix ἀ.

xenophobia: (strange + fear—ξεν + φοβ) fear of foreign people or things.

xerox: a method of dry printing that uses light, electricity, and powder, rather than ink.

xylophone: (wood + sound—ξυλ + φων) instrument constructed from strips of wood which, when hit, vibrate, producing musical sounds.

zodiac: diminutive of ζῷον (animal); a scheme in which animals (living things) are key symbols.

zone: something that girds or binds.

zoo: place for keeping live animals, as opposed to a museum.

zoology: (life + study—ζω + λογ) branch of science that studies animal life.

SECTION

4

Explanation of Greek Prefixes and Suffixes

In the following list, Greek prefixes and suffixes (listed in the far right column of the main Cognate List) are compared with English prefixes and suffixes to demonstrate the ways that a prefix or suffix can alter the meaning of a root. By learning how particular Greek prefixes and suffixes affect the meaning, the student will be able to determine the meaning of new words simply by attention to the attached prefixes and suffixes.

The prefixes and suffixes are listed in alphabetical order. Suffixes apply only to a particular part of speech (e.g., to a verb). That restriction is noted. Prefixes are not restricted in this manner. The general sense of the prefix or suffix is then given in bold letters. Then follows, in most cases, examples of comparable use of suffixes or prefixes in English. The suffix or prefix will first be given, followed by |, which is followed by actual English words that employ the suffix or prefix. Sometimes rather than adding a suffix or prefix, English uses a separate word. In such cases, examples are given. The final part of each entry consists of qualifying comments, where necessary.

One further note on prefixes. They are used extensively in compound words, much more so than in English. And they affect the meaning of the compound in a number of ways. Although sometimes prefixes add nothing to the meaning of the main root, more often there is some change. Prefixes often add emphasis to the main root. Often they add the full impact of a prefixed preposition. Sometimes, though, a change takes place for which no good explanation is possible. In summary, then, prefixes can affect the compound in the following ways:

(1) no change in the meaning
(2) the root is emphasized or intensified
(3) the full impact of the preposition is added to the root
(4) the meaning is changed, but the change cannot be explained by the added prefix.

The effect of verb endings sometimes is quite specific, though for the larger classes of verbs, generally no useful rule can be offered. There is, however, one somewhat regular pattern: *if a verb ending can mean both "to do" and "to be," the "to be" form will usually be a deponent* (i.e., middle or passive, rather than active, even though the meaning is active).

Endings of prepositions, conjunctions, particles, and often of adverbs contribute nothing to the meaning. Such endings are not included in column five of the Cognate Groups section. The space for suffixes will be left blank.

Some words listed as nouns in the Cognate Groups section actually have adjective endings. This happens when an adjective is used as a noun. English often uses adjectives as nouns too (e.g., *poor: the poor; blind: the blind*).

The list below is intended only as a tool for remembering Greek vocabulary. Any detailed study of cognates requires a more technical work.

ἀ [ἀν] — prefix — **negation** (e.g., *a-* | atheist; *an-* | anarchy; *non-* | nonproductive; un- | unable, undo; -less | reckless, spotless). [Note: when ἀ is prefixed to a word that begins with a vowel, the form will be lengthened to ἀν, as in "anarchy" above. The form will be identical to ἀν (shortened from ἀνα), which occurs when ἀνα is prefixed to a word that begins with a vowel. They do not mean the same thing.]

α — noun feminine first declension — (gen. ης or ας) [Since English does not indicate gender, no examples can be given here.]

α — adverb — no specified meaning.

ᾳ — adverb — no specified meaning.

αζω — verb — **to do / to cause / to be** (e.g., *-ize* | terrorize, memorize). If deponent, it usually means "to be." [Note: *z* is common to both English and Greek in the examples given. Usually, however, English does not use the *-ize* form to express this kind of intention.]

αινω — verb — **to cause; at times, to be.** If deponent, it usually means to be (e.g., *-en* | frighten; *en-* | enable; *em-* | empower; make | make wide). [Note: *n (m)* is common to both Greek and English.]

ακος — adjective — **characteristic of; pertaining to; like** (e.g., *-ac* | cardiac [Note: *-ac* is common to both Greek and English. Drop the case endings to see this more clearly. This form is for roots endings in ι. Otherwise ικος is used.]

αλος — adjective — **like / of x kind of character** (e.g., *-al* | ethical, magical). [Note: *-al* is common to both Greek and English. Drop the case endings to see this more clearly.]

αμφι — prefix — **around:** (e.g., *amphi-* | amphitheatre).

ἀνα [ἀν] — prefix — **up / again / back / intensifier** (e.g., *ana-* | anabaptist, analysis [a loosing up]; *re-* | repay, redo; up* | tie up, give up). *As in English, this prefix sometimes does not add much to the meaning of the root. [Note: when ἀνα is prefixed to a word that begins with a vowel, the form will be shortened to ἀν. This must be distinguished from ἀν (lengthened from ἀ) that occurs when ἀ is prefixed to a word that begins with a vowel.]

ἀντι [ἀντ / ἀνθ] — prefix — **against / opposition / replacement** (e.g., *anti-*| antidote, antiaircraft, Antichrist, Antarctic).

ανω — verb — **frequently a sense of gain / increase / getting,** primarily because most words in this group are based on the root λαμβάνω.

ἀπο [ἀπ ἀφ] — prefix — from / back / again / intensifier (e.g., *apo-* | apostasy) some-times in English with the prefix *re-*.

αριον — noun — (αριδιον) — small (e.g., *-let* | booklet; *-y* | puppy).

ας — noun masculine first declension — (gen. ου).

αω — to do / to be: "to do" is the more frequent.

δια [δι] — prefix — completion / intensifier / distribution / division: but often does not affect the meaning of the root (e.g., *dia-* | diagnosis [as in complete / full]; *dia-*| diaspora [as in distribution]; *dia-* | diameter [as in division]).

δυσ — prefix — bad / hard (e.g., *dys-* | dysentery lit. "bad entrails").

εια — noun feminine first declension — abstract (e.g., *-ity* | purity; *-ion* | starvation; *-ness* | truthfulness; *-ence* | disobedience; *-ance* | forbearance). Although often this ending indicates "quality," the only safe rule is that it will be an abstract noun.

ειον — noun neuter second declension — place (gen. ειου).

εἰς — prefix — into / to.

ἐκ [ἐξ] — prefix — from / intensifier: but quite often, no effect on meaning of root.

ἐν [ἐμ / ἐγ / ἐλ] — prefix — in; into but often this prefix does not alter meaning of root (e.g., *en-* | enclose; *em-* | employ; *in-* | inaugurate; *im-*| implant; in | live in, stay in). [Note: this Greek prefix never negates, unlike the English prefix *in- (im-)*, as in "impossible" or "inadmissible."]

ἐπι [ἐπ / ἐφ] — prefix — on / upon / intensifier (e.g., *epi-* | epidermis, epidemic, epi-center; "upon" | come upon). This is a light-weight prefix and often does not alter the meaning of root (e.g., καλέω and ἐπικαλέω both mean "name").

εὐ — prefix — well / good / full (e.g., *eu-* | euthanasia, eugenics, euphony; *-ful* | cheer-ful, useful; well | well known; good | good will).

ευς — noun masculine third declension — profession / position / doer (e.g., *-eus* | masseuse; *-er* | teacher; *-or* | actor).

ευω — verb — to be / to do: like εω below, though ευω verbs are far fewer. Often with τ, as in τευω.

εω — verb — to be / to do: Even when the "to be" form is not the normal expression in English, frequently a "be" form can be substituted so that the meaning is retained (e.g., grieve / be sad; love / be a friend; fear / be afraid; do / be active). But this is not the case often enough to be generally useful.

η — noun feminine first declension — (gen. ης). The most common feminine noun end-ing, with no meaning reflected often enough to offer a useful rule.

η — adverb — manner / location.

ἡμι — prefix — half (e.g., *hemi-* | hemisphere).

ην / ενος (ηνος) — noun — see ς.

ης / ες — adjective — quality.

ης — noun masculine first declension — agent (gen. ου) see της.

ητος — see τος.

θεν — adverb — place from where (e.g., from | from home). [This is opposite to the English suffix *-ward,* as in homeward.]

ια — noun feminine first declension — frequently quality, often an abstract idea (e.g., *-ia* | *-y* | *-ness* |). With σ (σια) often indicates action.

ιζω — verb — to do / to cause / to be (e.g., *-ize* | symbolize, characterize). Often the English equivalent will contain the suffix *-ize,* or an intelligible new English word could be created by using the related adjective or noun combined with the suffix *-ize.* About one half of the deponent forms are translated as "to be."

ικος / ικη / ικον — adjective — **characteristic of / pertaining to / like:** Adjective ending (e.g., *-ic* | metallic, plastic, despotic; *-ly* | worldly; *-al* | spiritual; pertaining to | pertaining to nature (i.e., natural). [Note: *-ic* is common to both Greek and English. Drop the case endings to see this more clearly. Also see τικος. Note: sometimes these forms are used as nouns.]

ικως — adverb — combination of endings ικος and ως.

ιμος / ιμη / ιμον — adjective — **fitness / ability** (e.g., *-able* | *-ed* | *-ful*).

ινος / ινη / ινον — adjective — **source / material** (e.g., *-in* | toxin; *-ine* | chlorine; *-en* | wooden, ethylene; of | of wood). [Note: *in* is common to both Greek and English. Drop the case endings to see this more clearly.]

ιον — noun neuter second declension — (gen. ιου) **diminutive / general.**

ιος / ια / ιον — adjective — **related to.**

ισμος — see μος.

ισσα — feminine noun ending: **profession / position** (e.g., *-ess* | goddess). [Note: vowel *i* / *e* plus double *ss* is common to both Greek and English. Drop case ending to see this more clearly.]

ιστα — adverb — **superlative:** neuter plural used as adverb.

ιστης — see της.

ιστος / ιστη / ιστον — adjective — **superlative** (e.g., *-est* | fast > fastest). [Note: *-ist* / *-est* is common to both Greek and English. Drop the case endings to see this more clearly.]

κατα [κατ / καθ] — prefix — **down / against / order / destructive.** This is the most negative of the Greek prefixes (except for the rare δυσ), though it does not always imply something negative.

κις — **one times indicator.**

κοντα — **ten times indicator.**

κοσιοι — **hundred times indicator.**

λος / λη / λον — adjective — **characterized by** (e.g., *-ful* | sinful).

μα — noun neuter third declension — **object / often result of action** (gen. ματος; e.g., *-ma* | drama, enigma; *-ion* | *-ing* | *-ment* | "something + past participle" | something spoken [i.e., a word] or something obscurely spoken [i.e., enigma]). Most common neuter noun ending.

μετα [μετ / μεθ] — prefix — **after / with / change** (e.g., *meta-* | metaphysics; metamorphosis).

μι — verb — **general.**

μος — noun masculine second declension — **action** (gen. μου) (e.g., *-ing* | Running is healthy, the dividing; *-ion* | the division (often σμος or ισμος).

μων / μον — adjective — **having quality of** *x* (e.g., *-ful*).

ξ — noun — see ς.

ον — noun neuter second declension — frequently an **object** (gen. ου) no general rule is adequate.

ον — adverb — from neuter singular adjective.

ος — noun masculine second declension (more rarely, feminine) —(gen. ου).

ος — noun neuter third declension — **object / concept.**

ος / η / ον — adjective — most common ending for adjectives; note two variations: (1) if the root ends in ρ, form will be ος α ον; (2) for some words, the neuter singular form is simply ο rather than ον.

οτης — noun feminine third declension — **quality** (gen. ητος).

ου − adverb − but not always an adverb.

ους / α / ουν − adjective − (= ε + ος) see ος η ov.

οω − verb − **to cause** (e.g., *en-* | widen; *en-* | enrich, enable; *em-* | empower; make | make rich, make able). Often best translated as "make" + adjective (e.g., strengthen / make strong). A few times, must be translated as "to be."

παρα [παρ] − prefix − **beside / disordered / negative** (e.g., *para-* | parallel, paramedic).

περ − **emphasis**, but often no observable change.

περι [περ] − prefix − **around / about / beyond / excessive:** almost always means one of the first two (e.g., *peri-* | perimeter; around | circumcise (i.e., cut around).

προ − prefix − **before** (e.g., *pro-* | prologue; before).

προς − **toward / to** (e.g., *pros-* | prosthesis).

ρ − noun − (similar to ς below).

ρος − adjective − **quality.**

ς − noun third declension − many third declension nouns end in ς or a blank in the nominative, and a genitive (of various forms) with an ending of ος ους ως.

σια − see ια.

σις − noun feminine third declension − **action or something that results from action** (gen. εως) (e.g., *-ing* | the educating, the forming; or the related *-tion* | formation, education.

σκω − verb − point at which something **begins or changes**; often with mental actions.

σμος − see μος.

σσω − verb − **to do.**

συν / συ / συγ / συλ / συμ / συσ] − prefix − **with / completely** almost always with sense of "with" in NT; otherwise probably means completely (e.g., *syn-* | synonym; *sym-* | sympathy; with | with the same meaning; up | break up; break completely).

συνη − noun feminine first declension − **quality.**

τερος / τερα / τερον − adjective − **comparative form er** (e.g., *-er* | small > smaller). [Note: this is roughly equivalent to English, where *-er* indicates comparative forms. Drop the case endings to see this more clearly.]

τερον − adverb − from neuter singular adjective above.

της − noun masculine first declension − **agent / instrument** (gen. ου).

τηρ − **agent / doer** (e.g., *-er* | teacher, mover, player; *-or* | actor). It can be translated as a relative clause. (e.g., teacher = the one who teaches). [Note: *-er* is common to both Greek and English.]

τηριον − noun neuter second declension − **place.**

της − noun masculine − **member of class / doer** (as in τηρ above).

της − see οτης.

τικος / τικη / τικον − adjective − **characteristic of / pertaining to / like** (e.g., *-tic* | semantic, therapeutic). [Note: *-tic* is common to both Greek and English. Drop the case endings to see this more clearly.] Also see ικος.

τικως − combination of τικος and ως.

τος / τη / τον − adjective − **possibility / actuality** (e.g., *-able* | believable; *-ible* | incredible; *-ing* | pleasing) (often: ητος).

τρια − noun feminine − **agent** (e.g., *-ess* | actress).

τρον − noun neuter second declension − **instrument** (e.g., *-tron* | cyclotron). [Note: *tron* is common to both Greek and English.]

τωρ − noun − **agent / doer** (e.g., *-or* | mediator, actor, arbitrator; *-er* | teacher, mover, player). It can be translated as a relative clause. (e.g., teacher = the one who teaches). [Note: *-or* is common to both Greek and English.]

υνω — verb — **to cause** / at times: **to be**; especially as deponent (e.g., *-en* | widen, enlighten, frighten; *en-* | enrich, enable; *em-* | empower; make | make rich, make able). [Note: *n (m)* is common to both Greek and English.]

ὑπερ — prefix — **over** / **excessive** (e.g., *hyper-* | hyperactive).

ὑπο [ὑπ / ὑφ] — prefix — **under** / **inferior** (e.g., *hypo-* | hypodermic).

υς εια υ — adjective — **quality.**

ω — verb — **the most common verb ending.**

ω — adverb — **from** / **place.**

ων — noun third declension — **object** (generally; masculine gen. ωνος or οντος; neuter gen. ονος).

ων ον — adjective — **comparative** / **quality** (neuter singular is sometimes used as an adverb).

ως — adverb — **manner** (e.g., *-ly* | slowly) almost always with an English equivalent ending in *-ly.*

5

Identical Greek/English Prefixes and Suffixes*

Greek	English	General Meaning	Example
ά-	a-	negation	*a*theist
-ακος**	-ac	pertaining to	cardi*ac*
-αλος**	-al	of *x* character	magic*al*
ἀμφι-	amphi-	around	*amphi*theatre
ἀνα-	ana-	up / back / again	*Ana*baptist
ἀντι-	anti-	against / opposition	*Anti*christ
ἀπο-	apo-	from	*apo*stasy
δια-	dia-	divided	*dia*meter
δυσ-	dys-	bad	*dys*function
ἐν-	en-	in / into	*en*close
ἐπι-	epi-	on / upon	*epi*dermis
εὐ-	eu-	well / good	*eu*thanasia
-ια	-ia	quality (abstract)	euthanas*ia*
-ιζω	-ize	do something to	terror*ize*
-ικος**	-ic	characteristic of	metall*ic*
-ινος**	-in	material / source	tox*in*
-ισμος**	-ism	belief in	Marx*ism*
-ιστης**	-ist	one who does	art*ist*
-ιστος**	-est	superlative	fast*est*
κατα-	cata-	down	*cata*ract
-μα	-ma	object (result)	enig*ma*
μετα-	meta-	after / change	*meta*morphosis
παρα-	para-	beside	*para*llel
περι-	peri-	around / about	*peri*meter

---

* A fuller discussion of Prefixes and Suffixes can be found in Section 4

** Delete case ending (ος or ης) to see the Greek / English parallel more clearly.

προ-	pro-	before	*pro*logue
προσ-	pros-	to / toward	*pros*thesis
-σις	-sis	action	metamorpho*sis*
συν-	syn-	with	*syn*onym
-τερος**	-er	comparative	small*er*
-τηρ	-er	doer	teach*er*
-τικος**	-tic	pertaining to	therapeu*tic*
-τρον	-tron	instrument	cyclo*tron*
-τωρ	-or	doer	act*or*
ὑπερ-	hyper-	over / excessive	*hyper*active
ὑπο-	hypo-	under	*hypo*dermic

APPENDIX: GRIMM'S LAW

From one of the brothers of German fairy-tale fame, Grimm's Law is a list of rules that helps to explain some of the relations between words of Indo-European languages and their Greek roots where there is not a direct letter-for-letter correspondence. In order to understand this "law," one needs first to learn a particular subdivision of consonants. In this case, we distinguish between SOFT, HARD, and ASPIRATE consonants. The rule is that where there is not an equivalent letter in an English word derived from the Greek, there may be a substitution of a related letter. The substitution, from Greek to English is: (1) SOFT (voiced); (2) HARD (voiceless); (3) ASPIRATED; (4) SOFT (voiced), as illustrated on the chart below. Simply find, on the chart below, the letter from the Greek word and replace it with the letter to the immediate right on the chart to find its English equivalent.

	1	2	3	4
GUTTURAL	γ → k	κ → h	χ → g	
LABIAL	β → p	π → f	φ → b	
DENTAL	δ → t	τ → th	θ → d	

Examples from the vocabulary list:

ἀγρ — acre
γεν — kind; kin
γνο — know
δε - tie
δεκα — ten
δυ — two
ἐργ οὐργ — work
θε — deity
θυγατηρ — daughter
θυρ — door
καρδ — heart

καρπ — fruit
μητηρ — mother
πατηρ — father
πιστ — faith
ποδ — foot
πολ — full
πορν — fornication
πυρ — fire
τρι — three
φερ — bear
χαρ — grace

COMMON PRONOUNS, ADJECTIVES, AND ADVERBS

CHART A

initial letter	Key Syllable	Relative ὁ	Interrogative π	Indefinite[1] π	Indefinite Relative o + indefinite	Demonstrative τ for π or δε
Place Where	ου	οὖ where	ποῦ where?	που somewhere	ὅπου wherever/whither	ὧδε here
Time When	οτε	ὅτε when	πότε when?	ποτε sometime	ὁπότε whenever	τότε then
Manner How	ως	ὥς as	πῶς how?	πως somehow	ὅπως that/in order that	οὕτως thus/so
Quantity[2] How much	οσ	ὅσος as much as	πόσος how much?	ποσος of some quantity	ὁπόσος of however much	τοσοῦτος so much
Quality[2] What kind	οι	οἷος such as	ποῖος what kind?	ποιος of some kind	ὁποῖος of whatever kind	τοιοῦτος such

CHART B

initial letter	Relative ὁ	Interrogative π	Indefinite[1] π	Indefinite Relative o + indefinite	Demonstrative often δε
Person[2] Who	ὅς who	τίς who?	τις someone	ὅστις whoever	ὅστος/ὅδε this
Thing[2] What	ὅς what	τίς what?	τις something	ὅστις whatever	ὅστος/ὅδε this

[1] English translation: "some" or "any."
[2] Only the masculine form is given on the chart

INDEX OF COGNATE GROUP TERMS*

ἀβαρής ές burdenless, 109
ἀγ—bring, lead, 23
ἀγαθ—good, 57
ἀγαθοεργέω do good, be generous, 57
ἀγαθοποιέω do good, be helpful, 57
ἀγαθοποιΐα ας good-doing, 57
ἀγαθοποιός οῦ good doer, 57
ἀγαθός ή όν good, useful, 57
ἀγαθουργέω do good, be kind, 57
ἀγαθωσύνη ης goodness, 57
ἄγαμος ου unmarried, single, 84
ἀγαπ—love, 32
ἀγαπάω love, 32
ἀγάπη ης love, 33
ἀγαπητός ή όν beloved, 33
ἀγγελ—message, 22
ἀγγελία ας message, news, 22
ἀγγέλλω tell, 22
ἄγγελος ου angel, messenger, 22
ἀγενεαλόγητος ον without genealogy, 13
ἀγενής ές insignificant, inferior, 13
ἀγι—holy, sacred, 34
ἀγιάζω make holy, purify, 34
ἀγιασμός οῦ consecration, 34
ἄγιος α ον holy, consecrated, 34
ἀγιότης ητος holiness, 34
ἀγιωσύνη ης holiness, consecration, 34
ἀγν—holy, sacred, 34
ἀγνεία ας moral purity, 34
ἀγνίζω purify (>holy + ize), 34
ἀγνισμός οῦ purification, 34
ἀγνοέω be ignorant, disregard, 24
ἀγνόημα ματος sin done in ignorance, 24
ἄγνοια ας ignorance, 24
ἀγνός ή όν holy, pure, 34
ἀγνότης ητος purity, sincerity, 34
ἀγνῶς purely, 34
ἀγνωσία ας lack of spiritual insight, 24
ἄγνωστος ον unknown, 24
ἀγορ—market, place of business transactions, 89
ἀγορά ᾶς market place, 89
ἀγοράζω buy, redeem, 89
ἀγοραῖος ου loafer, court session, 89
ἀγρ—field, wild, 95
ἀγράμματος ον uneducated, 30
ἀγραυλέω be outdoors, 95
ἀγρεύω trap, 95
ἀγριέλαιος ου wild olive tree, 95
ἄγριος α ον wild, 95
ἀγρός οῦ field, farm, 95
ἄγω lead, 23
ἀγωγ—bring, lead, 23
ἀγωγή ῆς manner of life, 23
ἀδελφ—brother, sister, 29
ἀδελφή ῆς sister, 29
ἀδελφός οῦ brother, countryman, 29
ἀδελφότης ητος brotherhood, 29
ἀδιάκριτος ον without favoritism, 19
ἀδιάλειπτος ον endless, constant, 58

ἀδιαλείπτως constantly, always, 58
ἀδικέω wrong, 33
ἀδίκημα ματος crime, sin, wrong, 33
ἀδικία ας wrongdoing, evil, 33
ἄδικος ον evil, sinful, 33
ἀδίκως unjustly, 33
ἀδόκιμος ον disqualified, worthless, 84
ἀδυνατεῖ it is impossible, 29
ἀδύνατος ον impossible, unable, 29
ἀδυσβάστακτος ον not difficult to bear, 106
ἄζυμος ον without yeast, 109
ἀθανασία ας immortality, 36
ἄθεος ον without God (>atheist), 11
ἄθεσμος ον morally corrupt, lawless, 31
ἀθετέω reject, ignore (>not put), 31
ἀθέτησις εως nullification (>not put), 31
ἀθυμέω become discouraged, 61
αἱμ—blood, 65
αἷμα τος blood, death, 65
αἱματεκχυσία ας shedding of blood, 65
αἱμορροέω hemorrhage, bleed, 65
αἰν—praise, 105
αἴνεσις εως praise, 105
αἰνέω praise, 105
αἶνος ου praise, 105
αἱρ—take away, seize (compare αἱρ), 89
αἱρ—take up, choose (compare αἱρ), 54
αἴρω take, 54
αἰσχ—shame, 87
αἰσχροκερδής ές greedy (>shameful in), 87
αἰσχροκερδῶς greedily, 88
αἰσχρολογία ας obscene speech, 88
αἰσχρός ά όν disgraceful, 88
αἰσχρότης ητος shameful behavior, 88
αἰσχύνη ης shame, shameful thing, 88
αἰσχύνομαι be ashamed, 88
αἰτ—ask, reason, cause, accusation, 57
αἰτέω ask, require, 57
αἴτημα ματος request, demand, 57
αἰτία ας reason, cause, charge, 57
αἴτιον ου guilt, reason, 57
αἴτιος ου cause, source, 57
αἰτίωμα ματος charge, accusation, 57
αἰων—age, 43
αἰών ῶνος age, eternity, 43
αἰώνιος ον eternal, 43
ἀκαθαρσία ας impurity, 63
ἀκάθαρτος ον unclean, 63
ἀκαιρέομαι be without opportunity, 65
ἀκαίρως untimely, 65
ἄκακος ον innocent, 60
ἄκαρπος ον barren, useless, 72
ἀκατάγνωστος ον above criticism, 24
ἀκατακάλυπτος ον uncovered, 78
ἀκατάκριτος ον uncondemned, 20
ἀκατάλυτος ον indestructible, 46
ἀκατάπαυστος ον unceasing, 89
ἀκαταστασία ας disorder, 18
ἀκατάστατος ον unstable, 18

---

*See also list of Identical Greek/English words, pp. 5–8.

ἀκλινής ἐς firm (not turned), 93
ἀκο—hear, 22
ἀκοή ῆς hearing, report, news, 22
ἀκολουθ—follow, 64
ἀκολουθέω follow, be a disciple, 64
ἀκου—hear, 22
ἀκούω hear, understand, 22
ἀκρασία ας lack of self control, 69
ἀκρατής ἐς uncontrolled, violent, 69
ἀκωλύτως unhindered, 111
ἁλ—salt, fish, 116
ἀλαλάζω wail, 32
ἀλάλητος ον inexpressible, 32
ἄλαλος ον unable to speak, dumb, 32
ἅλας ατος salt, 116
ἀληθ—true, 44
ἀλήθεια ας truth, truthfulness, 44
ἀληθεύω be truthful, honest, 44
ἀληθής ἐς true, truthful, genuine, 44
ἀληθινός ή όν real, true, genuine, 44
ἀληθῶς truly, actually, 44
ἁλι—salt, fish, 116
ἁλιεύς έως fisherman, 116
ἁλιεύω fish, 116
ἁλίζω salt, 116
ἀλλ—other, change, 14
ἀλλά but, 14
ἀλλάσσω change, 14
ἀλλαχόθεν at another place, 14
ἀλλαχοῦ elsewhere, 14
ἀλληγορέω speak allegorically, 89
ἀλλήλων οις ους one another, 14
ἀλλογενής ους foreigner, 14
ἄλλος η ο another, other, 14
ἀλλοτριεπίσκοπος busybody, 104
ἀλλότριος α ον of another, foreign, 14
ἀλλόφυλος ον foreign, 101
ἄλλως otherwise, 14
ἄλογος ον unreasoning, wild, 16
ἅλς ἁλός salt, 116
ἁλυκός ή όν salty, 116
ἀλυπότερος α ον freed from pain / sorrow, 91
ἀλυσιτελής ἐς of no advantage, no help, 46
ἀμαθής ἐς ignorant, 34
ἁμαρτ—sin, 36
ἁμαρτάνω sin, 36
ἁμάρτημα ματος sin, 36
ἁμαρτία ας sin, 36
ἀμάρτυρος ον without witness, 42
ἁμαρτωλός όν sinful, 36
ἄμαχος ον peaceable, 16
ἀμελέω disregard, neglect, 107
ἀμέριμνος ον free from worry, 107
ἀμετάθετος ον unchangeable, 31
ἀμεταμέλητος ον free from care or regret, 107
ἀμετανόητος ον unrepentant, 53
ἄμετρος ον immeasurable, 106
ἀμην—truly, 56
ἀμήν amen, truly, 56
ἀμήτωρ ορος without a mother, 70
ἀμπελ—grapevine, 102
ἄμπελος ου grapevine, 102
ἀμπελουργός οῦ vinedresser, gardener, 102
ἀμπελών ῶνος vineyard, 102
ἀμφιβάλλω cast a net, 28
ἀμφίβληστρον ου casting net, 28

ἄμφοδον ου street, 54
ἀν¹—particle indicating contingency, 43
ἄν (signals contingency), 43
ἀν²—up, again, 98
ἀνά (>acc.) up, each, 98
ἀναβαίνω go up, ascend, grow, 37
ἀναβάλλομαι postpone, 28
ἀναβιβάζω make to go, draw, drag, 37
ἀναβλέπω look up, regain sight, 44
ἀνάβλεψις εως restoration of sight, 44
ἀναβοάω cry out, 110
ἀναβολή ῆς delay, 28
ἀνάγαιον ου upstairs room, 23
ἀναγγέλλω tell, proclaim, 22
ἀναγεννάω give new birth to, 13
ἀναγινώσκω read, 24
ἀναγκ—necessity, 99
ἀναγκάζω force (>make necessary), 99
ἀναγκαῖος α ον necessary, forced, 99
ἀναγκαστῶς under compulsion, 99
ἀνάγκη ης necessity, distress, 100
ἀναγνωρίζομαι make known again, 24
ἀνάγνωσις εως reading, 24
ἀνάγω lead up, bring up, 23
ἀναδείκνυμι show clearly, appoint, 73
ἀνάδειξις εως public appearance, 73
ἀναδέχομαι receive, welcome, 50
ἀναδίδωμι deliver (i.e., give up), 17
ἀναζάω revive, 33
ἀναζητέω seek after, 48
ἀναζώννυμι bind up, 114
ἀναζωπυρέω stir into flame, 66
ἀνάθεμα ματος cursed, anathematized, 31
ἀναθεματίζω curse, anathematize, 31
ἀναθεωρέω observe closely, 70
ἀνάθημα ματος offering, gift, 31
ἀναίρεσις εως killing, murder, 89
ἀναιρέω do away with, take life, 89
ἀναίτιος ον not guilty (>no charge), 57
ἀνακαθίζω sit up, 48
ἀνακαινίζω renew, 86
ἀνακαινόω renew, remake, 86
ἀνακαίνωσις εως renewal, 86
ἀνακαλύπτω unveil, uncover, 78
ἀνάκειμαι be seated (lie) at a table, 70
ἀνακεφαλαιόω sum up, unite, 71
ἀνακλίνω seat at table, put to bed, 93
ἀνακράζω cry out, 76
ἀνακρίνω question, examine, 20
ἀνάκρισις εως investigation, 20
ἀναλαμβάνω take (up), 26
ἀνάλημψις εως ascension (>taking up), 26
ἀναλογία ας proportion, 16
ἀναλογίζομαι consider closely, 16
ἄναλος ον without salt, 116
ἀνάλυσις εως death (>releasing), 46
ἀναλύω come back, 46
ἀναμάρτητος ον sinless, 36
ἀναμένω wait expectantly, 41
ἀναμιμνήσκω remind, 57
ἀνάμνησις εως reminder, remembrance, 57
ἀνανεόω renew, make new, 92
ἀναντίρρητος ον undeniable, 90
ἀναντιρρήτως without objection, 90
ἀνάξιος ον unworthy, 82
ἀναξίως unworthily, 82

ἀνάπαυσις εως relief, rest, 89
ἀναπαύω relieve, refresh, rest, 89
ἀναπείθω incite, persuade, 71
ἀναπέμπω send, send back / up, 64
ἀναπίπτω sit, lean, 46
ἀναπληρόω meet requirements, 39
ἀναπολόγητος ον without excuse, 16
ἀνάπτω kindle, 94
ἀναρίθμητος ον innumerable, 112
ἀνασείω incite, stir up, 108
ἀνασκευάζω disturb, 98
ἀνάστασις εως resurrection, 18
ἀναστατόω agitate, incite a revolt, 18
ἀνασταυρόω crucify, crucify again, 74
ἀναστρέφω return (pass. live), 53
ἀναστροφή ῆς manner of life, 53
ἀνατάσσομαι compile, draw up, 58
ἀνατέλλω rise, 45
ἀνατίθεμαι lay before, present, 31
ἀνατολή ῆς rising, dawn, east, 45
ἀνατρέπω overturn, 82
ἀνατρέφω bring up, train, 100
ἀναφαίνω come into sight of, 51
ἀναφέρω offer (bring up), 40
ἀναφωνέω call out, 42
ἀνάχυσις εως flood, excess, 113
ἀναχωρέω withdraw, return, 52
ἀνάψυξις εως refreshment, 56
ἀναψύχω refresh (>cooled), 56
ἀνδρ—man, 40
ἀνδραποδιστής οῦ kidnaper, slave dealer, 40
ἀνδρίζομαι act like a man, 40
ἀνδροφόνος ου murderer, 40
ἀνέγκλητος ον beyond reproach, 21
ἀνεκδιήγητος ον indescribable, 23
ἀνεκλάλητος ον inexpressible in words, 32
ἀνέκλειπτος ον never decreasing, 58
ἀνελεήμων ον unmerciful, 74
ἀνέλεος ον merciless, 74
ἀνεμ—wind, 102
ἀνεμίζομαι be driven by wind, 102
ἄνεμος ου wind, 102
ἀνένδεκτος ον impossible, 50
ἀνεξίκακος ον tolerant, 60
ἀνεπαίσχυντος ον unashamed, 88
ἀνεπίλημπτος ον above reproach, 26
ἀνέρχομαι go (come) up, 11
ἄνεσις εως relief (>let up), 45
ἀνεύθετος ον unsuitable (>not well put), 31
ἀνευρίσκω find, 46
ἀνέχομαι tolerate (>hold up under), 15
ἀνήκει it is proper, 107
ἀνήμερος ον fierce, 25
ἀνηρ—man, 40
ἀνήρ ἀνδρός man, husband, 40
ἀνθίστημι resist, oppose, 18
ἀνθομολογέομαι give thanks, 16
ἀνθρωπ—man, 19
ἀνθρωπάρεσκος ον people-pleasing, 116
ἀνθρωπινος η ον human, 19
ἀνθρωποκτόνος ου murderer, 19
ἄνθρωπος ου man, person, 19
ἀνίημι loosen, stop, desert, 45
ἄνιπτος ον not (ritually) washed, 117
ἀνίστημι raise up, appoint, 18
ἀνόητος ον foolish, ignorant, 53

ἄνοια ας stupidity, foolishness, 53
ἀνοιγ—open, start, 71
ἀνοίγω open, 71
ἀνοικοδομέω rebuild, 26
ἄνοιξις εως opening, 71
ἀνομία ας lawlessness, wickedness, 38
ἄνομος ον lawless, 38
ἀνόμως lawlessly, without law, 38
ἀνοχή ῆς tolerance, 15
ἀντάλλαγμα ματος thing in exchange, 14
ἀνταναπληρόω complete (>make full), 39
ἀνταποδίδωμι repay, return, 17
ἀνταπόδομα ματος repayment, 17
ἀνταπόδοσις εως repayment, 17
ἀνταποκρίνομαι reply, 20
ἀντέχομαι be loyal to, hold firmly, 15
ἀντι—oppose, replace, 67
ἀντί (gen.) in place of, against, 67
ἀντιβάλλω exchange, 28
ἀντιδιατίθεμαι oppose, 31
ἀντίδικος ου opponent at law, enemy, 33
ἀντίθεσις εως antithesis, contradiction, 31
ἀντικαθίστημι resist, 18
ἀντικαλέω invite in return, 21
ἀντίκειμαι oppose, 70
ἄντικρυς (gen.) opposite, off, 67
ἀντιλαμβάνομαι help, 26
ἀντιλέγω object to, 16
ἀντίλημψις εως ability to help, helper, 26
ἀντιλογία ας argument, hatred, 16
ἀντίλυτρον ου ransom, 47
ἀντιμετρέω measure out in return, 106
ἀντιμισθία ας recompense, punishment, 95
ἀντιπαρέρχομαι pass by the other side, 11
ἀντιπέρα (gen.) opposite, 67
ἀντιπίπτω resist, fight against, 46
ἀντιστρατεύομαι war against, 81
ἀντιτάσσομαι resist, oppose, 58
ἀντίτυπος ον corresponding (n. copy), 118
ἀντίχριστος ου Antichrist, 67
ἀντοφθαλμέω head into, face, 65
ἄνυδρος ον waterless, desert, 72
ἀνυπόκριτος ον sincere, genuine, 20
ἀνυπότακτος disorderly, 58
ἄνω above, up, 98
ἄνωθεν from above, again, 98
ἀνωτερικός ή όν upper, inland, 98
ἀνώτερον first, above, 98
ἀνωφελής ές useless, 110
ἀξι—worthy, 82
ἄξιος α ον worthy, 82
ἀξιόω consider / make worthy, 82
ἀξίως worthily, 83
ἀόρατος ον invisible, unseen, 51
ἀπ—from, 17
ἀπαγγέλλω tell, proclaim, 22
ἀπάγω lead away, bring before, 23
ἀπαίδευτος ον ignorant (not learned), 55
ἀπαίρω take away, 54
ἀπαιτέω demand (in return), 57
ἀπαλλάσσω set free, 14
ἅπαν each, all, 12
ἀπάντησις εως meeting, 68
ἀπαράβατος ον permanent, 37
ἀπαρασκεύαστος ον unprepared, 98
ἀπαρτισμός οῦ completion, 117

ἀπαρχή ἦς first-fruits (>from beginning), 25
ἄπας each, all, 12
ἄπασα each, all, 12
ἀπάτωρ ορος the fatherless, 24
ἀπείθεια ας disobedience, 71
ἀπειθέω disobey, 71
ἀπειθής ές disobedient, 71
ἄπειμι be away, 10
ἀπείραστος ον unable to be tempted, 79
ἀπεκδέχομαι await, 50
ἀπεκδύομαι disarm, discard, 88
ἀπέκδυσις εως putting off, 88
ἀπελεύθερος ου freedman, 95
ἀπελπίζω expect in return, 71
ἀπέναντι (gen.) opposite, before, 68
ἀπέραντος ον endless, 100
ἀπερίτμητος ον uncircumcised, 79
ἀπέρχομαι go (away), 11
ἀπέχω receive in full, 15
ἀπιστέω fail to believe, 18
ἀπιστία ας unbelief, 18
ἄπιστος ον unfaithful, unbelieving, 18
ἀπο— from, 17
ἀπό from, 17
ἀποβαίνω get out, go from, 37
ἀποβάλλω throw off, 28
ἀποβλέπω keep one's eyes on, 44
ἀπόβλητος ον rejected, 28
ἀποβολή ἦς loss, rejection, 28
ἀπογίνομαι have no part in, 13
ἀπογραφή ἦς registration, census, 30
ἀπογράφω register, 30
ἀποδείκνυμι attest, proclaim, 73
ἀπόδειξις εως proof, demonstration, 73
ἀποδεκατόω tithe, make one tithe, 56
ἀπόδεκτος ον pleasing, 50
ἀποδέχομαι welcome, receive, 50
ἀποδημέω leave home, go away, 106
ἀπόδημος ον away from home, 106
ἀποδίδωμι give, pay, 17
ἀποδιορίζω cause divisions, 67
ἀποδοκιμάζω reject (after testing), 84
ἀποδοχή ἦς acceptance, 50
ἀπόθεσις εως removal, 31
ἀποθήκη ης barn, 31
ἀποθησαυρίζω acquire as a treasure, 109
ἀποθλίβω crowd in upon, 83
ἀποθνήσκω die, face death, 36
ἀποκαθίστημι reestablish, cure, 18
ἀποκαλύπτω reveal, 78
ἀποκάλυψις εως revelation, Apocalypse, 78
ἀποκαταλλάσσω reconcile, 14
ἀποκατάστασις εως restoration, 18
ἀπόκειμαι be stored away, 70
ἀποκεφαλίζω behead, 71
ἀποκλείω lock, close, 103
ἀποκόπτω cut off (mid. castrate), 94
ἀπόκριμα ματος sentence, 20
ἀποκρίνομαι answer, reply, 20
ἀπόκρισις εως answer, reply, 20
ἀποκρύπτω hide, keep secret, 89
ἀπόκρυφος ον hidden, secret, 89
ἀποκτείνω kill, 76
ἀπολαμβάνω receive, get back, 26
ἀπολείπω leave behind, 58
ἀπόλλυμι destroy, 63
ἀπολογέομαι speak in one's defense, 16

ἀπολογία ας defense (>apology), 16
ἀπολύτρωσις εως deliverance, 47
ἀπολύω release, send away, 47
ἀπονίπτω wash, 117
ἀποπίπτω fall from, 46
ἀποπλανάω mislead, deceive, 83
ἀποπλέω set sail, 68
ἀποπληρόω meet requirements, 39
ἀποπνίγω choke, drown, 25
ἀποσκίασμα ματος shadow, darkness, 78
ἀποστασία ας apostasy, 18
ἀποστάσιον ου notice of divorce, 18
ἀποστέλλω send, 35
ἀποστερέω defraud, deny, 104
ἀποστολή ἦς apostleship, 35
ἀπόστολος ου apostle, messenger, 35
ἀποστοματίζω question (>from mouth), 73
ἀποστρέφω turn away, remove, 53
ἀποσυνάγωγος ον excommunicated, 23
ἀποτελέω accomplish, 45
ἀποτίθημι throw (take) off, 31
ἀποτομία ας severity, 79
ἀποτόμως severely, 79
ἀποτρέπομαι avoid (>turn from), 82
ἀπουσία ας absence, 10
ἀποφέρω take, carry away, 40
ἀποφεύγω escape, 93
ἀποφορτίζομαι unload, 40
ἀπόχρησις εως process of being used, 67
ἀποχωρέω go away, leave, 52
ἀποχωρίζομαι separate, 52
ἀποψύχω faint, 56
ἀπρόσκοπος ον blameless, 94
ἀπροσωπολήμπτως impartially, 26
ἁπτ— light, touch, 94
ἅπτω kindle, ignite, 94
ἀπώλεια ας destruction, 63
ἀρ— then, therefore, 12
ἄρα then, therefore, thus, 12
ἀργέω be idle (>not working), 30
ἀργός ή όν idle, unemployed, 30
ἀργυ— money, silver, 100
ἀργύριον ου silver coin, money, 100
ἀργυροκόπος ου silversmith, 100
ἄργυρος ου silver, coin, 100
ἀργυροῦς ᾶ οῦν made of silver, 100
ἀρεσκ— please, 116
ἀρεσκεία ας desire to please, 116
ἀρέσκω (try to) please, 116
ἀρεστ— please, 116
ἀρεστός ή όν pleasing, 116
ἀριθμ— number, 112
ἀριθμέω number, count, 112
ἀριθμός οῦ number, total, 112
ἀρπ— seize, 105
ἁρπαγ— seize, 105
ἁρπαγή ἦς greed, seizure, 105
ἁρπαγμός οῦ booty, prize, 105
ἁρπάζω seize, 105
ἅρπαξ αγος robber (one who seizes), 105
ἄρρητος ον unutterable, (>not flowing), 90
ἀρτ¹— bread, 66
ἀρτ²— qualified, complete, 117
ἀρτι— now, 100
ἄρτι now, at once, 100
ἀρτιγέννητος ον newborn, 13
ἄρτιος α ον fully qualified, 117

ἄρτος ου bread, food, 66
ἀρχ—begin, old, rule, chief, 25
ἀρχάγγελος ου archangel, 22
ἀρχαῖος α ον old, ancient, former, 25
ἀρχή ῆς beginning, rule, 25
ἀρχηγός οῦ leader, founder, 25
ἀρχιερατικός όν high priestly, 25
ἀρχιερεύς έως high priest, 25
ἀρχιποίμην ενος chief shepherd, 25
ἀρχισυνάγωγος ου chief of a synagogue, 23
ἀρχιτελώνης ου tax superintendent, 111
ἀρχιτρίκλινος ου head steward, 93
ἄρχω govern, (mid. begin), 25
ἄρχων οντος ruler, 25
ἀσέβεια ας godlessness, 84
ἀσεβέω live in an impious way, 84
ἀσεβής ές godless, 84
ἄσημος ον insignificant, 69
ἀσθένεια ας weakness, 72
ἀσθενέω be weak, be sick, 72
ἀσθένημα ματος weakness, 72
ἀσθενής ές weak, sick, 72
ἀσιτία ας lack of appetite, 113
ἄσιτος ον without food, 113
ἄσοφος ον senseless, foolish, 75
ἀστατέω be homeless, wander, 19
ἀστερ—star, 94
ἀστηρ—star, 94
ἀστήρ έρος star, 94
ἀστήρικτος ον unsteady, 94
ἀστρ—star, 94
ἀστραπή ῆς lightning, ray, 94
ἀστράπτω flash, dazzle, 94
ἄστρον ου star, constellation, 94
ἀσύμφωνος ον in disagreement, 42
ἀσύνετος ον without understanding, 45
ἀσύνθετος ον faithless, disloyal, 31
ἀσχημ—shame, 88
ἀσχημονέω act improperly, 88
ἀσχημοσύνη ης shameless act, 88
ἀσχήμων ον unpresentable,, shameful, 88
ἀτακτέω be lazy (not ordered), 58
ἄτακτός ον lazy (not ordered), 58
ἀτάκτως lazily, 58
ἄτεκνος ον childless, 55
ἀτιμάζω dishonor, 49
ἀτιμία ας dishonor, shame, 49
ἄτιμος ον dishonored, despised, 49
ἄτομος ον indivisible, 79
ἄτοπος ον improper, 65
αὐλ—flute, courtyard, 114
αὐλέω play a flute, 114
αὐλή ῆς courtyard, house, 114
αὐλητής οῦ flute player, 114
αὐλίζομαι spend the night, 114
αὐλός οῦ flute, 114
αὐξ—grow, 108
αὐξάνω grow / increase, 108
αὔξησις εως growth, 108
αὐρ—tomorrow, 103
αὔριον tomorrow, soon, 103
αὐτ—this, 11
αὐτο—self, 9
αὐτοκατάκριτος ον self-condemned, 20
αὐτόματος η ον automatic, 9
αὐτός ή ό self, 9
αὐτόχειρ ος the doer, 43

ἀφ—from, 17
ἀφαιρέω take away, 89
ἀφανής ές hidden, 51
ἀφανίζω ruin, 51
ἀφανισμός οῦ disappearance, 51
ἄφαντος ον invisible, 51
ἄφεσις εως forgiveness, 45
ἀφθαρσία ας imperishability, 87
ἄφθαρτος ον imperishable, 87
ἀφθορία ας integrity, 87
ἀφίημι cancel, forgive, 45
ἀφιλάγαθος ον not good-loving, 57
ἀφιλάργυρος ον not money-loving, 100
ἀφίσταμαι leave, 19
ἀφόβως without fear, 49
ἀφομοιόω be like, 60
ἀφοράω fix one's eyes on, 51
ἀφορίζω separate, exclude, 67
ἀφροσύνη ης folly, 62
ἄφρων ον foolish, 62
ἄφωνος ον dumb, silent, 42
ἀχάριστος ον ungrateful, 36
ἀχειροποίητος ον not made by hands, 18
ἀχρειόομαι be worthless, 67
ἀχρεῖος ον worthless, mere, 67
ἄχρηστος ον of little use, useless, 67
ἄχρι—until, 80
ἄχρι (*gen.*) until, to, as, when, 80
ἀψευδής ές trustworthy, non-lying, 87
ἄψυχος ον inanimate, 56

βα—go, foot, 37
βαθμός οῦ standing, position, 37
βαιν—go, foot, 37
βαλ—throw, 28
βάλλω throw, 28
βαπτ—baptize, dip, 59
βαπτίζω baptize, 59
βάπτισμα ματος baptism, 59
βαπτισμός οῦ washing, baptism, 59
βαπτιστής οῦ Baptist (Baptizer), 59
βάπτω dip, 59
βαρ—burden, weight, 109
βαρέω burden, overcome, 109
βαρέως with difficulty, 109
βάρος ους burden, weight, 109
βαρύτιμος ον very expensive, 49
βαρύς εῖα ύ heavy, weighty, hard, 109
βασ—go, foot, 37
βασαν—torture, 116
βασανίζω torment, disturb, 116
βασανισμός οῦ torture, 116
βασανιστής οῦ torturer, jailer, 116
βάσανος ου torment, pain, 116
βασιλ—royal, 33
βασιλεία ας reign, kingdom, 33
βασίλειος ον royal, 33
βασιλεύς έως king, 33
βασιλεύω rule, reign, 33
βασιλικός ή όν royal, 33
βασίλισσα ης queen, 33
βάσις εως foot, (>base), 37
βαστ—carry, bear, 106
βαστάζω carry, bear, 106
βατταλογέω babble, 16
βεβαι—reliable, firm, 116
βεβαιο—reliable, firm, 116

βέβαιος α ον reliable, firm, 116
βεβαιόω confirm (>make firm), 116
βεβαίωσις εως confirmation, 116
βη—go, foot, 37
βῆμα ματος judgment bench, 37
βιβλ—book, 91
βιβλαρίδιον ου little book, 91
βιβλίον ου book, scroll, 91
βίβλος ου book, record, 91
βλασφημ—blaspheme (compare φα), 84
βλασφημέω blaspheme, 84
βλασφημία ας blasphemy, slander, 84
βλάσφημος ον blasphemous, 84
βλεμ—see, 44
βλέμμα ματος what is seen, sight, 44
βλεπ—see, 44
βλέπω see, look, 44
βλεψ—see, 44
βλη—throw, 28
βλητέος α ον must be put, poured, 28
βο—shout, 110
βοάω call, shout, 110
βοή ῆς shout, outcry, 110
βοηθ—shout, 110
βοήθεια ας help, aid, 110
βοηθέω help, 110
βοηθός οῦ helper, 110
βολ—throw, 28
βολή ῆς throw, 28
βολίζω measure depth, 28
βουλ—plan, 75
βουλεύομαι plan, consider, 75
βουλευτής οῦ councillor, 75
βουλή ῆς plan, intention, 75
βούλημα ματος plan, intention, desire, 75
βούλομαι plan, want, 75
βρω—food, 106
βρῶμα ματος food, 106
βρώσιμος ον eatable, 106
βρῶσις εως food, eating, 106

γαζοφυλάκιον ου treasury, offering box, 70
γαμ—marriage, 84
γαμέω marry, 84
γαμίζω give in marriage, 84
γαμίσκω give in marriage, 84
γάμος ου wedding, marriage, 84
γαρ—then, therefore, 12
γάρ for, since, then, 12
γε[1]—earth, 35
γε[2]—(particle adding emphasis), 103
γέ (used to add emphasis), 103
γεμ—full, 112
γεμίζω fill, 112
γέμω be full, 112
γεν—family, birth, 13
γενεά ᾶς generation, age, family, 13
γενεαλογέομαι to descend from, 13
γενεαλογία ας genealogy, 13
γενέσια ων (*pl.*) birthday party, 13
γένεσις εως birth, lineage, 13
γενετή ῆς birth, 13
γένημα ματος harvest, product, 13
γεννάω be father of, bear, 13
γέννημα ματος offspring, 13
γέννησις εως birth, 13
γεννητός ή όν born, 13

γένος ους family, race, 13
γεωργέω cultivate (>work earth), 35
γεώργιον ου field (>worked earth), 35
γεωργός οῦ farmer (>earth-worker), 35
γη—earth, 35
γῆ γῆς earth, land, region, 35
γιν—family, birth, 13
γίνομαι become, be, happen, 13
γινω—know, 24
γινώσκω know, learn, 24
γλωσσα—tongue, 86
γλῶσσα ης tongue, language, 86
γνο—know, 24
γνω—know, 24
γνώμη ης purpose, will, opinion, 24
γνωρίζω make known, know, 24
γνῶσις εως knowledge, 24
γνώστης ου one familiar with, 24
γνωστός ή όν known (acquaintance), 24
γομ—full, 112
γόμος ου cargo, 112
γον—family, birth, 13
γονεύς έως parent, 13
γραμ—write, 30
γράμμα ματος letter, Scripture, account, 30
γραμματεύς έως scribe, 30
γραπ—write, 30
γραπτός ή όν written, 30
γραφ—write, 30
γραφή ῆς Scripture, 30
γράφω write, 30
γρηγορ—raise, rouse, 45
γρηγορέω be awake, watch, 45
γυμν—exercise, naked, 111
γυμνάζω train, discipline, exercise, 111
γυμνασία ας training, 111
γυμνιτεύω be dressed in rags, 111
γυμνός ή όν naked, 111
γυμνότης ητος nakedness, poverty, 111
γυναικ—woman, 41
γυναικάριον ου foolish woman, 41
γυναικεῖος α ον female, 41
γυνη—woman, 41
γυνή αικός woman, wife, 41

δαιμ—demon, 74
δαιμονίζομαι be demon possessed, 74
δαιμόνιον ου demon, spirit, 74
δαιμονιώδης ες demonic, 74
δαίμων ονος demon, 74
δέ but, rather, 9
δε[1]—but, 9
δε[2]—bind, 81
δε[3]—lack, 52
δέησις εως prayer, request, 52
δεῖ it is necessary, 52
δειγ—show, example, 73
δεῖγμα ματος example, warning, 73
δειγματίζω disgrace, show publicly, 73
δεικ—show, example, 73
δείκνυμι show, explain, 73
δειξ—show, example, 73
δειπν—dine, 117
δειπνέω eat, dine, 117
δεῖπνον ου feast, supper, 117
δεκ—receive, 50
δεκα—ten, 56

δέκα ten, 56
δέκα ὀκτώ eighteen, 56
δεκαπέντε fifteen, 56
Δεκάπολις εως Decapolis (ten-city area), 56
δεκάτη ης tithe, 56
δεκατέσσαρες fourteen, 64
δέκατος η ον tenth, 56
δεκατόω collect (pay) tithes, 56
δεκτός ή όν acceptable, 50
δενδρ—tree, 111
δένδρον ου tree, 111
δεξ—right, 85
δεξιός ά όν right, 85
δέομαι ask, beg, 52
δεσμ—bind, imprison (compare δε²), 86
δεσμεύω bind, 86
δέσμη ης bundle, 86
δέσμιος ου prisoner, 86
δεσμός οῦ bond, chain, jail, 86
δεσμοφύλαξ ακος jailer, guard, 86
δεσμωτήριον ου jail, prison, 86
δεσμώτης ου prisoner, 86
δεσπότης despot, lord, 86
δευ—place to, hither, 116
δεῦρο hither (place to), 116
δεῦτε come hither (place to), 116
δευτερ—two, 44
δευτεραῖος α ον in two days, 44
δευτερόπρωτος ον the next, 44
δεύτερος α ον second, 44
δεχ—receive, 50
δέχομαι receive, take, 50
δέω bind, 81
δημ—people, home, 106
δημηγορέω make a speech, 89
δημιουργός οῦ builder, 30
δῆμος ου people, crowd, 106
δημόσιος α ον public, 106
δήποτε whatever, 21
δήπου of course, 43
δια—through, 17
διά (gen., acc.) through, on account of, 17
διαβαίνω cross, cross over, 37
διαβάλλω accuse (>throw against), 28
διαβεβαιόομαι speak confidently, 116
διαβλέπω see clearly, 44
διάβολος ον accusing (falsely), 28
διάβολος ου devil (the accuser), 28
διαγγέλλω preach, proclaim, 22
διαγίνομαι pass (of time), 13
διαγινώσκω investigate, decide, 24
διάγνωσις εως decision (>diagnosis), 24
διαγρηγορέω become fully awake, 45
διάγω lead, spend (a life), 23
διαδέχομαι receive possession of, 50
διάδημα ματος diadem, 81
διαδίδωμι distribute, 17
διάδοχος ου successor, 50
διαζώννυμι wrap around, 114
διαθήκη ης covenant, 31
διαίρεσις εως variety, difference, 89
διαιρέω divide, distribute, 89
διακαθαίρω clean out, 63
διακαθαρίζω clean out, 63
διακον—serve, 66
διακονέω serve, care for, 66
διακονία ας service, help, 66

διάκονος ου servant, deacon, 66
διακούω hear (legal cases), 22
διακρίνω evaluate (mid. doubt), 20
διάκρισις εως ability to discriminate, 20
διακωλύω prevent, 111
διαλαλέω discuss, 32
διαλέγομαι discuss, 16
διαλείπω cease, stop, 58
διάλεκτος ου language (>dialect), 16
διαλιμπάνω stop, quit, 58
διαλογίζομαι discuss, question, 16
διαλογισμός οῦ opinion, thought, 16
διαλύω scatter, 47
διαμαρτύρομαι declare solemnly, 42
διαμάχομαι protest violently, 96
διαμένω remain, stay, 41
διαμερίζω divide, 75
διαμερισμός οῦ division, 75
διανόημα ματος thought, 53
διάνοια ας mind, understanding, 53
διανοίγω open, 71
διανυκτερεύω spend the night, 80
διαπεράω cross, cross over, 100
διαπλέω sail across, 68
διαπορεύομαι go through, 38
διαπραγματεύομαι make a profit, 83
διαρπάζω plunder, 105
διασείω take money by force, 108
διασπείρω scatter, 62
διασπορά ᾶς dispersion, 62
διαστέλλομαι order, 35
διάστημα ματος interval, 19
διαστολή ῆς distinction, 35
διαστρέφω pervert, distort, 53
διασῴζω rescue, 61
διαταγή ῆς decree, 58
διάταγμα ματος order, decree, 58
διαταράσσομαι be deeply troubled, 115
διατάσσω command, 58
διατελέω continue, go, be, 45
διατηρέω keep, treasure up, 72
διατίθεμαι make (a covenant), 31
διατροφή ῆς food, 100
διαφέρω be superior, carry through, 40
διαφεύγω escape, 93
διαφημίζω spread around, 35
διαφθείρω decay, destroy, 87
διαφθορά ᾶς decay, 87
διαφυλάσσω protect, 70
διαχειρίζομαι seize and kill, 43
διαχωρίζομαι leave, 52
διδ—give, 17
διδακ—teach, 41
διδακτικός ή όν able to teach, 41
διδακτός ή όν taught, 41
διδασκ—teach, 41
διδασκαλία ας teaching, instruction, 41
διδάσκαλος ου teacher, 41
διδάσκω teach, 41
διδαχ—teach, 41
διδαχή ῆς instruction, 41
δίδωμι give, 17
διεγείρω awake, 45
διενθυμέομαι think over, 61
διέξοδος ου outlet, passage, 54
διέρχομαι go, come through, 11
διερωτάω learn, 59

διετής ές two years old, 85
διετία ας two-year period, 85
διηγέομαι tell fully, 23
διήγησις εως account, 23
διθάλασσος ον between the seas, 68
διΐστημι part, past time, 19
διϊσχυρίζομαι insist, 76
δικ—just, judgment, 33
δικαιοκρισία ας just judgment, 33
δίκαιος α ον just, right, 33
δικαιοσύνη ης righteousness, justice, 33
δικαιόω acquit, make righteous, 33
δικαίωμα ματος judgment, acquittal, 33
δικαίως justly, 33
δικαίωσις εως acquittal, 33
δικαστής οῦ judge, 33
δίκη ης justice, punishment, 33
δίλογος ον two-faced, 16
διο—therefore, 73
διό therefore, 73
διοδεύω go about, 54
διόπερ therefore (emphatic), 73
διότι because, for, therefore, 73
δίστομος ον double-edged, 79
διχοστασία ας division, 19
διχοτομέω cut in pieces, 79
δίψυχος ον undecided (>two minds), 56
διωγ—persecute, 83
διωγμός οῦ persecution, 83
διωκ—persecute, 83
διώκτης ου persecutor, 83
διώκω persecute, pursue, 83
δο—give, 17
δοκ¹—receive, 50
δοκ²—think, seem, 65
δοκέω think, seem, 66
δοκιμ—examine, 84
δοκιμάζω examine, discern, 84
δοκιμασία ας examination, test, 84
δοκιμή ῆς character, evidence, 84
δοκίμιον ου examination, testing, 84
δόκιμος ον approved, examined, 84
δομ—people, home, 106
δόμα ματος gift, 17
δοξ—glory, 39
δόξα ης glory, power, 39
δοξάζω praise, honor, 39
δόσις εως gift, 17
δότης ου giver, 17
δουλ—slave, 44
δουλαγωγέω bring under control, 44
δουλεία ας slavery, 44
δουλεύω serve, be enslaved, 44
δούλη ης female servant, 44
δοῦλος η ον slave-like, 44
δοῦλος ου servant, slave, 44
δουλόω enslave (>make a slave), 44
δοχ—receive, 50
δοχή ῆς reception, 50
δυ—clothe, 88
δυνα—power, ability, 29
δυναμ—power, ability, 29
δύναμαι be able, 29
δύναμις εως power, strength, 29
δυναμόω make strong, 29
δυνάστης ου ruler, 29
δυνατέω be able, be strong, 29

δυνατός ή όν able, possible, strong, 29
δυο—two, 44
δύο two, 44
δυσβάστακτος ον difficult to bear, 106
δυσνόητος ον difficult to understand, 53
δυσφημέω slander, 35
δυσφημία ας slander, 35
δω—give, 17
δώδεκα twelve, 56
δωδέκατος η ον twelfth, 56
δωδεκάφυλον ου the Twelve Tribes, 101
δωρ—gift, 94
δωρεά ᾶς gift, 94
δωρεάν without cost, 94
δωρέομαι give, 94
δώρημα ματος gift, 94
δῶρον ου gift, offering, 94
δωροφορία ας a bearing of gifts, 40

ε—let, send, 45
ἐάν if, even if, though, 14
ἐάνπερ if only, 14
ἑαυτοῦ ῆς οῦ himself, herself, itself, 9
ἐγγ—near, 74
ἐγγίζω approach, 74
ἐγγράφω write, record, 30
ἔγγυος ου guarantor, guarantee, 75
ἐγγύς near, 75
ἐγγύτερον nearer, 75
ἐγειρ—raise, rouse, 45
ἐγείρω raise, 45
ἐγερ—raise, rouse, 45
ἔγερσις εως resurrection, 45
ἐγκάθετος ου spy, 45
ἐγκαινίζω inaugurate, open, 86
ἐγκακέω become discouraged, 60
ἐγκαλέω accuse, 21
ἐγκαταλείπω forsake, leave, 58
ἐγκατοικέω live among, 26
ἐγκαυχάομαι boast, 80
ἔγκλημα ματος charge, accusation, 21
ἐγκοπή ῆς obstacle (>thing cutting in), 94
ἐγκόπτω prevent (>cut in), 94
ἐγκράτεια ας self-control, 69
ἐγκρατεύομαι be self-controlled, 69
ἐγκρατής ές self-controlled, 69
ἐγκρίνω class with, 20
ἐγκρύπτω place / mix / hide in, 89
ἐγχρίω rub on, 20
ἐγώ I (first person pronoun), 10
ἐγω—I, 10
ἐθν—nation, gentile, 48
ἐθνάρχης ου governor, ethnarch, 48
ἐθνικός ή όν pagan, Gentile, 48
ἐθνικῶς like a Gentile, 48
ἔθνος ους nation, Gentiles, 48
εἰ¹—be, exist, 10
εἰ²—if, 14
εἰ if, 14
εἰδέα ας appearance, form, 40
εἶδος ους visible form, sight, 40
εἰδωλ—image, idol, 102
εἰδωλεῖον ου idol's temple, 102
εἰδωλόθυτον ου meat offered to idols, 77
εἰδωλολάτρης ου idol worshipper, 99
εἰδωλολατρία ας idolatry, 99
εἴδωλον ου idol, image, 102

ἐμαυτοῦ ῆς myself, my own, 9
ἐμβαίνω get in, embark, 37
ἐμβάλλω throw, 28
ἐμβάπτω dip, 59
ἐμβλέπω look at, consider, 44
ἐμμένω remain faithful, 41
ἐμός ή όν my, mine, 75
ἐμπαιγμονή ῆς mockery, ridicule, 55
ἐμπαιγμός οῦ public ridicule, 55
ἐμπαίζω ridicule, trick, 55
ἐμπαίκτης ου mocker, 55
ἐμπεριπατέω live among, 34
ἐμπίμπλημι fill, satisfy, enjoy, 39
ἐμπίπτω fall into or among, 46
ἐμπνέω breathe, 25
ἐμπορεύομαι be in business, exploit, 38
ἐμπορία ας business, 38
ἐμπόριον ου market (>emporium), 38
ἔμπορος ου merchant, 38
ἔμπροσθεν (*gen.*) before, 15
ἐμφανής ές visible, revealed, 51
ἐμφανίζω inform, reveal, 51
ἔμφοβος ον full of fear, 49
ἐμφυσάω breathe on, 92
ἔμφυτος ον implanted, planted, 92
ἐν—in, 10
ἐν (*dat.*) in, 10
ἐνάλιον ου sea creature, 116
ἔναντι (*gen.*) before (in judgment of), 68
ἐναντίον (*gen.*) before (in judgment of), 68
ἐναντιόομαι oppose, contradict, 68
ἐναντίος α ον against, hostile, 68
ἐνάρχομαι begin, 25
ἐνδεής ές needy (>in need), 52
ἔνδειγμα ματος evidence, proof, 73
ἐνδείκνυμαι show, give indication, 73
ἔνδειξις εως evidence, indication, 73
ἔνδεκα eleven, 56
ἐνδέκατος η ον eleventh, 56
ἐνδέχεται it is possible, 50
ἐνδημέω be at home, be present, 106
ἐνδιδύσκω dress in, 88
ἔνδικος ον just, deserved, 34
ἐνδοξάζομαι receive glory, 39
ἔνδοξος ον glorious, fine, 39
ἔνδυμα ματος clothing, 88
ἐνδυναμόω strengthen, 29
ἔνδυσις εως wearing, 88
ἐνδύω clothe, wear (>endue), 88
ἔνειμι be in(side), 10
ἐνεκ—because of, 109
ἕνεκα (*gen.*) because of, 109
ἐνέργεια ας work (>energy), 30
ἐνεργέω work, 30
ἐνέργημα ματος working, activity, 30
ἐνεργής ές active, effective, 30
ἐνευλογέω bless, 16
ἐνέχω have grudge against, 15
ἐνθάδε here, in this place, 10
ἔνθεν from here, 10
ἐνθυμέομαι think about, think, 61
ἐνθύμησις εως thought, idea, 61
ἐνίστημι be present, 19
ἐνισχύω strenghten, 76
ἔννοια ας attitude, thought, 53
ἔννομος ον legal, subject to law, 38
ἔννυχα in the night, 80

ἐνοικέω live in, 27
ἐνορκίζω place under oath, 117
ἐνότης ητος unity, 26
ἐνοχλέω trouble (>crowd in), 46
ἐνταλ—commandment, 72
ἔνταλμα ματος commandment, 72
ἐντέλλομαι command, order, 72
ἔντιμος ον valuable, esteemed, 49
ἐντολ—commandment, 72
ἐντολή ῆς commandment, 72
ἐντόπιος α ον local (*pl.* residents), 65
ἐντός (*gen.*) within, 10
ἐντρέπω make ashamed, 82
ἐντρέφομαι live on, feed oneself on, 100
ἐντροπή ῆς shame, 82
ἐντυγχάνω intercede, plead, appeal, 112
ἐντυπόω engrave, carve, 118
ἐνωπ—before, 60
ἐνώπιον (*gen.*) before, 60
ἐξ—out, from, 13
ἐξ—six, 111
ἔξ six, 111
ἐξαγγέλλω tell, proclaim, 22
ἐξαγοράζω set free, 89
ἐξάγω lead, bring out, 23
ἐξαιρέω pull out, rescue, 89
ἐξαίρω remove, drive out, 54
ἐξαιτέομαι ask, demand, 57
ἐξακολουθέω follow, be obedient, 64
ἑξακόσιοι αι α six hundred, 111
ἐξανάστασις εως resurrection, 19
ἐξανατέλλω sprout, spring up, 45
ἐξανίστημι have, stand up, 19
ἐξαποστέλλω send off, 35
ἐξαρτίζω be completed, 117
ἐξαστράπτω flash (like lightning), 94
ἐξαυτῆς at once, 9
ἐξεγείρω raise, 45
ἐξέρχομαι come / go out, escape, 11
ἔξεστι it is proper / possible, 10
ἐξηγέομαι tell, explain, 23
ἑξήκοντα sixty, 111
ἐξίστημι be amazed, amaze, 19
ἐξισχύω be fully able, 76
ἔξοδος ου departure (>Exodus), 54
ἐξομολογέω agree, consent, admit, 16
ἐξορκίζω put under oath, 117
ἐξορκιστής οῦ exorcist, 117
ἐξουσ—authority, 63
ἐξουσία ας authority, official, 63
ἐξουσιάζω have power over, 63
ἐξουσιαστικός ή όν authoritative, 63
ἔξω (*gen.*) out, outside, 13
ἔξωθεν (*gen.*) from outside, 13
ἐξωθέω drive out, run aground, 13
ἐξώτερος α ον outer, 13
ἑορτ—feast, 109
ἑορτάζω observe a festival, 109
ἑορτή ῆς festival, feast, 109
ἐπαγγελία ας promise, decision, 22
ἐπαγγέλλομαι promise, confess, 22
ἐπάγγελμα ματος promise, 22
ἐπάγω bring upon, 23
ἐπαινέω praise, commend, 105
ἔπαινος ου praise, approval, 105
ἐπαίρω raise, lift up, 54
ἐπαισχύνομαι be ashamed, 88

ἐπαιτέω beg, 57
ἐπακολουθέω follow, 64
ἐπακούω hear, listen to, 22
ἐπάν when, 43
ἐπάναγκες necessarily, 100
ἐπανάγω return, put out, 23
ἐπαναμιμνήσκω remind, 57
ἐπαναπαύομαι rest / rely upon, 89
ἐπανέρχομαι return, 11
ἐπανίσταμαι turn against, rebel, 19
ἐπάνω (gen.) on, above, over, 15
ἐπαρχεία ας province (>thing led), 25
ἔπαυλις εως house (>on the court), 114
ἐπαύριον next day, 103
ἐπεγείρω stir up, 45
ἐπει– since, 99
ἐπεί since, because, as, 99
ἐπειδή since, because, for, en, 99
ἐπειδήπερ inasmuch as, since, 99
ἐπεισαγωγή ῆς bringing in, 23
ἐπεισέρχομαι come upon, 11
ἐπέκεινα (gen.) beyond, 28
ἐπεκτείνομαι stretch toward, 104
ἐπενδύομαι put on, 88
ἐπενδύτης ου outer garment, 88
ἐπέρχομαι come, come upon, 11
ἐπερωτάω ask, ask for, 59
ἐπερώτημα ματος promise, answer, 59
ἐπέχω notice, 15
ἐπι– on, 15
ἐπί (gen., dat., acc.) upon, on, over, 15
ἐπιβαίνω embark, arrive, 37
ἐπιβάλλω lay (hands) on, 28
ἐπιβαρέω be a burden, 109
ἐπιβλέπω look upon (with care), 44
ἐπιβουλή ῆς plot, 75
ἐπιγαμβρεύω marry, 84
ἐπίγειος ον earthly, 35
ἐπιγίνομαι spring up, come on, 13
ἐπιγινώσκω know, perceive, 24
ἐπίγνωσις εως knowledge, 24
ἐπιγραφή ῆς inscription (>epigraph), 30
ἐπιγράφω write on, 30
ἐπιδείκνυμι show, 73
ἐπιδέχομαι receive, welcome, 50
ἐπιδημέω visit, live, 106
ἐπιδιατάσσομαι add to (a will), 58
ἐπιδίδωμι deliver, give way, 17
ἐπιζητέω seek, desire, 48
ἐπιθανάτιος ον sentenced to death, 36
ἐπίθεσις εως laying on (of hands), 31
ἐπιθυμέω desire, covet, lust for, 61
ἐπιθυμητής οῦ one who desires, 61
ἐπιθυμία ας desire, lust, 61
ἐπικαθίζω sit, sit on, 48
ἐπικαλέω call, name, 21
ἐπικάλυμμα ματος covering, pretext, 78
ἐπικαλύπτω cover (sin), 78
ἐπίκειμαι lie on, crowd, 70
ἐπικρίνω decide, 20
ἐπιλαμβάνομαι take, seize, help, 26
ἐπιλανθάνομαι forget, overlook, 118
ἐπιλέγω call, name, 16
ἐπιλείπω run short, 58
ἐπίλοιπος ον remaining, 58
ἐπίλυσις εως interpretation, 47
ἐπιλύω explain, settle, 47

ἐπιμαρτυρέω witness, declare, 42
ἐπιμέλεια ας care, attention, 107
ἐπιμελέομαι take care of, 107
ἐπιμελῶς carefully, 107
ἐπιμένω remain, continue, 42
ἐπίνοια ας intent, purpose, 53
ἐπιορκέω break an oath, 117
ἐπίορκος ου oath-breaker, perjurer, 117
ἐπιπίπτω fall upon, close in on, 46
ἐπιπλήσσω reprimand, 110
ἐπιποθέω desire, 97
ἐπιπόθησις εως longing, 97
ἐπιπόθητος ον longed for, 97
ἐπιποθία ας desire, 97
ἐπιπορεύομαι come to, 38
ἐπισείω urge on, stir up, 108
ἐπίσημος ον well known, 69
ἐπισιτισμός οῦ food, 113
ἐπισκέπτομαι visit, care for, 104
ἐπισκευάζομαι prepare, make ready, 98
ἐπισκηνόω rest upon, live in, 97
ἐπισκιάζω overshadow, 78
ἐπισκοπέω see to it, take care, 104
ἐπισκοπή ῆς visitation, episcopate, 104
ἐπίσκοπος ου overseer, bishop, 104
ἐπισπείρω sow in addition, 62
ἐπίσταμαι know, understand, 19
ἐπίστασις εως pressure, stirring up, 19
ἐπιστάτης ου master, 19
ἐπιστέλλω write, 35
ἐπιστήμων ον understanding, 19
ἐπιστηρίζω strengthen, 104
ἐπιστολή ῆς letter, 35
ἐπιστομίζω make silent, 73
ἐπιστρέφω turn back, 53
ἐπιστροφή ῆς conversion, 53
ἐπισυνάγω gather, 23
ἐπισυναγωγή ῆς assembly, 23
ἐπισυντρέχω gather rapidly, close in, 102
ἐπισχύω insist, 76
ἐπιταγή ῆς command, authority, 58
ἐπιτάσσω order, 58
ἐπιτελέω complete, 45
ἐπιτίθημι put on, place, 31
ἐπιτιμάω order, rebuke, 49
ἐπιτιμία ας punishment, 49
ἐπιτρέπω let, allow, 82
ἐπιτροπή ῆς commission, 82
ἐπίτροπος ου steward, guardian, 82
ἐπιτυγχάνω obtain, 112
ἐπιφαίνω appear, give light, 51
ἐπιφάνεια ας appearance, coming, 51
ἐπιφανής ές glorious, 51
ἐπιφέρω bring upon, inflict, 40
ἐπιφωνέω shout, 42
ἐπιφώσκω dawn, draw near, 67
ἐπιχειρέω undertake, 43
ἐπιχέω pour on, 114
ἐπιχρίω smear, 20
ἐποικοδομέω build on / build up, 27
ἐπονομάζομαι call oneself, 39
ἐποπτεύω see, observe, 60
ἐπόπτης ου observer, eyewitness, 60
ἐπουράνιος ον heavenly, 34
ἑπτ– seven, 68
ἑπτά seven, 68
ἑπτάκις seven times, 68

ἑπτακισχίλιοι αι α seven thousand, 68
ἑπταπλασίων ον seven times as much, 68
ἐργ—work, 30
ἐργάζομαι work, do, 30
ἐργασία ας gain, doing, 30
ἐργάτης ου worker, 30
ἔργον ου work, action, 30
ἐρημ—desert, 83
ἐρημία ας desert, 83
ἐρημόομαι to be made waste, 83
ἔρημος ον lonely, desolate, 83
ἐρήμωσις εως desolation, 83
ἐρχ—come, 11
ἔρχομαι come, 11
ἐρωτ—ask, 59
ἐρωτάω ask, 59
ἐσ—be, exist, 10
ἐσθι—eat, 76
ἐσθίω eat, 76
ἔσοπτρον ου mirror, 60
ἐσχατ—last, final, 85
ἔσχατος η ον last, final, 85
ἐσχάτως finally, 85
ἔσω—into, 10
ἔσω inside, 10
ἔσωθεν from within, 10
ἐσώτερος α ον inner (adj.); behind / in (prep.), 10
ἐτ—year, 85
ἑτερ—other, different, 66
ἑτερόγλωσσος ον with strange language, 86
ἑτεροδιδασκαλέω teach different doctrine, 41
ἕτερος α ον other, different, 66
ἑτέρως otherwise, differently, 66
ἔτι—still, yet, 48
ἔτι still, yet, 48
ἑτοιμ—ready, prepare, 80
ἑτοιμάζω prepare, make ready, 80
ἑτοιμασία ας readiness, equipment, 80
ἕτοιμος η ον ready, 80
ἑτοίμως readily, 80
ἔτος ους year, 85
εὐαγγελίζω evangelize, 22
εὐαγγέλιον ου good news, gospel, 22
εὐαγγελιστής οῦ evangelist, 22
εὐαρεστέω please, be pleasing to, 116
εὐάρεστος ον pleasing, 116
εὐαρέστως pleasingly, 116
εὐγενής ές high born (>eugenics), 13
εὐδ—sleep, 114
εὐδοκέω be pleased, choose, will, 66
εὐδοκία ας good will, pleasure, 66
εὐεργεσία ας service, kind act, 30
εὐεργετέω do good, 30
εὐεργέτης ου benefactor, 30
εὐθ—immediate, straight, 65
εὔθετος ον suitable (>well placed), 31
εὐθέως immediately, soon, 65
εὐθυμέω take courage, be happy, 61
εὔθυμος ον encouraged, 61
εὐθύμως cheerfully, 61
εὐθύνω make straight, 65
εὐθύς immediately, 65
εὐθύς εῖα ύ straight, (up)right, 65
εὐθύτης ητος uprightness, justice, 65
εὐκαιρέω have time, spend time, 65
εὐκαιρία ας opportune moment, 65
εὔκαιρος ον suitable, timely, 65

εὐκαίρως when the time is right, 65
εὐκοπώτερος α ον easier, 88
εὐλάβεια ας godly fear, reverence, 26
εὐλαβέομαι act in reverence, 26
εὐλαβής ές reverent, 26
εὐλογέω bless (>eulogize), 16
εὐλογητός ή όν blessed, praised, 16
εὐλογία ας blessing (>eulogy), 16
εὐμετάδοτος ον liberal, generous, 17
εὐνοέω make friends, 53
εὔνοια ας good will, eagerness, 53
εὐοδόομαι have things go well, 54
εὐπειθής ές open to reason, 71
εὐπερίστατος ον holding on tightly, 19
εὐποιΐα ας doing of good, 18
εὐπορέομαι have financial means, 38
εὐπορία ας wealth, 38
εὐπρόσδεκτος ον acceptable, 50
εὐπροσωπέω make a good showing, 74
εὑρ—find, 46
εὑρίσκω find, 46
εὐρύχωρος ον wide, spacious, 52
εὐσέβεια ας godliness, religion, 84
εὐσεβέω worship, 85
εὐσεβής ές godly, religious, 85
εὐσεβῶς in a godly manner, 85
εὔσημος ον intelligible, 69
εὔσπλαγχνος ον kind, 111
εὐφημία ας good reputation, 35
εὔφημος ον worthy of praise, 35
εὐφορέω produce good crops, 40
εὐφραίνω make glad, 62
εὐφροσύνη ης gladness, 62
εὐχ—pray, 55
εὐχαριστέω thank, be thankful, 36
εὐχαριστία ας thanksgiving eucharist, 36
εὐχάριστος ον thankful, 36
εὐχή ῆς prayer, vow, 55
εὔχομαι pray, 56
εὔχρηστος ον useful, 67
εὐψυχέω be encouraged, 56
ἐφευρετής οῦ inventor, 46
ἐφημερία ας division, 25
ἐφήμερος ον daily, 25
ἐφίστημι come to, approach, 19
ἐφοράω take notice of, 51
ἐχ—have, hold, 15
ἐχθρ—enemy, 98
ἔχθρα ας hostility, hatred, 98
ἐχθρός ά όν hated (*as noun*: enemy), 98
ἔχω have, 15
ἕως—until, 52
ἕως (*gen.*) until, 52

ζα—life, 33
ζάω live, 33
ζηλ—zealous, jealous, 96
ζηλεύω be zealous, 96
ζῆλος ου zeal, jealousy, 96
ζηλόω be jealous, 96
ζηλωτής οῦ someone zealous, 96
ζητ—seek, discuss, 48
ζητέω seek, try, 48
ζήτημα ματος question, 48
ζήτησις εως discussion, 48
ζυμ—yeast, 109
ζύμη ης yeast, 109

ζυμόω make / cause to rise, 109
ζω—life, 33
ζωή ῆς life, 33
ζων—fasten, bind, 114
ζώνη ης belt, 114
ζώννυμι fasten, 114
ζωογονέω save life, 33
ζῷον ου animal (>living thing), 33
ζῳοποιέω make alive, 33

ἤ—or, than, 31
ἤ or, than, 31
ἡ—the, 9
ἡγ—govern (compare with ἀγ), 86
ἡγεμ—govern, 86
ἡγεμον—govern, 86
ἡγεμονεύω be governor, rule, 86
ἡγεμονία ας reign, rule, 86
ἡγεμών όνος governor, ruler, 86
ἡγέομαι lead, rule, consider, 86
ἤδη—now, already, 82
ἤδη now, already, 82
ἡκ—be present, 107
ἥκω have come, be present, 107
ἡλι—sun, 96
ἡλικία ας age, years, 96
ἥλιος ου sun, 96
ἡμερ—day, 25
ἡμέρα ας day, 25
ἡμιθανής ές half dead, 36
ἡμίωρον ου half an hour, 63
ἤπερ than, 31
ἤτοι or, 31

θαλλασ—sea, 68
θάλασσα ης sea, 68
θαν—death, 36
θανάσιμον ου deadly poison, 36
θανατηφόρος ον deadly, 36
θάνατος ου death, 36
θανατόω kill (>make dead), 36
θαυμ—wonder, 86
θαῦμα ματος wonder, miracle, 86
θαυμάζω marvel, 86
θαυμάσιος α ον wonderful, 86
θαυμαστός ή όν marvelous, astonishing, 86
θε¹—god, 11
θε²—put, place, 31
θεα—see, 69
θεά ᾶς goddess, 11
θεάομαι see, observe, 70
θεατρίζω expose to public shame, 70
θέατρον ου theatre, spectacle, 70
θει—god, 11
θεῖος α ον divine, 11
θειότης ητος deity, 11
θελ—will, 36
θέλημα ματος will, desire, 36
θέλησις εως will, 36
θέλω wish, want, 36
θεμελι—foundation, 114
θεμέλιον ου foundation, 114
θεμέλιος ου foundation, 114
θεμελιόω establish (>make firm), 114
θεο—god, 11
θεοδίδακτος ον taught by God, 41
θεομάχος ον God-opposing, 11

θεόπνευστος ον God-inspired, 11
θεός οῦ God, 11
θεοσέβεια ας religion, 11
θεοσεβής ές religious, 11
θεοστυγής ές God-hating, 11
θεότης ητος deity, 11
θερ—warm, harvest, 91
θεραπ—healing, service, 91
θεραπεία ας healing, house servants, 91
θεραπεύω heal, serve, 91
θεράπων οντος servant, 91
θερίζω harvest, gather, 91
θερισμός οῦ harvest, crop, 91
θεριστής οῦ reaper, 91
θερμ warm, harvest, 91
θερμαίνομαι warm oneself, 91
θέρμη ης heat, 91
θέρος ους summer, 91
θεωρ—see, 69
θεωρέω see, observe, 70
θεωρία ας sight, 70
θη—put, place, 31
θήκη ης sheath, 31
θηρ—wild animal, 90
θήρα ας trap, 90
θηρεύω catch, 90
θηριομαχέω fight wild beasts, 90
θηρίον ου animal, 90
θησαυρ—treasure, 109
θησαυρίζω save, store up, 109
θησαυρός οῦ treasure, storeroom, 109
θλιβ—trouble, crowd, 83
θλίβω crush, press, 83
θλιψ—trouble, crowd, 83
θλῖψις εως trouble, 83
θνη—death, 36
θνήσκω die, 36
θνητός ή όν mortal, 36
θρον—throne, 81
θρόνος ου throne, 81
θυ—sacrifice, 77
θυγατηρ—daughter, 105
θυγάτηρ τρός daughter, woman, 105
θυγάτριον ου little daughter, 105
θυγατρ—daughter, 105
θυμ—feelings (emotions), 61
θυμομαχέω be very angry, 61
θυμόομαι be furious, 61
θυμός οῦ anger, 61
θυρ—door, 91
θύρα ας door, 92
θυρίς ίδος window, 92
θυρωρός οῦ doorkeeper, 92
θυσ—sacrifice, 77
θυσία ας sacrifice, 77
θυσιαστήριον ου altar (>place of sacrifice), 77
θύω sacrifice, kill, 77

ια—heal, 98
ἴαμα ματος healing, 98
ἰάομαι heal, 98
ἴασις εως healing, 98
ιατρ—heal, 98
ἰατρός οῦ physician, healer, 98
ιδ—see, 40
ἴδε Behold! here is, 40
ιδι—own, 59

ἴδιος α ον one's own, personal, 59
ἰδιώτης ου untrained person, 59
ἰδού Behold! here is, 40
ἱερ—priest, 59
ἱερατ—priest, 59
ἱερατεία ας priestly office, 59
ἱεράτευμα ματος priesthood, 59
ἱερατεύω serve as a priest, 59
ἱερεύς έως priest, 59
ἱερόθυτος ον sacrificial, 59
ἱερόν οὖ temple, 59
ἱεροπρεπής ές reverent, 59
ἱερός ά όν sacred, 59
ἱεροσυλέω commit sacrilege, 59
ἱερόσυλος ου sacrilegious person, 59
ἱερουργέω work as a priest, 59
ἱερωσύνη ης priesthood, 60
ἱη—let, send, 45
ἱκαν—able, 94
ἱκανός ή όν able, worthy, 94
ἱκανότης ητος capability, capacity, 94
ἱκανόω make fit, make able, 94
ἱματ—clothe, 80
ἱματίζω clothe, dress, 80
ἱμάτιον ου clothing, coat, 80
ἱματισμός οὖ clothing, 80
ἱνα—in order that, 16
ἵνα in order that, 16
ἱνατί why? 16
ἱππ—horse, 117
ἱππεύς έως horseman, 117
ἱππικόν οὖ cavalry, 118
ἵππος ου horse, 118
ἰσάγγελος ον angel-like, 22
ἰσότιμος ον equally valuable, 49
ἰσόψυχος ον sharing same feelings, 56
ἰστη—stand, 18
ἵστημι set, stand, 19
ἰσχυ—strong, 76
ἰσχυρός ά όν strong, 76
ἰσχύς ύος strength, 76
ἰσχύω be able, 76
ἰχθυ—fish, 114
ἰχθύδιον ου small fish, fish, 114
ἰχθύς ύος fish, 114

κἀγώ and I; I also, 9
καθ¹—down, according to, 20
καθ²—sit (compare with κατ), 48
καθαιρ—clean, 63
καθαίρεσις εως destruction, 89
καθαιρέω take down, destroy, 89
καθαίρω clean, prune, 63
καθάπερ as, just as, 21
καθάπτω fasten on, 94
καθαρ—clean, 63
καθαρίζω cleanse, 63
καθαρισμός οὖ cleansing, 63
καθαρός ά όν clean, pure, 63
καθαρότης ητος purification, purity, 63
καθεδρ—sit (compare with κατ), 48
καθέδρα ας chair, 48
καθέζομαι sit, 48
καθεύδω sleep, 114
καθηγητής οὖ teacher, 23
κάθημαι sit, live, 48
καθημερινός ή όν daily, 25

καθίζω sit, 48
καθήημι let down, 45
καθίστημι put in charge, 19
καθό as, according as, 21
καθόλου completely, altogether, 61
καθοράω perceive clearly, 51
καθώς as, just as, 14
καθώσπερ as, just as, 14
και—and, 9
καί and, also, but, 9
καιν—new, 86
καινός ή όν new, 87
καινότης ητος newness, 87
καίπερ though, 9
καιρ—time, 65
καιρός οὖ time, age, 65
καίτοι yet, though, 9
καίτοιγε yet, though, 9
κακ—bad, 60
κἀκεῖ and there, 28
κἀκεῖθεν from there, 28
κἀκεῖνος η ο and that one, 28
κακία ας evil, trouble, 60
κακοήθεια ας meanness, 60
κακολογέω speak evil of, curse, 60
κακοπάθεια ας suffering, endurance, 60
κακοπαθέω suffer, endure, 60
κακοποιέω do evil, 60
κακοποιός οὖ criminal, wrong doer, 60
κακός ή όν evil, bad, 60
κακοῦργος ου criminal, 60
κακουχέομαι be treated badly, 60
κακόω treat badly, harm, 60
κακῶς badly, 60
κάκωσις εως oppression, suffering, 60
καλ¹—good, proper, 54
καλ²—call, 21
καλέω call, name, 21
καλλιέλαιος ου cultivated olive tree, 108
κάλλιον very well, 54
καλοδιδάσκαλος ον teaching what is good, 41
καλοποιέω do what is good, 54
καλός ή όν good, proper, 54
καλυμ—hide, 78
κάλυμμα ματος veil, 78
καλυπτ—hide, 78
καλύπτω cover, hide, 78
καλυψ—hide, 78
καλῶς well, 54
κἄν (καὶ ἐάν) even if, 43
καρδ—heart, 48
καρδία ας heart, 48
καρδιογνώστης ου knower of hearts, 48
καρπ—fruit, 72
καρπός οὖ fruit, 72
καρποφορέω be fruitful / productive, 73
καρποφόρος ον fruitful, 73
κατ—down, according to, 20
κατά (gen., acc.) down, according to, 21
καταβαίνω descend, fall, 37
καταβάλλω knock down, 28
καταβαπτίζομαι wash oneself, 59
καταβαρέω be a burden to, 109
καταβαρύνομαι be very heavy, 109
κατάβασις εως descent, slope, 37
καταβολή ῆς beginning, foundation, 28
καταγγελεύς έως proclaimer, 22

καταγγέλλω proclaim, 22
καταγινώσκω condemn, 24
καταγράφω write, 31
κατάγω bring (down), 23
καταδέω bandage, bind up, 81
καταδικάζω condemn, 34
καταδίκη ης sentence, condemnation, 34
καταδιώκω search for diligently, pursue, 83
καταδουλόω make a slave of, 44
καταδυναστεύω oppress, 29
κατάθεμα ματος God-cursed thing, 11
καταθεματίζω curse, 31
καταισχύνω put to shame, 88
κατακαλύπτομαι cover one's head, 78
κατακαυχάομαι be proud, despise, 80
κατάκειμαι lie, be sick, 70
κατακλάω break in pieces, 92
κατακλείω lock up (in prison), 103
κατακλίνω cause to recline, dine, 93
κατακολουθέω follow, accompany, 64
κατακόπτω cut badly, beat, 95
κατάκριμα ματος condemnation, 20
κατακρίνω condemn, judge, 20
κατάκρισις εως condemnation, 20
κατακυριεύω have power over, 15
καταλαλέω slander (>speak against), 32
καταλαλιά ᾶς slander, 32
κατάλαλος ου slanderer, 32
καταλαμβάνω obtain, attain, overtake, 26
καταλέγω enroll (>catalogue), 16
καταλείπω leave, forsake, 58
καταλιθάζω stone, 74
καταλλαγή ῆς reconciliation, 14
καταλλάσσω reconcile, 14
κατάλοιπος ον rest, remaining, 58
κατάλυμα ματος room, guest room, 47
καταλύω destroy, stop, 47
καταμανθάνω consider, observe, 34
καταμαρτυρέω witness against, 42
καταμένω remain, stay, live, 42
κατανοέω consider, 53
καταντάω come, arrive, 68
κατάνυξις εως stupor, numbness, 80
καταξιόω make / count worthy, 83
καταπατέω trample on, despise, 34
κατάπαυσις εως place of rest, rest, 89
καταπαύω cause to rest, prevent, 89
καταπίνω swallow (>drink down), 73
καταπίπτω fall (down), 46
καταπλέω sail, 68
καταργέω destroy, 30
καταριθμέω number, 112
καταρτίζω mend, make adequate, 117
κατάρτισις εως adequacy, 117
καταρτισμός οῦ adequacy, 117
κατασείω move, make a sign, 108
κατασκευάζω prepare, make ready, 98
κατασκηνόω nest, live, dwell, 97
κατασκήνωσις εως nest, 97
κατασκοπέω spy on, 104
κατάσκοπος ου spy, 104
κατασοφίζομαι take advantage of, 75
καταστέλλω quiet, 35
κατάστημα ματος behavior, 19
καταστρέφω overturn, 53
καταστροφή ῆς ruin (>catastrophe), 53
κατασφραγίζω seal, 103

κατατίθημι lay, place, 31
κατατομή ῆς mutilation, 79
κατατρέχω run down, 102
καταφέρω bring against, 40
καταφεύγω flee, 94
καταφθείρω corrupt, ruin, 87
καταφιλέω kiss, 77
καταφρονέω despise, 62
καταφρονητής οῦ scoffer, 62
καταχέω pour over, 114
καταχράομαι use, use fully, 67
καταψύχω cool, refresh, 56
κατείδωλος ον full of idols, 102
κατέναντι (gen.) opposite, 68
κατεξουσιάζω rule over, 63
κατεργάζομαι do, accomplish, 30
κατέρχομαι come / go down, 11
κατεσθίω eat up, devour, 76
κατευθύνω direct, guide, 65
κατευλογέω bless, 16
κατεφίστημι attack, set upon, 19
κατέχω hold fast, keep, 15
κατηγορέω accuse (bring against), 23
κατηγορία accusation, 23
κατήγορος ου accuser, 23
κατήγωρ ορος accuser, 23
κατισχύω have strength, defeat, 76
κατοικέω live, inhabit, 27
κατοίκησις εως home, 27
κατοικητήριον ου house, home, 27
κατοικία ας place where one lives, 27
κατοικίζω place, put, 27
κατοπτρίζω behold, 60
κάτω down, below, 21
κατώτερος α ον lower, 21
κατωτέρω under, 21
καυχα—proud, 80
καυχάομαι be proud, boast, 80
καυχη—proud, 80
καύχημα ματος pride, boasting, 80
καύχησις εως pride, boasting, 80
κει—lie, 70
κεῖμαι lie, be laid, be, 70
κελευ—command, 109
κέλευσμα ματος command, 109
κελεύω command, 109
κενο—empty, 112
κενοδοξία ας conceit (>empty glory), 39
κενόδοξος ον conceited, 39
κενός ή όν empty, senseless, 112
κενοφωνία ας foolish (empty) talk, 42
κενόω make empty / powerless, 112
κενῶς in vain, 112
κερδ—gain, 118
κερδαίνω gain, profit, 118
κέρδος ους gain, 118
κεφαλ—head, sum, 71
κεφάλαιον ου main point, summary, 71
κεφαλή ῆς head, 71
κεφαλιόω beat over the head, 71
κηρυγ—preach, 77
κήρυγμα ματος message, kerygma, 77
κηρυξ—preach, 77
κῆρυξ υκος preacher, 77
κηρυσσ—preach, 77
κηρύσσω preach, proclaim, 77
κλα—break, 92

κλάδος ου branch, 92
κλαι—weep, 91
κλαίω weep, 91
κλάσις εως breaking (of bread), 92
κλάσμα ματος fragment, piece, 92
κλαυ—weep, 91
κλαυθμός οῦ bitter crying, 91
κλάω break, 92
κλει—lock, close, 103
κλείς κλειδός key, 103
κλείω lock, shut, close, 103
κλεμ—steal, 103
κλέμμα ματος theft, 103
κλεπτ—steal, 103
κλέπτης ου thief, 103
κλέπτω steal, 103
κλη—call, 21
κλῆμα ματος branch, 92
κληρ—share, choose, 80
κληρονομέω receive, share (in), 81
κληρονομία ας property, 81
κληρονόμος ου heir, 81
κλῆρος ου lot, share, 81
κληρόω choose, 81
κλῆσις εως call, calling, 21
κλητός ή όν called, invited, 21
κλιν—recline, incline, turn, 93
κλινάριον ου small bed, 93
κλίνη ης bed, 93
κλινίδιον ου bed, 93
κλίνω lay, put to flight, 93
κλισία ας group, 93
κλοπ—steal, 103
κλοπή ῆς theft, 103
κοιλ—stomach, 113
κοιλία ας stomach, appetite, 113
κοιν—common, 77
κοινός ή όν common, profane, 77
κοινόω defile (>make common), 77
κοινων—common, 77
κοινωνέω share, participate, 77
κοινωνία ας fellowship, 77
κοινωνικός ή όν liberal, generous, sharing, 77
κοινωνός οῦ partner, 77
κοπ—work, 88
κοπή ῆς slaughter, defeat, 88
κοπιάω work, grow tired, 88
κόπος ου work, trouble, 88
κοπτ—cut, 94
κόπτω cut (mid. mourn), 95
κοσμ—world, order, 42
κοσμέω adorn, put in order, 42
κοσμικός ή όν worldly, man-made, 42
κόσμιος ον well-behaved, ordered, 42
κοσμοκράτωρ ορος world-ruler, 42
κόσμος ου world, universe, 42
κραζ—shout, 76
κράζω shout, call out, 76
κρατ—strong, power, 69
κραταιόομαι become strong, 69
κραταιός ά όν strong, 69
κρατέω hold, seize, 69
κράτιστος η ον most excellent, 69
κράτος ους strength, power, 69
κραυγ—shout, 76
κραυγάζω shout, call out, 76
κραυγή ῆς shout, 76

κρι—judge, 19
κρίμα τος judgment, decision, 20
κρίνω judge, consider, 20
κρίσις εως judgment, 20
κριτήριον ου court (judgment hall), 20
κριτής οῦ judge, 20
κριτικός ή όν able to judge, 20
κρυπτ—hide, 89
κρύπτη ης hidden place, cellar, 89
κρυπτός ή όν hidden, secret, 89
κρύπτω hide, cover, 89
κρυφ—hide, 89
κρυφαῖος α ον hidden, secret, 89
κρυφῇ secretly, 89
κτ—create, 96
κτειν—kill, 76
κτίζω create, make, 96
κτισ—create, 96
κτίσις εως creation, 96
κτίσμα ματος creation, 97
κτίστης ου creator, 97
κυρι—lord, power, 15
κυρία ας lady, 16
κυριακός ή όν belonging to the Lord, 16
κυριεύω rule, have power, 16
κύριος ου lord, master, 16
κυριότης ητος power, authority, 16
κωλυ—hinder, 111
κωλύω hinder, 111
κωμ—town, 107
κώμη ης small town, 107
κωμόπολις εως town, 107

λα—people, 52
λαβ—take, receive, 26
λαθ—forget, 118
λάθρα secretly, quietly, 118
λαλ—speak, 32
λαλέω speak, 32
λαλιά ᾶς what is said, accent, 32
λαμβ—take, receive, 26
λαμβάνω take, receive, 26
λαμπ—lamp, 105
λαμπάς άδος lamp, 105
λαμπρός ά όν bright, fine, 105
λαμπρότης ητος brightness, 105
λαμπρῶς splendidly, 105
λάμπω shine, 105
λανθαν—forget, 118
λανθάνω be hidden, ignore, 118
λαός οῦ people, nation, 52
λατομέω cut, hew (of rock), 79
λατρ—worship, 99
λατρεία ας worship, service, 99
λατρεύω worship, serve, 99
λεγ—say, word, 16
λέγω say, 16
λειμ—leave, lack, 58
λεῖμμα ματος remnant, 58
λειπ—leave, lack, 58
λείπω lack, leave, 59
λειτουργ—serve, worship (compare with ἐργ), 118
λειτουργέω serve, worship, 118
λειτουργία ας service, worship, 118
λειτουργικός ή όν ministering, 118
λειτουργός οῦ servant, minister, 118
λεκτ—say, word, 16

λευκ—white, 109
λευκαίνω make white, 109
λευκός ή όν white, shining, 109
λήθη ης forgetfulness, 118
λημ—take, receive, 26
λῆμψις εως receiving, 26
λιθ—stone, 74
λιθάζω stone, 74
λίθινος η ον made of stones, 74
λιθοβολέω stone (>throw stones), 74
λίθος ου stone, 74
λιθόστρωτον ου pavement, 74
λιμ—leave, lack, 58
λογ—say, word, 16
λόγια ων oracles, words, 16
λογίζομαι count, consider, 16
λογικός ή όν rational, spiritual, 17
λόγιος α ον eloquent, learned, 17
λογισμός οῦ thought, reasoning, 17
λογομαχέω fight about words, 17
λογομαχία ας quarrel about words, 17
λόγος ου word, message, 17
λοιπ—leave, lack, 58
λοιπός ή όν rest, remaining, 59
λυ—loose / redeem, 46
λυπ—pain, 91
λυπέω pain, grieve, be sad, 91
λύπη ης grief, pain, 91
λύσις εως separation (loosed from), 47
λυτρ—loose / redeem, 46
λύτρον ου means of release, 47
λυτρόομαι redeem, set free, 47
λύτρωσις εως redemption, 47
λυτρωτής οῦ liberator, 47
λυχν—lamp, 110
λυχνία ας lampstand, 110
λύχνος ου lamp, 110
λύω loose, free, 47

μαθ—learn, 34
μαθητεύω make a disciple, 34
μαθητής οῦ disciple, pupil, 34
μαθήτρια ας woman disciple, 34
μακαρ—blessed, 84
μακαρίζω consider blessed, 84
μακάριος α ον blessed, happy, 84
μακαρισμός οῦ blessing, happiness, 84
μακρ—long, 85
μακράν far, at a distance, 85
μακρο—long, 85
μακρόθεν far, at a distance, 85
μακροθυμέω be patient, 85
μακροθυμία ας patience, 85
μακροθύμως patiently, 85
μακρός ά όν long, distant, 85
μακροχρόνιος ον long-lived, 85
μαλ—more, 68
μάλιστα most of all, 68
μαλλ—more, 68
μᾶλλον more, 69
μανθ—learn, 34
μανθάνω learn, discover, 34
μαρτυρ—witness, 42
μαρτυρέω testify, affirm, 42
μαρτυρία ας witness, testimony, 42
μαρτύριον ου witness, testimony, 42
μαρτύρομαι witness, testify, urge, 42

μάρτυς μάρτυρος witness, martyr, 43
μαχ—fight, 96
μάχαιρα ης sword, 96
μάχη ης fight, 96
μάχομαι fight, 96
μεγ—great, 41
μεγαλ—great, 41
μεγαλεῖον ου great / mighty act, 41
μεγαλειότης ητος greatness, majesty, 41
μεγαλύνω enlarge, 41
μεγάλως greatly, 41
μεγαλωσύνη ης greatness, majesty, 41
μέγας μεγάλη μέγα great, large, 41
μέγεθος ους greatness, 41
μεγιστάν ᾶνος person of high position, 41
μέγιστος η ον very great, greatest, 41
μεθίστημι remove, mislead, 19
μεθοδεία ας trickery, 54
μειζ—greater, 90
μείζων ον greater, 90
μελ¹—concern, care, 107
μελ²—part, 101
μέλει it concerns (imper.), 107
μελλ—about, 63
μέλλω be going, be about, 63
μέλος ους part, member, 101
μέν (used to show contrast), 43
μεν¹ [particle of contrast], 43
μεν²—wait, remain, 41
μενοῦν rather, 43
μέντοι but, 43
μένω remain, 42
μερ—part, 75
μερίζω divide, 75
μεριμν—worry, 107
μέριμνα ης worry, care, 107
μεριμνάω worry, 107
μερίς ίδος part, 75
μερισμός οῦ distribution, division, 75
μεριστής οῦ one who divides, 75
μέρος ους part, piece, 75
μεσι—middle, 76
μεσιτεύω mediate, 76
μεσίτης ου mediator, 76
μεσο—middle, 76
μεσονύκτιον ου midnight, 76
Μεσοποταμία ας Mesopotamia, 76
μέσος η ον middle, 76
μεσότοιχον ου dividing wall, 76
μεσουράνημα τος mid-heaven, 76
μεσόω be in the middle, 76
μετα—with, after, 23
μετά (gen., acc.) with, after, 23
μεταβαίνω leave, move, 37
μεταβάλλομαι change one's mind, 28
μετάγω guide, direct, 23
μεταδίδωμι give, share, 17
μετάθεσις εως removal, change, 31
μεταίρω leave, 54
μετακαλέομαι send for, invite, 21
μεταλαμβάνω receive, share in, 26
μετάλημψις εως receiving, accepting, 26
μεταλλάσσω exchange, 14
μεταμέλομαι regret, 107
μετανοέω repent, 53
μετάνοια ας repentance, 53
μεταξύ (gen.) between, among, 23

μεταπέμπομαι send for, 64
μεταστρέφω change, alter, 53
μετατίθημι remove, change, 31
μετατρέπω turn, change, 82
μετέχω share in, eat, have, 15
μετοικεσία ας carrying off, 27
μετοικίζω deport / send off, 27
μετοχή ῆς partnership, 15
μέτοχος ου partner, 15
μετρ—measure, 106
μετρέω measure, give, 106
μετρητής οῦ measure, 106
μετριοπαθέω be gentle with, 97
μετρίως greatly, 106
μέτρον ου measure, quantity, 106
μέτωπον ου forehead, 60
μέχρι (gen.) until, to, 80
μη—not, 12
μή not, 12
μήγε otherwise, 12
μηδαμῶς no, by no means, 12
μηδέ nor, 12
μηδείς μηδεμία μηδέν no one, 26
μηδέποτε never, 21
μηκέτι no longer, 48
μήποτε lest, whether, never, 21
μήτε and not, 12
μητηρ—mother, 70
μήτηρ τρός mother, 70
μήτι (negative answer), 12
μητρ—mother, 70
μήτρα ας womb, 70
μητρολῴας ου mother-murderer, 70
μια—one, 26
μικρ—small, 91
μικρόν a little while, 91
μικρός ά όν small, insignificant, 91
μιμν—remember, 56
μιμνήσκομαι remember, 57
μισ—hate, 97
μισέω hate, be indifferent to, 97
μισθ—pay, 95
μισθαποδοσία ας reward, punishment, 95
μισθαποδότης ου rewarder, 95
μίσθιος ου hired man, laborer, 95
μισθόομαι hire (>make a payee), 95
μισθός οῦ pay, 95
μίσθωμα ματος expense, rent, 95
μισθωτός οῦ hired man, laborer, 95
μν—remember, 56
μνεία ας remembrance, mention, 57
μνη—remember, 56
μνημ—remember, 56
μνῆμα ματος grave, tomb (memorial), 57
μνημεῖον ου grave, monument, 57
μνήμη ης remembrance, memory, 57
μνημονεύω remember, 57
μνημόσυνον ου memorial, 57
μογιλάλος ον mute, dumb, 32
μοιχ—adultery, 107
μοιχαλίς ίδος adulteress, 107
μοιχάομαι commit adultery, 107
μοιχεία ας adultery, 107
μοιχεύω commit adultery, 107
μοιχός οῦ adulterer, 107
μον—wait, remain, 41
μονή ῆς room, 42

μονο—only, 57
μονογενής ές only begotten, unique, 13, 58
μόνον only, alone, 58
μονόομαι be left alone, 58
μόνος η ον only, alone, 58
μυστηρ—mystery, 108
μυστήριον ου secret, mystery, 108
μυωπάζω be shortsighted, 60
μωρ—foolish, 115
μωραίνω make foolish, 115
μωρία ας foolishness, 115
μωρολογία ας foolish talk, 115
μωρός ά όν foolish, 115

να—temple, 92
ναι—yes, 101
ναί yes, 101
ναός οῦ temple, 92
νε—new, 92
νεα—new, 92
νεανίας ου young man, 92
νεανίσκος ου young man, 92
νεκρ—death, 55
νεκρός ά όν dead, 55
νεκρόω put to death, make dead, 55
νέκρωσις εως death, barrenness, 55
νεο—new, 92
νεομηνία ας new moon, 92
νέος α ον new, young, 92
νεότης ητος youth, 92
νεόφυτος ον new convert (neophyte), 92
νεφ—cloud, 110
νεφέλη ης cloud, 110
νέφος ους cloud, 110
νεω—new, 92
νεωτερικός ή όν youthful, 92
νηστ—hunger, 108
νηστεία ας hunger, fasting, 108
νηστεύω fast, 108
νῆστις ιδος hungry, 108
νικ—victory, 101
νικάω conquer, 101
νίκη ης victory, 101
νῖκος ους victory, 101
νιπτ—wash, 117
νιπτήρ ῆρος washbasin, 117
νίπτω wash, 117
νο—mind, 53
νοέω understand, 53
νόημα τος mind, thought, 53
νομ—law, 38
νομίζω think, suppose, 38
νομικός ή όν legal, 38
νομίμως lawfully, 38
νόμισμα ματος coin (>legal tender), 38
νομοδιδάσκαλος ου teacher of law, 38
νομοθεσία ας giving of the law, 38
νομοθετέομαι be given the law, 38
νομοθέτης ου lawgiver, 38
νόμος ου law, 38
νουθεσία instruction, 53
νουθετέω instruct (>place in mind), 53
νουνεχῶς wisely, 53
νυ—night, 80
νυκ—night, 80
νυμφ—bride, 107
νύμφη ης bride, daughter-in-law, 108

νυμφίος ου bridegroom, 108
νυμφών ῶνος wedding hall, 108
νυν—now, 47
νῦν now, 47
νυνί now, 47
νύξ νυκτός night, 80
νυσ—night, 80
νυστάζω be asleep, drowsy, idle, 80
νυχ—night, 80
νυχθήμερον ου a night and a day, 80

ξεν—strange, guest, 103
ξενία ας place of lodging, room, 103
ξενίζω entertain strangers, 103
ξενοδοχέω be hospitable, 103
ξένος η ον strange, foreign, 103
ξηρ—dry, 113
ξηραίνω dry up, 113
ξηρός ά όν dry, withered, 113
ξυλ—wood, 115
ξύλινος η ον wooden, 115
ξύλον ου wood, tree, club, 115

ὁ—the, 9
ὁ ἡ τό the, 9
ὁδ—way, travel, 54
ὅδε ἥδε τόδε this, 9
ὁδεύω travel, 54
ὁδηγέω lead, guide, 54
ὁδηγός οῦ guide, leader, 54
ὁδοιπορέω travel, 54
ὁδοιπορία ας journey, 54
ὁδός οῦ way, journey, 54
οι—such, as, 87
οἰδ—know, 32
οἶδα know, 32
οἰκ—house, 26
οἰκεῖος ου family member, 27
οἰκετεία ας household, 27
οἰκέτης ου house servant, 27
οἰκέω live, dwell, 27
οἴκημα ματος prison cell, 27
οἰκητήριον ου home, dwelling, 27
οἰκία ας home, family, 27
οἰκιακός οῦ member of household, 27
οἰκοδεσποτέω run a household, 27
οἰκοδεσπότης ου master, householder, 27
οἰκοδομέω build, encourage, 27
οἰκοδομή ῆς structure, 27
οἰκοδόμος ου builder, 27
οἰκονομέω be a manager, steward, 27
οἰκονομία ας task, responsibility, 27
οἰκονόμος ου manager, steward, 27
οἶκος ου house, 27
οἰκουμένη ης world, oikomenia, 27
οἰκουργός όν domestic, 27
οἰν—wine, 97
οἰνοπότης ου drinker, drunkard, 97
οἶνος ου wine, 97
οἰνοφλυγία ας drunkenness, 97
οἷος α ον such, such as, 87
ὀκταήμερος ον on the eighth day, 25
ὀλ—whole, all, 61
ὀλιγ—little, few, 95
ὀλιγοπιστία ας little faith, 18
ὀλιγόπιστος ον of little faith, 18
ὀλίγος η ον little, few, 95

ὀλιγόψυχος ον faint-hearted, 95
ὀλιγωρέω think lightly of, 95
ὀλίγως barely, just, 95
ὀλλ—destroy, 63
ὅλος η ον whole, all, 61
ὁλοτελής ές wholly, 62
ὅλως at all, actually, 62
ὀμ—swear, 110
ὀμν—swear, 110
ὀμνύω swear, vow, 110
ὁμο—same, like, 60
ὁμοθυμαδόν with one mind, 61
ὅμοι—same, like, 60
ὁμοιάζω resemble, 60
ὁμοιοπαθής ές similar (>of same feelings), 60
ὅμοιος α ον like, 60
ὁμοιότης ητος likeness, 60
ὁμοιόω make like, compare, 61
ὁμοίωμα ματος likeness, 61
ὁμοίως too, in the same way, 61
ὁμοίωσις εως likeness, 61
ὁμολογέω confess, declare, 17
ὁμολογία ας confession, 17
ὁμολογουμένως undeniably, 17
ὁμοῦ together, 61
ὁμόφρων ον of one mind, 62
ὅμως even, 61
ὀνομ—name, 39
ὄνομα ματος name, 39
ὀνομάζω name, call, 39
ὀντ—be, exist, 10
ὄντως really, 10
ὀπ—see, 60
ὀπισ—behind, after, 95
ὄπισθεν behind, 95
ὀπίσω behind, after, 95
ὁποῖος α ον as, such as, 87
ὁπότε when, 21
ὅπου where, 43
ὀπτ—see, 60
ὀπτάνομαι appear (>gain sight of), 60
ὀπτασία ας vision, 60
ὅπως that, in order that, 14
ὀρ—boundary, 67
ὀρ—hill, 81
ὀρα—see, 51
ὅραμα ματος vision, sight, 51
ὅρασις εως vision, appearance, 51
ὁρατός ή όν visible, 51
ὁράω see, perceive, 51
ὀργ—anger, 90
ὀργή ῆς anger, punishment, 90
ὀργίζομαι be angry, 90
ὀργίλος η ον quick-tempered, 90
ὀρεινή ῆς hill country, 81
ὀρθοποδέω be consistent, 63
ὁρίζω decide, determine, 67
ὅριον ου territory, vicinity, 67
ὁρκ—oath, 117
ὁρκίζω adjure, 117
ὅρκος ου oath, 117
ὁρκωμοσία ας oath, 117
ὁροθεσία ας limit, boundary, 67
ὅρος ου limit, boundary, 67
ὄρος ους mountain, hill, 81
οσ—much, many, 51
ὅς ἥ ὅ who, which, what, 9

ὅσος η ον as much as, as great as, 51
ὅσπερ ἥπερ ὅπερ who, which, 9
ὅστις ἥτις ὅ τι whoever, whichever, 12
ὅταν when, whenever, 21
ὅτε when, while, 21
οτε—when, 21
ὅτι—that, because, 12
ὅτι that, because, 12
οὐ—no, 10
οὖ no, 10
οὐ not, 10
οὑ—where, 43
οὖ where, 43
οὐαι—woe, 92
οὐαί woe, 92
οὐδαμῶς by no means, 10
οὐδέ neither, nor, 10
οὐδέποτε never, 21
οὐδέπω not yet, 106
οὐκ—no, 10
οὐκέτι no longer, 48
οὐκοῦν so, then, 22
οὐν—therefore, 22
οὖν therefore, 23
οὔπω not yet, 106
οὐραν—heaven, 34
οὐράνιος ον heavenly, 34
οὐρανόθεν from heaven, 34
οὐρανός οῦ heaven, 34
οὐργ—work, 30
οὐσ—be, exist, 10
οὖς—ear, 100
οὖς ὠτός ear, 100
οὐσία ας property, 10
οὖτ—this, 11
οὔτε not, nor, 10
οὗτος αὕτη τοῦτο this, this one, 11
οὕτως [οὕτω] thus (>in this way), 11
οὐχ—no, 10
οὐχί not, no (emphatic), 10
ὀφειλ—debt, 88
ὀφειλέτης ου debtor, offender, 88
ὀφειλή ῆς debt, 88
ὀφείλημα ματος debt, 88
ὀφείλω owe, ought, 88
ὄφελος ους gain, benefit, 110
ὀφθαλμ—eye, 65
ὀφθαλμοδουλία ας eye-service, 65
ὀφθαλμός οῦ eye, 65
οχ—have, 15
ὀχλ—crowd, mob, 46
ὀχλέομαι crowd, trouble, harass, 46
ὀχλοποιέω gather a crowd, 46
ὄχλος ου crowd, mob, 16
ὀψ—late, 113
ὀψέ late, after, 113
ὀψία ας evening, 113
ὄψιμος ου late rain, spring rain, 113
ὀψώνιον ου pay (>given late in day), 113

παθ—feel, desire, 97
πάθημα ματος suffering, passion, 97
παθητός ή όν subject to suffering, 97
πάθος ους lust, passion, 97
παι—child, education, 55
παιδ—child, education, 55
παιδαγωγός οῦ instructor (>pedagogue), 55

παιδάριον ου boy, 55
παιδεία ας discipline, instruction, 55
παιδευτής οῦ teacher, 55
παιδεύω instruct, correct, 55
παιδιόθεν from childhood, 55
παιδίον ου child, infant, 55
παιδίσκη ης maid, slave, 55
παίζω play, dance, 55
παῖς παιδός child, servant, 55
παλ—again, 54
παλαι—old, 102
πάλαι long ago, formerly, 102
παλαιός ά όν old, former, 102
παλαιότης ητος age, 102
παλαιόω make old, 102
παλιγγενεσία ας rebirth, new age, 13
πάλιν again, once, 54
παμπληθεί together, 39
παν—all, 12
πανδοχεῖον ου inn (>receive all), 50
πανδοχεύς έως inn-keeper, 50
πανοικεί with one's household, 27
πανουργία ας trickery, 30
πανοῦργος ον tricky, 30
παντ—all, 12
πανταχῇ everywhere, 12
πανταχοῦ everywhere, 12
παντελής ές complete, 45
πάντη in every way, 12
πάντοθεν from all directions, 12
παντοκράτωρ ορος the All-Powerful, 69
πάντοτε always, at all times, 21
πάντως by all means, 12
παρα—by, 43
παρά (gen., dat., acc.) by, with, 43
παραβαίνω break, disobey, 37
παραβάλλω arrive, 28
παράβασις εως disobedience, 37
παραβάτης ου one who disobeys, 37
παραβολεύομαι risk, 28
παραβολή ῆς parable, symbol, 28
παραγγελία ας order, instruction, 22
παραγγέλλω command, order, 22
παραγίνομαι come, appear, stand by, 13
παράγω pass by (away), 23
παραδειγματίζω expose to ridicule, 73
παραδέχομαι accept, receive, welcome, 50
παραδίδωμι hand over, deliver, 17
παράδοξος ον incredible (>paradox), 66
παράδοσις εως tradition, 17
παραζηλόω make jealous, 96
παραθαλάσσιος α ον by the sea or lake, 68
παραθεωρέω overlook, 70
παραθήκη ης something entrusted, 31
παραινέω advise, 105
παραιτέομαι ask for, excuse, 57
παρακαθέζομαι sit, 49
παρακαλέω beg, encourage, 21
παρακαλύπτομαι be hidden, 78
παράκειμαι be present, 70
παράκλησις εως encouragement, help, 21
παράκλητος ου helper (the Paraclete), 21
παρακοή ῆς disobedience, disloyalty, 22
παρακολουθέω follow closely, 64
παρακούω refuse to listen, disobey, 22
παραλαμβάνω take (along), receive, 26
παράλιος ου coastal district, 116

παραλλαγή ῆς variation, change, 14
παραλογίζομαι deceive, 17
παραλύομαι be paralyzed, 47
παραλυτικός οῦ paralytic, 47
παραμένω remain, stay, 42
παραμυθέομαι console, 61
παραμυθία ας comfort, 61
παραμύθιον ου comfort, 61
παρανομέω act contrary to the law, 38
παρανομία ας offense, 38
παραπίπτω apostatize (>fall away), 46
παραπλέω sail past, 68
παραπορεύομαι pass by, go, 38
παράπτωμα ματος sin, 46
παραρρέω drift away, 90
παράσημος ον marked by a figurehead, 69
παρασκευάζω prepare, make ready, 98
παρασκευή ῆς day of preparation, 98
παρατείνω prolong, 104
παρατηρέω keep, watch, observe, 72
παρατήρησις εως observation, 72
παρατίθημι place before, give, 31
παρατυγχάνω happen to be present, 112
παραφέρω remove, carry away, 40
παραφρονέω be insane, 62
παραφρονία ας insanity, 62
παραχρῆμα immediately, 67
πάρειμι be present, 10
παρεισάγω bring in, 23
παρεισέρχομαι come in, 11
παρεισφέρω exert, 40
παρεκτός (*gen.*) except, 13
παρεμβάλλω set up, 28
παρεμβολή ῆς barracks, camp, 28
παρενοχλέω add extra difficulties, 46
παρεπίδημος ου refugee, 106
παρέρχομαι pass (by, away), 11
παρέχω cause, 15
παρίημι neglect, 45
παρίστημι present, 19
πάροδος ου passage, 54
παροικέω live in, live as a ranger, 27
παροικία ας stay, visit, 27
πάροικος ου alien, stranger, 27
πάροινος ου drunkard, 97
παρομοιάζω be like, 61
παρόμοιος ον like, similar, 61
παροργίζω make angry, 90
παροργισμός οῦ anger, 90
παρουσία ας coming, parousia, 10
παρρησία ας openness (>all flowing), 90
παρρησιάζομαι speak boldly, 90
πασ—all, 12
πᾶς πᾶσα πᾶν each, all, 12
πασχ—suffer, 78
πάσχα Passover, 78
πάσχω suffer, 78
πατ—walk, 34
πατέω walk, trample, 34
πατήρ πατρός father, 24
πατρ—father, 24
πατριά ᾶς family, nation, 24
πατριάρχης ου patriarch, 24
πατρικός ή όν paternal, 24
πατρίς ίδος homeland, 24
πατροπαράδοτος ον handed from ancestors, 17
πατρῷος α ον belonging to ancestors, 25

παυ—stop, 89
παύω stop, 90
πεδ—foot, 63
πέδη ης chain (for feet), 64
πεδινός ή όν level (ground), 64
πεζ—foot, 63
πεζεύω travel by land, 64
πεζῇ on foot, by land, 64
πειθ—persuade, 71
πειθαρχέω obey, 71
πειθός ή όν persuasive, 71
πείθω persuade, 71
πειθώ οῦς persuasiveness, 71
πειν—hunger, 112
πεινάω be hungry, 112
πειρ—test, 79
πεῖρα ας attempt, 79
πειράζω test, tempt, 79
πειράομαι try, attempt, 79
πειρασμός οῦ trial, period of testing, 79
πεισμονή ῆς persuasion, 71
πεμπ—send, 64
πέμπω send, 64
πεντ—five, 90
πεντάκις five times, 90
πεντακισχίλιοι five thousand, 90
πεντακόσιοι αι α five hundred, 90
πέντε five, 90
πεντεκαιδέκατος fifteenth, 90
πεντήκοντα fifty, 90
περα—far, end, 100
περαιτέρω further, 100
πέραν beyond, across, 100
πέρας ατος end, boundary, 100
περι—around, 32
περί (*gen., acc.*) about, concerning, 32
περιάγω go around, travel over, 23
περιαιρέω take away, remove, 89
περιάπτω kindle, 94
περιαστράπτω flash around, 94
περιβάλλω put on, clothe, 28
περιβλέπομαι look around, 44
περιβόλαιον ου cloak, covering, 28
περιδέω wrap, bind, 81
περιεργάζομαι be a busybody, 30
περίεργος ου busybody, 30
περιέρχομαι go around, 11
περιέχω seize, contain, 15
περιζώννυμι wrap around, 114
περίθεσις εως wearing (of jewelry), 31
περιΐστημι stand around, 19
περικάθαρμα ματος rubbish, 63
περικαλύπτω cover, conceal, 78
περίκειμαι be placed around, 70
περικεφαλαία ας helmet, 71
περικρατής ές in control of, 69
περικρύβω keep in seclusion, 89
περιλάμπω shine around, 105
περιλείπομαι remain, 59
περίλυπος ον very sad, 91
περιμένω wait for, 42
πέριξ around, 32
περιοικέω live in neighborhood, 27
περίοικος ου neighbor, 27
περιούσιος ον special, 10
περιπατέω walk, move about, live, 34
περιπείρω pierce through, 79

περιπίπτω encounter, 46
περιποιέομαι obtain, preserve, 18
περιποίησις εως obtaining, possession, 18
περισσ—abundance, 69
περισσεία ας abundance, 69
περίσσευμα ματος abundance, 69
περισσεύω be left over, abound, 69
περισσός ή όν more, 69
περισσότερος α ον greater, more, 69
περισσοτέρως all the more, 69
περισσῶς all the more, 69
περιτέμνω circumcise, 79
περιτίθημι put around, 32
περιτομή ῆς circumcision, 79
περιτρέπω drive insane, 82
περιτρέχω run about, 102
περιφέρω carry about, bring, 40
περιφρονέω esteem lightly, disregard, 62
περίχωρος ου neighborhood, 52
πίμπλημι fill, end, 39
πιν—drink, 73
πίνω drink, 73
πιπτ—fall, 46
πίπτω fall, 46
πιστ—belief, faith, 18
πιστεύω believe, 18
πιστικός ή όν genuine, 18
πίστις εως faith, trust, belief, 18
πιστόομαι firmly believe, entrust, 18
πιστός ή όν faithful, believing, 18
πλαν—error, wandering, 83
πλανάω lead astray, 84
πλάνη ης error, deceit, 84
πλανήτης ου wanderer, 84
πλάνος ον deceitful, 84
πλασσ—plague, strike, 110
πλε—sail, 68
πλει—more, 70
πλεῖστος η ον most, large, 70
πλείων ον more, 70
πλεον—more, 70
πλεονάζω increase, grow, 70
πλεονεκτέω take advantage of, 70
πλεονέκτης ου one who is greedy, 70
πλεονεξία ας greed (>have more), 70
πλέω sail, 93
πλη—full, 39
πληγ—plague, strike, 110
πληγή ῆς plague, blow, 110
πληθ—full, 39
πλῆθος ους crowd, 39
πληθύνω increase, 39
πλήκτης ου violent person, 110
πλήμμυρα ης flood, 39
πλην—but, 104
πλήν but, nevertheless, 104
πληρ—full, 39
πλήρης ες full, 39
πληροφορέω accomplish, 39
πληροφορία ας certainty, 39
πληρόω fulfill (>make happen), 39
πλήρωμα ματος fullness, 39
πλησμονή ῆς satisfaction, 39
πλησσ—plague, strike, 110
πλήσσω strike, 110
πλο—sail, 68
πλοιάριον ου boat, 68

πλοῖον ου boat, 68
πλου—rich, 79
πλοῦς πλοός voyage, 68
πλούσιος α ον rich, 79
πλουσίως richly, 79
πλουτέω be rich, prosper, 79
πλουτίζω make rich, 79
πλοῦτος ου wealth, 79
πν—spirit, wind, breath, 25
πνευ—spirit, wind, breath, 25
πνεῦμα ματος spirit, self, wind, 25
πνευματικός ή όν spiritual, 25
πνευματικῶς spiritually, symbolically, 25
πνέω blow, 25
πνίγω choke, drown, 26
πνικτός ή όν strangled, 26
πνοή ῆς wind, breath, 26
πο¹—foot, 63
πο²—drink, river (compare πιν), 79
ποδ—foot, 63
ποθ—feel, desire, 97
πόθεν from where, where, 43
ποι—make, do, 18
ποιέω make, do, 18
ποίημα ματος something made, 18
ποίησις εως undertaking, 18
ποιητής οῦ one who does; doer, 18
ποιμ—sheep, 97
ποιμαίνω tend, rule, 97
ποιμήν ένος shepherd, 97
ποιμν—sheep, 97
ποίμνη ης flock, 97
ποίμνιον ου flock, 97
ποῖος α ον what, what kind of, 87
πολεμ—war, 111
πολεμέω fight, be at war, 111
πόλεμος ου war, conflict, polemic, 111
πολι—city, 47
πόλις εως city, town, 47
πολιτάρχης ου city official, 47
πολιτεία ας citizenship, state, 47
πολίτευμα ματος place of citizenship, 47
πολιτεύομαι live, be a citizen, 47
πολίτης ου citizen, 47
πολλ—much, many, 29
πολλάκις often, 29
πολλαπλασίων ον more, 29
πολυ—much, many, 29
πολυλογία ας many words, 29
πολυμερῶς many times, bit by bit, 29
πολυποίκιλος ον in varied forms, 29
πολύς πολλή πολύ much, many, 29
πολύσπλαγχνος ον very compassionate, 29
πολυτελής ές expensive, 29
πολύτιμος ον expensive, 29
πολυτρόπως in many ways, variously, 29
πονηρ—evil, 47
πονηρία ας wickedness, 47
πονηρός ά όν evil, 47
πορ—journey, 38
πορεία ας journey, 38
πορεύομαι journey, go, live, 38
πορν—evil, 47
πορνεία ας fornication, 47
πορνεύω commit fornication, 47
πόρνη ης prostitute, 47
πόρνος ου immoral person, 47

πόρρω far away, 38
πόρρωθεν from a distance, 38
πορρώτερον farther, 38
ποσάκις how often? 51
πόσις εως drink, 79
πόσος η ον how much, how many, 51
ποτ—drink, river (compare πιν), 79
ποταμ—drink, river (compare πιν), 79
ποταμός οῦ river, 79
ποταμοφόρητος ον swept away, 79
ποτέ once, ever, 21
πότε when? 21
ποτήριον ου cup (>place for water), 80
ποτίζω give to drink, water, 80
πότος ου drunken orgy, 80
πού somewhere, 43
ποῦ where? 43
πούς ποδός foot, 64
πραγ—matter, event, something done, 83
πρᾶγμα ματος matter, event, 83
πραγματεῖαι ῶν (*pl.*) affairs, 83
πραγματεύομαι trade, do business, 83
πρᾶξις εως deed, practice, 83
πρασ—matter, event, something done, 83
πράσσω do, 83
πρεσβυ—old, elderly, 77
πρεσβυτέριον ου body of elders, 77
πρεσβύτερος ου elder, presbyter, 77
πρεσβύτης ου old man, 77
πρεσβῦτις ιδος old woman, 77
πρίν before, 37
προ—before, first, 37
πρό (*gen.*) before, 37
προάγω go before, 23
προαιρέομαι decide, 54
προαιτιάομαι accuse beforehand, 57
προακούω hear before, 22
προαμαρτάνω sin previously, 36
προαύλιον ου gateway, forecourt, 114
προβαίνω go on, 37
προβάλλω put forward, 28
προβατ—sheep, 96
προβατικός ή όν pertaining to sheep, 96
προβάτιον ου lamb, sheep, 96
πρόβατον ου sheep, 96
προβλέπομαι provide, 44
προγίνομαι happen previously, 13
προγινώσκω know already, 24
πρόγνωσις εως foreknowledge, purpose, 24
πρόγονος ου parent (>progenitor), 13
προγράφω write beforehand, 31
προδίδωμι give first, 18
προδότης ου traitor, 18
προελπίζω be the first to hope, 71
προενάρχομαι begin, begin before, 25
προεπαγγέλλομαι promise before, 22
προέρχομαι go ahead, 11
προετοιμάζω prepare beforehand, 80
προευαγγελίζομαι evangelize before, 22
προέχομαι be better off, 15
προηγέομαι outdo, lead the way, 23
πρόθεσις εως purpose, plan, 32
προθυμία ας willingness, zeal, 61
πρόθυμος ον willing, 61
προθύμως willingly, eagerly, 61
προΐστημι be a leader, manage, 19
προκαλέομαι irritate, 21

προκαταγγέλλω announce before, 22
προκαταρτίζω prepare in advance, 117
προκατέχω have previously, 15
πρόκειμαι be set before, be esent, 70
προκηρύσσω preach beforehand, 77
προκοπή ῆς progress, 88
προκόπτω advance, progress, 88
πρόκριμα ματος prejudice (>pre-judging), 20
προλαμβάνω do (take) ahead of me, 26
προλέγω say, warn (>prologue), 17
προμαρτύρομαι predict, 43
προμελετάω prepare ahead of time, 107
προμεριμνάω worry beforehand, 107
προνοέω plan, 53
πρόνοια ας provision, 54
προοράω see ahead of time, 51
προπάσχω suffer previously, 78
προπάτωρ ορος forefather, 25
προπέμπω send on one's way, escort, 64
προπορεύομαι go before, 38
προσ—to, toward, 15
πρός (*acc.*) to, toward, 15
προσάγω bring to or before, 23
προσαγωγή ῆς access, 24
προσαιτέω beg, 57
προσαίτης ου beggar, 57
προσαναβαίνω move up, 37
προσαναπληρόω supply, provide, 39
προσανατίθεμαι go for advice, add to, 32
προσανέχω approach, 15
προσδέομαι need, 52
προσδέχομαι wait for, expect, receive, 50
προσδοκάω wait for, expect, 50
προσδοκία ας expectation, 50
προσεγγίζω come near, 75
προσεργάζομαι make more, 30
προσέρχομαι come to, agree with, 11
προσευχή ῆς prayer, 56
προσεύχομαι pray, 56
προσέχω pay close attention to, 15
πρόσκαιρος ον temporary, 65
προσκαλέομαι summon, invite, 21
προσκεφάλαιον ου pillow, 71
προσκληρόομαι join, 81
προσκλίνομαι join, 93
πρόσκλισις εως favoritism, 93
προσκοπή ῆς obstacle, offense, 95
προσκόπτω stumble, be offended, 95
προσκυν—worship, 82
προσκυνέω worship, 82
προσκυνητής οῦ worshiper, 82
προσλαλέω speak to, 32
προσλαμβάνομαι welcome, accept, 26
προσλέγω answer, reply, 17
πρόσλημψις εως acceptance, 26
προσμένω remain (with), 42
προσοφείλω owe, 88
πρόσπεινος ον hungry, 112
προσπίπτω fall at someone's feet, 46
προσποιέομαι pretend, 18
προσπορεύομαι come to, 38
προστάσσω command, 58
προστάτις ιδος helper (>stand before), 19
προστίθημι add, increase, continue, 32
προστρέχω run up (to someone), 102
προσφέρω offer, do, 40
προσφιλής ές pleasing, 77

προσφορά ᾶς offering, sacrifice, 40
προσφωνέω call to, address, 42
προσωπ—face, 74
προσωπολημπτέω show favoritism, 74
προσωπολήμπτης ου shower of favoritism, 74
προσωπολημψία ας favoritism, 74
πρόσωπον ου face, 74
προτείνω tie up, 104
πρότερος α ον former, earlier, 37
προτίθεμαι plan, intend, 32
προτρέπομαι encourage, 82
προτρέχω run on ahead, 102
προϋπάρχω exist previously, 25
προφέρω progress, produce, 40
προφητεία ας prophesying, preaching, 35
προφητεύω preach, prophesy, 35
προφήτης ου prophet, 35
προφητικός ή όν prophetic, 35
προφῆτις ιδος prophetess, 35
προχειρίζομαι choose in advance, 43
προχειροτονέω choose in advance, 44
πρω—before, first, 37
πρωΐ morning, 37
πρωΐα ας morning, 37
πρωϊνός ή όν morning, 37
πρῷρα ης prow, bow, 37
πρωτ—before, first, 37
πρωτεύω have first place, 37
πρωτοκαθεδρία ας place of honor, 49
πρωτοκλισία ας place of honor, 93
πρῶτον in the first place, earlier, 37
πρῶτος η ον first, earlier, leading, 37
πρωτοστάτης ου ring-leader, 37
πρωτοτόκια ων birthright, 37
πρωτότοκος ον first-born, 38
πρώτως for the first time, firstly, 38
πτω—fall, 46
πτῶμα ματος body, corpse, 46
πτῶσις εως fall, 46
πτωχ—poor, 98
πτωχεία ας poverty, 98
πτωχεύω become poor, 98
πτωχός ή όν poor, 98
πυλ—gate, door, 108
πύλη ης gate, door, 108
πυλών ῶνος gate, entrance, porch, 108
πυρ—fire, 66
πῦρ ός fire, 66
πυρά ᾶς fire, 66
πυρέσσω be sick with fever, 66
πυρετός οῦ fever, 66
πύρινος η ον fiery red (color), 66
πυρόομαι burn, 66
πυρράζω be red (for sky), 66
πυρρός ά όν red (color), 66
πύρωσις εως burning, ordeal, 66
πω—yet, 106
πωλ—sell, 115
πωλέω sell, 115
πώποτε ever, at any time, 21
πῶς how? in what way? 14
πώς somehow, in some way, 14

ῥαδιούργημα ματος wrongdoing, 30
ῥαδιουργία ας wrongdoing, 30
ῥε—flow, 90

ῥέω flow, 90
ῥη¹—flow, 90
ῥη²—word, 78
ῥῆμα ματος word, thing, event, 79
ῥητ—word, 78
ῥήτωρ ορος lawyer, spokesperson, 79
ῥητῶς expressly, 79
ῥιζ—root, 115
ῥίζα ης root, descendant, source, 115
ῥιζόομαι be firmly rooted, 115
ῥυ—flow, 90
ῥύσις εως flow, hemorrhage, 90

σ—you, 12
σαλπ—trumpet, 112
σάλπιγξ ιγγος trumpet, 112
σαλπίζω sound a trumpet, 112
σαλπιστής οῦ trumpeter, 112
σαρκ—flesh, 49
σαρκικός ή όν belonging to the world, 49
σάρκινος η ον belonging to the world, 49
σαρξ—flesh, 49
σάρξ σαρκός flesh, physical body, 49
σεαυτοῦ ῆς yourself, 9
σεβ—worship, piety, religion, 84
σεβάζομαι worship, reverence, 85
σέβασμα ματος object / place of worship, 85
σεβαστός ή όν imperial, 85
σέβομαι worship, 85
σει—quake, 108
σεισμός οῦ earthquake, storm, 108
σείω shake, excite, 108
σημ—sign, indication, 69
σημαίνω indicate, 69
σημεῖον ου sign, miracle, 69
σημειόομαι take / make note of, 69
σήμερον today, 25
σθενόω strengthen, 72
σι—silence, 115
σιγ—silence, 115
σιγάω keep silent, 115
σιγή ῆς silence, 115
σιτ—food, fat, 113
σιτευτός ή όν fattened, 113
σιτίον ου grain, food (*pl.*), 113
σιτιστός ή όν fattened, 113
σιτομέτριον ου ration (>measure of food), 113
σῖτος ου grain, 113
σιωπάω be silent, 115
σκ—dark, 78
σκανδαλ—scandal, 93
σκανδαλίζω scandalize, 93
σκάνδαλον ου scandal, 93
σκεπ—view, 104
σκευ—prepare, 98
σκευή ῆς gear, 98
σκεῦος ους thing, container, 98
σκην—tent, 97
σκηνή ῆς tent, 97
σκηνοπηγία ας Feast of Tabernacles, 98
σκηνοποιός οῦ tent-maker, 98
σκῆνος ους tent, 98
σκηνόω live, dwell, 98
σκήνωμα ματος body, dwelling place, 98
σκιά ᾶς shadow, shade, 78
σκληροκαρδία ας hardheartedness, 48

σκοπ—view, 104
σκοπέω pay attention to, 104
σκοπός οῦ goal, 104
σκοτ—dark, 78
σκοτεινός ή όν dark, 78
σκοτία ας darkness, 78
σκοτίζομαι become dark, 78
σκοτόομαι become dark, 78
σκότος ους darkness, sin, 78
σκυθρωτός ή όν sad, 60
σός σή σόν your, yours, 12
σοφ—wisdom, 75
σοφία ας wisdom, 75
σοφίζω give wisdom, 75
σοφός ή όν wise, experienced, 75
σπειρ—scatter, 62
σπείρω sow, 62
σπερ—scatter, 62
σπέρμα ματος seed, offspring, 62
σπερμολόγος ου gossiper (>word scatter), 62
σπευδ—speed, eagerness, 99
σπεύδω hurry, 99
σπλαγχν—pity, 111
σπλαγχνίζομαι have pity, 111
σπλάγχνον ου affection, feeling, compassion, 111
σπορ—scatter, 62
σπορά ᾶς seed, origin, 62
σπόριμα ων (*pl.*) grainfields, 62
σπόρος ου seed, 62
σπουδ—speed, eagerness, 99
σπουδάζω do one's best, work hard, 99
σπουδαῖος α ον earnest, 99
σπουδαίως eagerly, 99
σπουδή ῆς earnestness, zeal, 99
στα—stand, 18
στασιαστής οῦ rebel, 19
στάσις εως dispute, revolt, 19
σταυρ—cross, 73
σταυρός οῦ cross, 74
σταυρόω crucify, 74
στελ—send, equip, 35
στέλλομαι avoid, 35
στενοχωρέομαι be held in check, 52
στενοχωρία ας distress, 52
στερε—firm, solid, 104
στερεός ά όν firm, solid, 104
στερεόω make strong, 104
στερέωμα ματος firmness, 104
στεφαν—crowd, reward, 117
στέφανος ου crown, 117
στεφανόω crown, reward, 117
στη—stand, 18
στήκω stand, 19
στηρε—firm, solid, 104
στηριγμός οῦ firm footing, 104
στηρίζω strengthen, 104
στολ—send, equip, 35
στομ—mouth, 73
στόμα ματος mouth, 73
στρατ—army, 81
στρατεία ας warfare, fight, 81
στράτευμα ματος troops, army, 81
στρατεύομαι serve as a soldier, battle, 81
στρατηγός οῦ chief officer, 81
στρατιά ᾶς army, 81
στρατιώτης ου soldier, 81

στρατολογέω enlist soldiers, 81
στρατοπεδάρχης ου officer, 81
στρατόπεδον ου army, 81
στρεβλόω distort, twist, 53
στρεφ—turn, 53
στρέφω turn, 53
στροφ—turn, 53
σύ you, 12
συγγένεια ας relatives, 13
συγγενής οῦς relative, 13
συγγενίς ίδος female relative, 14
συγγνώμη ης permission, 24
συγκάθημαι sit with, 49
συγκαθίζω sit together with, 49
συγκακοπαθέω share in hardship, 97
συγκακουχέομαι suffer with, 60
συγκαλέω call together, summon, 21
συγκαλύπτω cover up, 78
συγκαταβαίνω come down with, 37
συγκατάθεσις εως agreement, 32
συγκατατίθεμαι agree with, 32
συγκλείω make / keep a prisoner, 103
συγκληρονόμος ον sharing, 81
συγκοινωνέω take part in, 77
συγκοινωνός οῦ sharer, 77
συγκρίνω compare, interpret, 20
συγχαίρω rejoice with, 53
συγχέω confound, stir up, 114
συγχράομαι associate with, 67
σύγχυσις εως confusion, 114
συζάω live with, 33
συζητέω discuss, argue, 48
συζήτησις εως discussion, argument, 48
συζητητής οῦ skillful debater, 48
συζωοποιέω make alive together, 18
συκ—fig, 115
συκάμινος ου mulberry tree, 115
συκῆ ῆς fig tree, 115
συκομορέα ας sycamore tree, 115
σῦκον ου fig, 115
συλαγωγέω make captive, 24
συλλαλέω talk with, 32
συλλαμβάνω seize, arrest, 26
συλλογίζομαι discuss, 17
συλλυπέομαι feel sorry for, 91
συμβαίνω happen, come about, 37
συμβάλλω meet, discuss, 28
συμβασιλεύω live together as kings, 33
συμβιβάζω bring together, 37
συμβουλεύω advise, 75
συμβούλιον ου plan, plot, 75
σύμβουλος ου counselor, 75
συμμαθητής οῦ fellow disciple, 34
συμμαρτυρέω testify in support of, 43
συμμερίζομαι share with, 75
συμμέτοχος ου sharer, 15
συμπαθέω sympathize with, 97
συμπαθής ές sympathetic, 97
συμπαραγίνομαι assemble, 14
συμπαρακαλέομαι be encouraged together, 21
συμπαραλαμβάνω take / bring along with, 26
συμπάρειμι be present with, 10
συμπάσχω suffer together, 78
συμπέμπω send along with, 64
συμπεριλαμβάνω embrace, hug, 26
συμπίνω drink with, 73

συμπίπτω collapse, fall, 46
συμπληρόω draw near, end, 39
συμπολίτης ου fellow citizen, 47
συμπορεύομαι go along with, 38
συμπόσιον ου group (>symposium), 73
συμπρεσβύτερος ου fellow-elder, 77
συμφέρω be helpful, useful, 40
σύμφημι agree with, 35
σύμφορον ου advantage, benefit, 40
συμφυλέτης ου fellow countryman, 101
συμφύομαι grow up with, 92
σύμφυτος ον sharing in, 92
συμφωνέω agree with, 42
συμφώνησις εως agreement, 42
συμφωνία ας music (symphony), 42
σύμφωνον ου mutual consent, 42
σύμψυχος ον united in spirit, 56
συν—with, 83
σύν (*dat.*) with, 83
συνάγω gather, 24
συναγωγή ῆς synagogue, 24
συναίρω settle, 54
συνακολουθέω follow, accompany, 64
συναλλάσσω reconcile, 14
συναναβαίνω come up together, 37
συνανάκειμαι sit at table with, 70
συναναπαύομαι have a time of rest with, 90
συναντάω meet, happen, 68
συναντιλαμβάνομαι (come to) help, 26
συναπάγομαι be carried away, 24
συναποθνήσκω die with, 36
συναπόλλυμαι perish with, 63
συναποστέλλω send along with, 35
συναρπάζω seize, drag, 105
συναυξάνομαι grow together, 108
συνδέομαι be in prison with, 81
σύνδεσμος ου bond, chain, 86
συνδοξάζομαι share in glory, 39
σύνδουλος ου fellow-slave (servant), 44
συνεγείρω raise together, 45
συνειδη—conscience, 106
συνείδησις εως conscience, 106
σύνειμι be with, be present, 10
συνεισέρχομαι enter in, 11
συνέκδημος ου travelling companion, 107
συνεπιμαρτυρέω add further witness, 43
συνεπιτίθεμαι join in the attack, 32
συνεργέω work with, 30
συνεργός οῦ fellow-worker, 30
συνέρχομαι come together, 11
συνεσθίω eat with, 76
συνευδοκέω approve of, 66
συνεφίστημι join in an attack, 19
συνέχω surround, control, 15
συνηλικιώτης ου contemporary, 96
συνθλίβω crowd, press upon, 83
συνίστημι recommend, show, 19
συνοδεύω travel with, 55
συνοδία ας group (>synod), 55
σύνοιδα share knowledge with, 32
συνοικέω live with, 27
συνοικοδομέω build together, 107
συνοράω realize, learn, 51
συντάσσω direct, instruct, 58
συντέλεια ας end, completion, 45
συντελέω end, complete, 45
συντέμνω cut short, 79

συντηρέω protect, 72
συντίθεμαι agree, arrange, 32
συντρέχω run together, join with, 102
σύντροφος ου close friend, 100
συντυγχάνω reach, 112
συνυποκρίνομαι act insincerely with, 20
συνυπουργέω join in, help, 30
σύσσωμος ον of same body, 51
συσταυρόομαι be crucified together, 74
συστέλλω carry out, 35
συστρατιώτης ου fellow-soldier, 81
σφραγι—seal, 103
σφραγίζω seal, acknowledge, 103
σφραγίς ῖδος seal, evidence, 103
σωζ—save, 61
σῴζω save, rescue, preserve, 61
σωμα—body, physical, 51
σῶμα ματος body, substance, 51
σωματικός ή όν physical, 51
σωματικῶς in bodily (human) form, 51
σωτηρ—salvation, 76
σωτήρ ῆρος savior, 77
σωτηρία ας salvation, release, 77
σωτήριον ου salvation, 77
σωτήριος ον saving, 77
σωφρονέω be sane, sensible, 62
σωφρονίζω train, teach, 62
σωφρονισμός οῦ sound judgment, 62
σωφρόνως sensibly, 62
σωφροσύνη ης good sense, 62
σώφρων ον sensible, 62

ταγ—order, 58
τάγμα ματος proper order, 58
τακ—order, 58
τακτός ή όν appointed, fixed, 58
ταξ—order, 58
τάξις εως order, division, 58
ταπειν—humble, 101
ταπεινός ή όν humble, poor, 101
ταπεινοφροσύνη ης (false) humility, 101
ταπεινόφρων ον humble, 101
ταπεινόω make humble, 101
ταπείνωσις εως humble state, 101
ταρασσ—trouble, 115
ταράσσω trouble, disturb, 115
ταραχ—trouble, 115
ταραχή ῆς disturbance, trouble, 116
τάραχος ου confusion, 116
τασσ—order, 58
τάσσω appoint, 58
ταχ¹—order, 58
ταχ²—quick, 99
ταχέως quickly, 99
ταχινός ή όν soon, swift, 99
τάχιον quickly, 99
τάχιστα as soon as possible, 99
τάχος ους speed, 99
ταχύ quickly, 99
ταχύς εῖα ύ quick, 99
τειν—extend, stretch, 104
τεκν—child, 55
τεκνίον ου little child, 55
τεκνογονέω have children, 55
τεκνογονία ας childbirth, 55
τέκνον ου child, 55
τεκνοτροφέω bring up children, 55

τελ—end, far, 45
τέλειος α ον complete, 45
τελειότης ητος completeness, 45
τελειόω make perfect, 45
τελείως fully, 45
τελείωσις εως fulfillment, 45
τελειωτής οῦ perfecter, 45
τελεσφορέω produce mature fruit, 45
τελευτάω die, 45
τελευτή ῆς death, 46
τελέω finish (make an end), 46
τέλος ους end, 46
τελων—tax, 111
τελώνης ου tax-collector, 111
τελώνιον ου tax (office), 111
τεμν—cut, 79
τεν—extend, stretch, 104
τεσσαρ—four, 64
τεσσαράκοντα forty, 64
τέσσαρες α four, 64
τεσσαρεσκαιδέκατος fourteenth, 64
τεσσαρακονταετής ές forty years, 85
τεταρ—four, 64
τεταρταῖος α ον on the fourth day, 64
τέταρτος η ον fourth, 64
τετρα—four, 64
τετρααρχέω be tetrarch, be ruler, 64
τετραάρχης ου tetrarch (ruler), 64
τετράγωνος ον squared (>four-angled), 64
τετράδιον ου squad (of four men), 64
τετρακισχίλιοι αι α four thousand, 64
τετρακόσιοι αι α four hundred, 64
τετράμηνος ου period of four months, 64
τετραπλοῦς ῆ οῦν four times as much, 64
τετράπουν ποδος animal (>four-footed), 64
τηρ—keep, observe, 72
τηρέω keep, observe, 72
τήρησις εως custody, keeping, 72
τι—who, what, any, 12
τιθ—put, place, 31
τίθημι put, place, lay, 32
τικ—child, 55
τίκτω give birth to, yield, 55
τιμ—honor, price, 49
τιμάω honor, 49
τιμή ῆς honor, price, 49
τίμιος α ον precious, respected, 50
τιμιότης ητος wealth, abundance, 50
Τιμόθεος ου Timothy, 50
τιν¹—extend, stretch, 104
τιν²—who, what, any, 12
τις—who, what, any, 12
τὶς τὶ anyone, anything, 12
τίς τί who? what? (why? τι), 12
το—the, 9
τοιγαροῦν therefore, then, 23
τοίνυν therefore, then, 47
τοιοῦτος αύτη οῦτον such, similar, 11
τοκ—child, 55
τόκος ου interest (>child of money), 55
τομ—cut, 79
τομός ή όν sharp, cutting, 79
τον—extend, stretch, 104
τοπ—place, 65
τόπος ου place, 65
τοσοῦτος αύτη οῦτον so much, so great, 51
τότε then, 21

τουναντίον on the contrary, 68
τουτ—this, 11
τρεῖς τρία three, 50
τρεπ—turn, 82
τρεφ—feed, support, 100
τρέφω feed, support, 100
τρεχ—run, 102
τρέχω run, 102
τρι—three, 50
τριάκοντα thirty, 50
τριακόσιοι αι α three hundred, 50
τριετία ας period of three years, 50
τρίμηνον ου three months, 50
τρίς three times, a third time, 50
τρίστεγον ου third floor, 50
τρισχίλιοι αι α three thousand, 50
τρίτον the third time, 50
τρίτος η ον third, 50
τροπ—turn, 82
τροπή ῆς turning, change, 82
τρόπος ου way, manner, 82
τροποφορέω put up with, 82
τροφ—feed, support, 100
τροφή ῆς food, keep, 100
τροφός οῦ nurse, 100
τροφοφορέω care for, 40
τροχ—run, 102
τροχιά ᾶς path, 102
τροχός οῦ wheel, cycle, 102
τυγχ—obtain, 112
τυγχάνω obtain, 112
τυπ—type, example, 118
τύπος ου example, pattern, 118
τυφλ—blind, 86
τυφλός ή όν blind, 86
τυφλόω make blind, 86
τυχ—obtain, 112

ὑγι—health, 113
ὑγιαίνω be healthy, be sound, 113
ὑγιής ές healthy, whole, 113
ὑδρ—water, 72
ὑδρία ας water jar, 72
ὑδροποτέω drink water, 72
ὑδρωπικός ή όν suffering from dropsy, 72
ὕδωρ ὕδατος water, 72
υἱ—son, 29
υἱοθεσία ας adoption, sonship, 29
υἱός οῦ son, descendant, 29
ὑπάγω go (away), 24
ὑπακοή ῆς obedience, 22
ὑπακούω obey, 22
ὕπανδρος ον married (>under + man), 40
ὑπαντάω meet, fight, oppose, 68
ὑπάντησις εως meeting, 68
ὕπαρξις εως possession, 25
ὑπάρχω be under one's rule, 25
ὑπεναντίος α ον against, 68
ὑπερ—over, 49
ὑπέρ (gen., acc.) over, 49
ὑπεραίρομαι be puffed up with pride, 54
ὑπεράνω (gen.) far above, above, 49
ὑπεραυξάνω grow abundantly, 108
ὑπερβαίνω do wrong to, 37
ὑπερβαλλόντως much more, 28
ὑπερβάλλω surpass (>overthrow), 28

ὑπερβολή ῆς the extreme (>hyperbole), 28
ὑπερέκεινα (gen.) beyond, 28
ὑπερεκπερισσοῦ with all earnestness, 69
ὑπερεκτείνω go beyond, 104
ὑπερεκχύννομαι run over, 114
ὑπερεντυγχάνω intercede, 112
ὑπερέχω surpass, govern, 15
ὑπερηφανία ας arrogance, 51
ὑπερήφανος ον arrogant, 52
ὑπερνικάω be completely victorious, 101
ὑπεροράω overlook, 51
ὑπεροχή ῆς position of authority, 15
ὑπερπερισσεύω increase abundantly, 69
ὑπερπερισσῶς completely, 69
ὑπερπλεονάζω overflow, 70
ὑπερυψόω raise to highest position, 85
ὑπερφρονέω hold high opinion of, 62
ὑπερῷον ου upstairs room, 49
ὑπέχω undergo, suffer, 15
ὑπήκοος ον obedient, 22
ὑπηρετ—serve, 113
ὑπηρετέω serve, 113
ὑπηρέτης ου attendant, helper, 113
ὑπο—under, by means of, 41
ὑπό (gen., acc.) under, by means of, 41
ὑποβάλλω bribe, 28
ὑπογραμμός οῦ example, 31
ὑπόδειγμα τος example, copy, 73
ὑποδείκνυμι show, warn, 73
ὑποδέομαι put on shoes, 82
ὑποδέχομαι receive as a guest, 50
ὑπόδημα ματος sandal, 82
ὑπόδικος ον answerable to, 34
ὑποζώννυμι strengthen, brace, 114
ὑποκάτω (gen.) under, 21
ὑποκρίνομαι pretend, be a hypocrite, 20
ὑπόκρισις εως hypocrisy, 20
ὑποκριτής οῦ hypocrite, 20
ὑπολαμβάνω suppose, take away, 26
ὑπόλειμμα ματος remnant, 59
ὑπολείπω leave, 59
ὑπολιμπάνω leave, 59
ὑπομένω endure (>stay under), 42
ὑπομιμνήσκω remind, 57
ὑπόμνησις εως remembrance, 57
ὑπομονή ῆς endurance (>stay under), 42
ὑπονοέω suppose, suspect, 54
ὑπόνοια ας suspicion, 54
ὑποπλέω sail under the shelter, 68
ὑποπνέω blow gently, 26
ὑποπόδιον ου footstool, 64
ὑπόστασις εως conviction, confidence, 19
ὑποστέλλω draw back, hold back, 35
ὑποστολή ῆς shrinking / turning back, 35
ὑποστρέφω return, 53
ὑποταγή ῆς obedience, submission, 58
ὑποτάσσω subject, 58
ὑποτίθημι risk (>place under), 32
ὑποτρέχω run under the shelter, 102
ὑποτύπωσις εως example, 118
ὑποφέρω endure, bear up under, 40
ὑποχωρέω withdraw, go away, 52
ὑπωπιάζω control (>under the eye of), 60
ὑσ—last, lack, 96
ὑστερέω lack, need, 96
ὑστέρημα ματος what is lacking, 96
ὑστέρησις εως lack, need, 96

ὕστερον later, afterwards, then, 96
ὕστερος α ον later, last, 96
ὑψ—high, 85
ὑψηλός ή όν high, 85
ὑψηλοφρονέω be proud, 85
ὕψιστος η ον highest, 85
ὕψος ους height, heaven, 85
ὑψόω exalt (>make high), 85
ὕψωμα ματος height, stronghold, 85

φα—say, report, 35
φαιν—display, appear, 51
φαίνω shine, appear, 52
φαν—display, appear, 51
φανερ—display, appear, 51
φανερός ά όν known, visible, plain, 52
φανερόω make known, reveal, 52
φανερῶς openly, clearly, 52
φανέρωσις εως disclosure, 52
φανός οῦ lantern, 52
φαντζομαι appear, 52
φαντασία pomp, 52
φάντασμα ματος phantom ghost, 52
φάσις εως news, report, 35
φάσκω claim, assert, 35
φερ—bring, bear, carry, 39
φέρω bring, carry, 40
φευγ—flee, 93
φεύγω flee, 94
φη—say, report, 35
φημ—say, report, 35
φήμη ης report, news, 35
φημί say, 35
φθαρ—decay, 87
φθαρτός ή όν perishable, mortal, 87
φθειρ—decay, 87
φθείρω corrupt, ruin, 87
φθινοπωρινός ή όν of late autumn, 87
φθορ—decay, 87
φιλ—love, 77
φιλάγαθος ον good-loving, 57
φιλαδελφία ας brotherly love, 29
φιλάδελφος ον brother-loving, 29
φίλανδρος ον husband-loving, 40
φιλανθρωπία ας kindness, 19
φιλανθρώπως considerately, 19
φιλαργυρία ας love of money, 100
φιλάργυρος ον money-loving, 100
φίλαυτος ον selfish, 9, 78
φιλέω love, like, kiss, 78
φίλημα ματος kiss, 78
φιλία ας love, friendship, 78
φιλόθεος ον God-loving, 11
φιλοξενία ας hospitality, 103
φιλόξενος ον hospitable, 103
φιλοπρωτεύω desire to be first, 38
φίλος ου friend, 78
φιλοσοφία ας philosophy, 75
φιλόσοφος ου philosopher, teacher, 75
φιλότεκνος ον loving one's children, 55
φιλοτιμέομαι aspire, 78
φιλοφρόνως kindly, 62
φοβ—fear, 49
φοβέομαι fear, be afraid, respect, 49
φοβερός ά όν fearful, 49
φόβητρον ου fearful thing, 49
φόβος ου fear, 49

φον—murder, 99
φονεύς έως murderer, 99
φονεύω murder, put to death, 99
φόνος ου murder, killing, 99
φορ—bring, bear, carry, 39
φορέω wear, 40
φόρος ου tax (>burden), 40
φορτίζω burden, load, 40
φορτίον ου burden, cargo, 40
φρ—think, 62
φρήν φρενός thought, understanding, 62
φρο—think, 62
φρον—think, 62
φρονέω think, 62
φρόνημα ματος way of thinking, mind, 62
φρόνησις εως insight, wisdom, 62
φρόνιμος ον wise, 62
φρονίμως wisely, 62
φροντίζω concentrate upon, 62
φρουρέω guard, 51
φυ—natural, growth, planted, 92
φυγ—flee, 93
φυγή ῆς flight, 94
φυλ—tribe, 101
φυλακ—guard, 70
φυλακή ῆς prison, 71
φυλακίζω imprison, 71
φυλακτήριον ου phylactery, 71
φύλαξ ακος guard, 71
φυλασσ—guard, 70
φυλάσσω guard, keep, obey, 71
φυλή ῆς tribe, nation, 101
φυσ—natural, growth, planted, 92
φυσικός ή όν natural, 92
φυσικῶς naturally, 92
φυσιόω make conceited, 93
φύσις εως nature, 93
φυσίωσις εως conceit, 93
φυτ—natural, growth, planted, 92
φυτεία ας plant, 93
φυτεύω plant, 93
φύω grow, 93
φων—voice, 42
φωνέω call, 42
φωνή ῆς voice, sound, 42
φωσ—light, 67
φῶς φωτός light, fire, 67
φωστήρ ῆρος light, star, 67
φωσφόρος ου morning star, 67
φωτ—light, 67
φωτεινός ή όν full of light, 67
φωτίζω give light, shine on, 67
φωτισμός οῦ light, revelation, 67

χαιρ—rejoice, 53
χαίρω rejoice, 53
χαρ—rejoice, 53
χαρά ᾶς joy, 53
χαρι—gift, 36
χαρίζομαι give, forgive, 36
χάριν for sake of, because of, 36
χάρις ιτος grace, favor, kindness, 36
χάρισμα ματος gift, 36
χαριστ—gift, 36
χαριτόω give freely (>make a gift), 36
χε—pour, 113
χειρ—hand, 44

χείρ χειρός hand, 44
χειραγωγέω lead by the hand, 24
χειραγωγός οῦ one who leads, 24
χειρόγραφον ου record of debt, 31
χειροποίητος ον hand / man-made, 18
χειροτονέω appoint, choose, 104
χηρ—widow, 110
χήρα ας widow, 110
χιλι—thousand, 101
χιλίαρχος ου tribune, officer, 25
χιλιάς άδος a thousand, 101
χίλιοι αι α thousand, 101
χορτ—food, 105
χορτάζω feed, satisfy, 105
χόρτασμα ματος food, 105
χόρτος ου grass, vegetation, 105
χρα—need, use, 67
χράομαι use, 67
χρει—need, use, 67
χρεία ας need, 67
χρεοφειλέτης ου debtor, 88
χρη—need, use, 67
χρή it ought, 67
χρήζω need, 67
χρῆμα ματος possessions, wealth, 67
χρήσιμον ου good, value, 67
χρῆσις εως sexual intercourse, 67
χρι—anoint, 20
χρισ—anoint, 20
χρῖσμα ματος anointing, 20
Χριστιανός οῦ Christian, 20
Χριστός οῦ Christ, 20
χρίω anoint, 20
χρον—time, 82
χρονίζω delay (>use time), 82
χρόνος ου time, 82
χρονοτριβέω spend time, 82
χρυσ—gold, 93
χρυσίον ου gold, 93
χρυσοδακτύλιος ον wearing a gold ring, 93
χρυσόλιθος ου chrysolite, 93
χρυσόπρασος ου chrysoprase (gem), 93
χρυσός οῦ gold, 93
χρυσοῦς ῆ οῦν golden, 93
χρυσόω make golden, 93
χυ—pour, 113
χωρ—place, 52
χώρα ας country, land, 52
χωρέω make room for, accept, 52
χωρίζω separate, leave, 52
χωρίον ου field, piece of land, 52
χωρίς without, separately (*dat.*), 52

ψευδ—false, 87
ψευδάδελφος ου false brother, 29
ψευδαπόστολος ου false apostle, 87
ψευδής ές false, 87
ψευδοδιδάσκαλος ου false teacher, 87
ψευδολόγος ου liar, 87
ψεύδομαι lie, 87
ψευδομαρτυρέω give false witness, 87
ψευδομαρτυρία ας false witness, 87
ψευδόμαρτυς υρος false witness, 87
ψευδοπροφήτης ου false prophet, 35
ψεῦδος ους lie, imitation, 87
ψευδόχριστος ου false Christ, 20
ψευδώνυμος ον so-called, 39

ψεῦσμα ματος   lie, untruthfulness, 87
ψεύστης ου   liar, 87
ψυχ—self, soul / cold (unspiritual), 56
ψυχή ῆς   self, person, 56
ψυχικός ή όν   unspiritual, material, 56
ψύχομαι   grow cold, 56
ψῦχος ους   cold, 56
ψυχρός ά όν   cold, 56

ὧδε—here, 81
ὧδε   here, 81
ωπ—see, 60
ὠρ—time, hour, 63

ὥρα ας   moment, time, 63
ὡραῖος α ον   timely, welcome, 63
ὡς—as, how (manner), 14
ὡς   as, like, 14
ὡσαύτως   likewise, 14
ὡσεί   like, as, 14
ὥσπερ   as, just as, 15
ὡσπερεί   as (though), 15
ὥστε   that, so that, thus, 15
ὠτ—ear, 100
ὠφελ—gain, 110
ὠφέλεια ας   advantage, benefit, 110
ὠφελέω   gain, help, 110
ὠφέλιμος ον   valuable, beneficial, 110